DEATH IN THE EVERGLADES

DEATH IN THE EVERGLADES

Accidents, Foolhardiness, and Mayhem in South Florida

RANDI MINETOR

Essex, Connecticut

An imprint of Globe Pequot, the Trade Division of
The Rowman & Littlefield Publishing Group, Inc.
4501 Forbes Blvd., Ste. 200
Lanham, MD 20706
www.rowman.com
Distributed by NATIONAL BOOK NETWORK

British Library Cataloguing in Publication Information available

Library of Congress Cataloging-in-Publication Data
Names: Minetor, Randi, author.
Title: Death in the Everglades : accidents, foolhardiness, and mayhem in
  South Florida / Randi Minetor.
Description: Guilford, Connecticut : Lyons Press, [2022] | Includes
  bibliographical references and index.
Identifiers: LCCN 2022011603 (print) | LCCN 2022011604 (ebook) | ISBN
  9781493065981 (paperback ; alk. paper) | ISBN 9781493070039 (ebook)
Subjects: LCSH: Violent deaths—Florida—Everglades—History—20th
  century—Popular works. | Violent
  deaths—Florida—Everglades—History—21st century—Popular works. |
  Violent deaths—Florida, South—History—20th century—Popular works. |
  Violent deaths—Florida, South—History—21st century—Popular works.
Classification: LCC F317.E9 M528 2022 (print) | LCC F317.E9 (ebook) | DDC
  975.9/39—dc23/eng/20220321
LC record available at https://lccn.loc.gov/2022011603
LC ebook record available at https://lccn.loc.gov/2022011604

Contents

To my Mom, Annette Bassow (1927–2017),
who lived in Fort Lauderdale for twenty-four years and feared everything.
It turns out you weren't wrong.

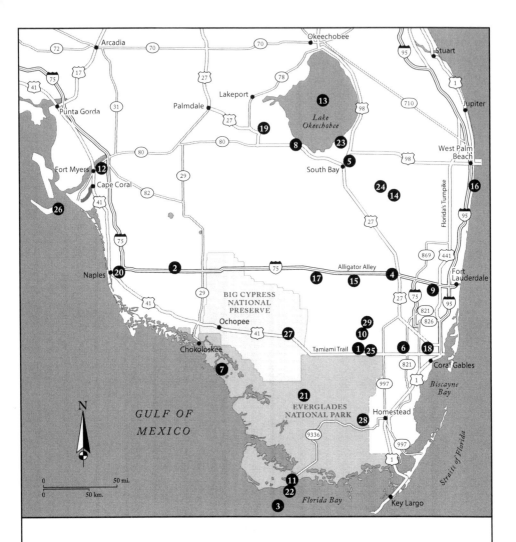

1. 1937 Bus Accident
2. Alan Stuart Marsh found
3. Al Snider disappearance
4. Andytown
5. Belle Glade
6. Braniff 971 crash site
7. Chatham Bend
8. Clewiston
9. Davie
10. Eastern 401 crash site
11. Flamingo Campground
12. Fort Myers
13. Lake Okeechobee
14. Lew Gene Harvey body dump site
15. Lorraine Hatzakorzian found
16. Manalapan
17. Marissa Karp found
18. Miami International Airport
19. Moore Haven
20. Naples
21. Northwest Orient 705 crash site
22. Oyster Keys
23. Pelican Bay
24. Poor Boy Slim's bus crash
25. Robert Steward Hall found
26. Sanibel Island
27. Tamiami Trail (US 41)
28. Thomas Wentz found
29. ValuJet 592 crash site

Note

About Casual Racism in Florida Historical Documents

Many news accounts and histories written in Florida from the early 1800s through the late twentieth century refer to "colored people," "Negros," "Indians," "braves," using ethnic group terms that were part of the vernacular of the time. Many news stories do not bother to give names to people of color, continuing to refer to them by their ethnicity—implying that they are interchangeable with others of their race. References to people of color as less intelligent or trustworthy than white people are also frequent in the press.

In some cases, accused felons attempt to frame people of color for crimes they themselves committed . . and in more than one case, they very nearly get away with this.

The casual racism in the media of the time is inappropriate and unacceptable and must be repudiated as such, so I have done my best to point it out wherever this is appropriate. My purpose is to showcase this kind of racism from a historical perspective. If you are offended, rest assured that I am as well.

Acknowledgments

Writing is a solitary process but publishing is a business, and for this I am very grateful to the supremely talented team at Lyons Press for their work on all of the books in this series. For *Death in the Everglades* I thank Rick Rinehart, who had the foresight to commission the first book decades ago—*Death in Yellowstone*, by Lee Whittlesey—and who now sees the potential in broadening this series beyond the confines of specific national parks. As always, the crack Lyons team—this time, production editor Jessica Thwaite, layout artist Joanna Beyer, and cover artist Ponderosa Pine Design—have done an excellent job in bringing this book to fruition.

I contacted many sources in attempting to verify information I found about various crimes, accidents, and other incidents, but only a few responded: Tully Lehman at the National Insurance Crime Bureau; Tammy Sapp and Melody Kilbourn at the Florida Fish and Wildlife Conservation Commission; Col. James Vitali, undersheriff in the DeSoto County Sheriff's Office; Mona Rzeszewski, office specialist, Central Records Bureau, Collier County Sheriff's Office; and Tacita Barrera, archivist assistant at Ripley's Believe It Or Not! Others did me the courtesy of responding to let me know they could not help me, including Jacquie Weisblum, vice president of communications and engagement at the Everglades Foundation, and Karie Partington, media relations bureau manager at the Collier County Sheriff's Office. An astonishing number of others did not acknowledge my requests for information, but I have found this to be par for the course in writing a book of this nature.

In addition, my old high school friend Lawrence Margolis, Miami attorney, did me the favor of sorting out how a uniquely Everglades-based insurance fraud scheme works so I could warn my readers about it. The upshot: Run a check on the vehicle identification number (VIN) before you buy a used car.

It's long past time that I give tribute to the amazing service offered by Newspapers.com, which provides online access to the archives of more than twenty thousand newspaper titles, including all of the major newspapers in Florida. This service has made it possible for me to find information that had been locked away in morgues of clippings for many decades, key ingredients in telling a complete story and sorting out fact from fiction.

My agent, dear friend, and advisor Regina Ryan made the connections that brought me into this series, and I cannot say enough about her guidance and friendship over the last sixteen years. I was lucky to find her when I made the decision to become a travel writer; this relationship changed my life for the better. Thank you again, pal.

To the friends who are forever ready to hear my stories as I sit in my little office and write and who are equally ready with drinks and celebration when a manuscript is delivered, you have no idea what your support means to me. Ken Horowitz and Rose-Anne Moore, Lisa Jaccoma, Kevin Hyde, Bruce Barton, Martha and Peter Schermerhorn, Ruth Watson and John King, Cindy Blair, my cousins Paula and Rich Landis, and Diane and Chris Hardy always have my back.

And finally, and always, my husband, Nic Minetor, sits through the gruesome descriptions over dinner of the nasty stuff I discover, makes sure that I eat and take days off, supports my writing habit, and remains my rock after thirty-seven years. No one takes the brunt of these books like he does, and for this I am eternally grateful. On to the next.

Introduction

It's Not What You Think

I really thought this book would be about alligators.

Whenever someone has a violent encounter with an alligator, it becomes a top news story nationwide—so it seems like people fall prey to these prehistoric-looking reptiles on a regular basis. As I began a book about causes of death in the Florida Everglades, I assumed that I would find dozens of stories about people challenging the beasts, goading them into attack . . . or at least stepping into the path of one unexpectedly and losing a limb.

If not alligators, snakes rose to the top of the list of hazards I expected to uncover. Venomous snakes do indeed share the world with residents of South Florida, but miraculously, deaths by snakebite are nearly unheard of. The recent infestation of Burmese pythons also leaves humans pretty much to their own devices, as these invasive serpents choose small mammals, birds, and the occasional baby alligator for their meals.

So if not alligators or snakes, what kills people in the Everglades? Certainly not the kinds of things to which visitors lose their lives in the other places I've written about: Glacier, Zion, Acadia, and Rocky Mountain National Parks, as well as Mount Washington in New Hampshire and Mount Katahdin in Maine. After all, there are no mountains in the Everglades; the highest point in the entire region is just twenty feet. No one dies here by falling off some high precipice or by stumbling into a deep chasm. Even exposure to the elements takes very few lives in South Florida, where temperatures rarely rise so high that they might sap away a visitor's vitality, and they almost never drop below freezing. People do not venture into the backcountry accidentally here, as trails do not lead far before they give way to water. To go any farther, you need a boat, supplies, and a plan.

In short, the Everglades do not qualify for a book that chronicles the deaths of rugged adventurers, foolish hikers who ignore rangers' advice, or people who just run into bad luck on a trail, encounter fierce wildlife in a campground, or don't see an approaching change in the weather. The Everglades are something else entirely.

Before you assume that this book's subtitle could have been *The Further Adventures of Florida Man*, let me clarify that the vast majority of people whose deaths are detailed in the following pages did not die because of some stunt, or because they trusted their own poor judgment over common sense. Thousands drowned during the hurricanes of 1926 and 1928 when floods wiped out entire towns. A staggering number perished in accidents on the early versions of roads that crossed the region from east to west—two-lane blacktops that turned into ribbons of light-sucking blackness from dusk to dawn. Hundreds died in four commercial airline crashes, some of which had no survivors. A handful disappeared into the wilderness on boats or wandered off and became lost in vegetation that closed in over their head.

And far too many were murdered.

WHEN WE SAY EVERGLADES . . .

Let's be clear on the region covered in this book. The Florida Everglades, the only ecosystem of its type in the world, stretches from the Kissimmee Chain of Lakes in central Florida to Lake Okeechobee and then across the entire southern tip of Florida, south from Cape Coral on the west coast and West Palm Beach on the east. This book focuses on the wilderness and agricultural areas, not on the urban centers of Fort Lauderdale, Miami, Naples, Fort Myers, Everglades City, Homestead, and others, except for the boundaries of these municipalities that lie in open, unpopulated areas.

This book departs from the rest of the volumes in this series in that it does not focus exclusively on Everglades National Park or on the smaller national park properties in the area: Biscayne National Park and Big

Cypress National Preserve. Research has revealed that these are among the safest parks in the National Park Service system, with very few deaths that are not by natural causes. Everglades National Park does see its share of fatal auto accidents on the road that traverses the park to Flamingo, but these are infrequent; occasionally, someone goes missing among the backcountry islands and vanishes forever.

Instead, *Death in the Everglades* casts a wider net, exploring the nearly eleven thousand square miles of South Florida that the Everglades once contained. Originally the Everglades watershed south of Orlando ran into wide and shallow Lake Okeechobee, filling its 730-square-mile basin but maintaining a depth of just nine feet. The lake regularly overflowed in wet seasons, but this predictable course of events did no damage as the water ran out into what environmental advocate Marjory Stoneman Douglas called the "river of grass," some sixty miles wide and about one hundred miles long. From here, the water continued to flow slowly southward into Florida Bay. The natural flow acted to cleanse the water and enrich the soil, and the lack of settlements, towns, and farms throughout the southern portion of the peninsula allowed this annual refreshment to go on unabated and undisturbed.

Before the 1880s, the only inhabitants of the Everglades were indigenous people—in particular, the Seminole nation. Many Seminole were forced out of Florida by U.S. Army troops led by Andrew Jackson, a general during the First Seminole War in 1817. Florida was still under Spanish dominion then, but Jackson and his troops gained access because escaped Black slaves from Georgia often ran to Seminole villages in Florida, where they received refuge from people who knew what it was to be oppressed by white landowners. Jackson was charged by the U.S. government with retrieving these slaves and bringing them back to their owners.

When Jackson invaded and destroyed Seminole villages under this pretext, many Seminoles retreated south into the Everglades, an environment so dense and forbidding that the American soldiers could not gain a military advantage there. The native people's lot grew even more fraught with peril in 1819, when Florida became a U.S. territory and Jackson could wage war against them with few restrictions.

Jackson became the nation's seventh president in 1829, giving him the power he needed to pass legislation and carry out his plan of removing all native Americans from the southern states. With this deed done, he could award their land to rich plantation owners and industry. Jackson signed the Indian Removal Act in 1830, and some Seminoles recognized the inevitable and agreed to move west—but others could not imagine being forced to live on a reservation with their historic rivals, the Creeks, so they stayed put as long as they could.

American soldiers rode into Florida in 1835 to supervise the move, but the Seminoles who resisted initiated a seven-year conflict known as the Second Seminole War. While many of their kinsmen and their families obeyed the orders and left Florida for Oklahoma, some took refuge in the Everglades, making themselves virtually impossible to find. The U.S. government gave up on moving them out in 1842 with the realization that it had already spent nearly $40 million in its attempt to scrub all the Seminoles out of the state, with very limited success. Peace settled in for a few years, but war erupted a third time in the late 1850s—after which the U.S. military totaled its losses and decided the cost did not justify the result. Only a few hundred Seminoles had been removed after all that effort. The rest remained in the Everglades, where their descendants maintain a community to this day.

When They Nearly Killed the Everglades

After the Civil War and passage of the Homestead Act, opening land across the Midwest to ownership and agriculture, rampant development throughout the United States kept the wide-open land at the tip of South Florida in the public consciousness, no matter how impenetrable it appeared. What could be done to turn this fertile, ever-temperate "swamp" into habitable, farmable agricultural land?

Hamilton Disston, a developer from Pennsylvania, took on this challenge in 1881 by making the first attempt to change the course of the Everglades' water, allowing some land to emerge from the gently flowing slough. He bought up 4 million acres—that's roughly the size of the state of Connecticut—and built canals, and his aggressive interest in the region spurred others to get involved as well. The Everglades experienced the first of several land booms, with industrialists buying up areas that became the towns of Gulfport, Kissimmee, St. Cloud, and Tarpon Springs. Nearby, St. Petersburg saw an indirect jump in interest, with many people moving there from parts north. Never mind that Disston's canals didn't work and he ended up selling off his land at a fraction of his original purchase price; by the end of the nineteenth century, the Everglades were in the sights of many other developers. Disston's efforts led to the construction of two railroads in the state: one down the east coast and another along the western edge. Railroads led to opulent resorts on both coasts and finally to an east-west line from Tampa to Sanford, the first transportation across the marshland of south-central Florida.

The failure of Disston's canals did not deter others from attempting another audacious takeover of the region. An op-ed piece in the *Daytona Gazette-News* in 1901 noted,

> *Now the Everglades will soon become one of the richest portions of a rapidly developing state that allows nothing to stand idle—a company has been chartered which will probably drain it by cutting a ship canal, and another incorporated to cross it with a railroad and telegraph line from the Gulf to the Atlantic. Therefore the visitor of a few years hence will find a new scenic route opened for his exploitation . . . He can sweep across the state in a grand circle and return at his leisure to wonder how and why it was supposed the southern end of the state was once considered uninhabitable as well as uninhabited.*

Soon speculators like Richard Bolles, an entrepreneur from New Mexico, turned up in the Everglades and purchased nearly 1 million acres, launching development of drainage operations. Large investors bought up the land and threw the doors open to small farmers, calling their offering "the greatest land movement in the history of this country" in a 1910 advertisement. By that time, 9,300 Everglades farms had already been sold as "wet prairie." The Everglades Land Sales Company, based in Chicago, offered 5-, 10-, 20-, and 40-acre properties for one dollar per acre per month for twenty-nine months. Everyday citizens with a little savings to spend bought up the land in droves, ready to wait out the canal-building process until their land would be drained enough to begin farming. The more they bought, the more the price skyrocketed—up to fifteen dollars per acre by the 1920s.

If you've seen the Marx Brothers movie *The Cocoanuts* or if you've ever heard a tall tale that ends with "And if you believe that, I've got some swampland in Florida to sell you," then you have an inkling of what happened next. Massive storms in the 1920s (see chapter 4) wiped out so much new construction that developers began to ditch their building plans in droves. Small investors were stuck with land they could sell only at a considerable loss.

The government shifted its focus from drainage to flood control, so the Army Corps of Engineers arrived to attempt a massive flood control project, a network of levees, canals, pumps, and gates that diverted more than 1 billion gallons of water every day into the Atlantic Ocean. In the span of a few short years, the natural flow of the Everglades became so disrupted that entire species began to die out. Where water flow had once fed a unique ecosystem, only drought-stricken fields remained. Natural bacteria in the Everglades muck, exposed to oxygen for the first time, began to feed on the nutrients in the soil and wipe them out. The fertile topsoil turned to dust.

Enter the Central and Southern Florida Project for Flood Control and Other Purposes (C&SF Project), approved by Congress in 1948. The C&SF Project built levees, basins and canals, and pumping stations that moved water into and out of the area in times of drought and flooding. The newly dedicated Everglades National Park, however, fell prey to a drought caused by this system, and everything from alligators to raccoons left the park to search for water north of the Tamiami Trail. Crossing this main road put thousands of animals in peril, so much so that alligator numbers dropped into the endangered species range. Wading birds became victims of drought as well, their populations experiencing a ninety percent drop by the 1960s.

The final straw came in 1968 when developers proposed a new airport in the middle of the Big Cypress Swamp—one that would be larger than the major airports in Chicago; Washington, DC; New York City; and Los Angeles combined—to be positioned just six miles north of Everglades National Park.

Environmental organizations were outraged by the proposal and took action, demanding studies that eventually determined that the airport would dump four million gallons of raw sewage per day into the Everglades—among other noxious effects. One of the most dedicated campaigners against this project was Marjory Stoneman Douglas, whose efforts to educate the public about the Everglades' uniqueness in the world had already led to the establishment of the national park. Douglas created the Friends of the Everglades organization and recruited thousands of members, and their objections to the project finally reached the ears of President Richard Nixon. He came out on the side of environmental protection, established Big Cypress National Preserve, and killed any further discussion of an airport in the Everglades.

...AND WHEN THEY SAVED IT

After this near disaster, the entire world took notice of the one-of-a-kind ecosystem at work at the southern tip of Florida. In 1998, U.S. Secretary of the Interior Bruce Babbitt arrived in Florida with good news for families that still held their acreage in the Everglades: He brought $30 million with which to begin to buy back nineteen thousand acres along the edges of Big Cypress National Preserve and the eastern Everglades. The land the government purchased would help to restore the natural water flow through a northeastern section of the region. This followed a purchase the previous December of fifty thousand acres of sugar plantation near Lake Okeechobee, a $133.5 million investment announced by Vice President Al Gore.

Two years later, Florida governor Jeb Bush signed the Save Our Everglades Trust Fund, promising $200 million per year for the next ten years for "preserving Florida's quality of life by protecting our resources and avoiding further destruction to America's Everglades."

So the region narrowly escaped death—a level of destruction that would have crippled South Florida's water systems and natural environments, devastated populations of birds and animals, and wiped out the only ecosystem of its kind in the world.

Today's water management system, however, drains none of the mystery out of the Everglades.

People still take airboat tours to see what lies within the stretches of open water lined with seven-foot-tall sawgrass, ready for a taste of undisturbed wilderness they cannot reach on their own. Visitors seeking adventure take small watercraft through the Ten Thousand Islands National Wildlife Refuge to fish, look for bird species like mangrove cuckoo and roseate spoonbill, and enjoy an area that few people ever see. They drive the Tamiami Trail and Alligator Alley, the only two highways that cross South Florida from east to west, sometimes getting distracted by interesting wildlife or taking unnecessary chances in passing slower vehicles. Some folks wander along the edges of the region near their own homes and have encounters with animals that have the power to tear off a limb or take a life. And criminals take full advantage of the canals to hide their deeds, whether they push their stolen cars into deep water or use the waterways to dump a dead body.

Death in the Everglades tells just a handful of their stories. I've made the choice not to enumerate every one of the hundreds of auto accidents that still take place on the Tamiami Trail or Alligator Alley, as a few choice examples make the most important points about the hazards these roads can present. I also followed the example of my favorite television series, *Law and Order*, and only tell stories of murders that have a beginning, a middle, and an end—limiting the tales to bodies with positive identifications and killers that had their day in court. I dedicate an entire chapter to four major commercial airline crashes rather than listing the dozens of small, private planes that have met disaster in the Everglades, because these four serve as fine illustrations of the kinds of pre- and in-flight errors that end lives. The rest—alligator attacks, airboat disasters, and people who vanish into the wilderness—are the kinds of things that can only happen in this place, where the tip of the Florida peninsula makes its gradual descent into the sea.

In other books in this series, I have endeavored to be exhaustive in accounting for every death in a national or state park with as complete a list as I could compile. This simply was not possible for *Death in the Everglades*. It became clear as I researched this that many deaths involve the discovery of corpses that have never been identified, and still more were the result of catastrophic events in which hundreds or even thousands perished, their names long since lost to history. So you will not find a neat table of names, ages, dates, and causes of death in the back of this book.

Even though the Everglades have seen far more than their share of death over the last two centuries, there is no reason to think of this part of Florida as more dangerous than any other. My husband Nic Minetor and I have visited the region dozens of times without experiencing more than a few mosquito bites and a little sunburn, and there is no reason to believe that you will encounter any more hazards than we have. Stay on roads and trails, apply sunscreen and bug spray, use all of the navigation tools available to you if you venture into the backcountry, and don't poke alligators with a stick. Beyond these simple precautions, if you're not running illegal rum, playing fast and loose with the lawless, or trying to ride out a category 5 hurricane in the mangrove swamps, your visit will most likely be as pleasant an adventure as you could wish.

Just be careful out there.

The Desperado of Chatham Bend

So MUCH RUMOR AND LEGEND HAVE BEEN WOVEN INTO THE STORY OF farmer and entrepreneur Edgar J. Watson that it would take a trip back in time to determine which misdeeds attributed to him were actually his. His tale spans several states, more than twenty years of mayhem, three wives, and a trail of dead bodies—and while plenty of townsfolk on Chokoloskee Island and in Everglades City could list his victims, he managed to avoid ever serving time for murdering a single one of them.

Described as blue-eyed, red-haired, and quick to anger, Watson was born in South Carolina in 1855. He was still a young child when his mother packed up both of her children—the other was a sister named Minnie—and moved them to Fort White, Florida, to save them from their abusive father. Watson grew up in Fort White and soon showed signs that he had inherited his father's short fuse and proclivity for violence. He picked fights with his peers and eventually committed his first murders, killing one or more of his cousins—a crime heinous enough that he left the state to dodge law enforcement and seek his fortune elsewhere.

So far he had managed to escape the notice of the press, but Watson first rose to public consciousness in 1889 because of an even more reckless outlaw, the notorious Belle Starr. His brush with Starr set the course for much of the rest of his life.

Born Myra Maybelle Shirley in 1848 in Carthage, Missouri, Belle lived among neighbors whose names would become legend a few years later: Jesse James, one of the most famous of all western outlaws, and his scofflaw compatriots the Younger brothers. Belle and her parents moved to Scyene, Texas, in 1863, but the family maintained their relationship with these young men, and they became influential figures in their daughter's life. Belle was in her teens when she fell in love with an outlaw named Jim Reed, a comrade-in-arms during the Civil War with James, his brother Frank, and the Youngers when they served with Confederate bushwhackers known as Quantrill's Raiders.

Reed was not a criminal when he and Belle were married, but he soon befriended Tom Starr, an ostracized Cherokee whose murderous tendencies labeled him "an embarrassment to the Cherokee Nation," according to historian Richard D. Arnott. Reed cast his lot with the Starr clan, a band of horse and whisky thieves. Despite an attempt to settle in Paris, Texas, and become a farmer, Reed could not resist the outlaw life, and before long Reed and the Starrs were wanted for a stagecoach robbery between San Antonio and Austin where the robbers absconded with about $2,500. "One of the robbers was a woman," an account in the *Tahlequah Arrow* in Oklahoma notes, and many years later, Belle would take credit for being there.

In August 1874, police officers tracking Reed came upon him eating dinner at his home in Paris, Texas, and shot him dead. Myra—widowed and now known as Belle—had developed quite a resume of her own by this time. Newspapers wrote of her fine wardrobe, her ability as a crack shot while riding sidesaddle, and her genius in devising strategies for successful robberies and rustling operations. She earned the nickname "Bandit Queen" in the press, and as her legend grew, so did the credit she received for a wide range of crimes—whether or not she had any hand in them. "She has been credited with stealing from the rich and giving to the poor, cleaning out crooked poker games with her six-shooters, and galloping down city streets with pistols blazing," her www.historynet.com biography claims.

So the loss of her first husband did not slow her life of crime for more than a moment. Belle quickly married into the Starr family and settled with them in Oklahoma, and for the next decade she led "a more adventurous life than generally falls to the lot of women," she noted in an account she penned herself and gave to a reporter at the *Tahlequah*

Arrow in 1887. By the time she put pen to paper to capture her own tale, she was widowed once again and had settled in "a place of picturesque beauty on the Canadian River" in Oklahoma, where she "hoped to pass the remainder of my life in peace and quietude."

This was not to be, however—while she had chosen a spot where few people would happen upon her, she said, "it soon became noised around that I was a woman of some notoriety from Texas, and from that time on my home and actions have been severely criticized." Indeed, Jesse James himself visited her at her little ranch and apparently others of her previous cohorts followed, much to the chagrin of neighbors she described as "a low down class of shoddy whites who have made the Indian country their home to evade paying tax on their dogs, and who I will not permit to hunt on my premises."

Nonetheless, the string of outlaws visiting her property came to the attention of the Cherokee Tribal Council, who told Belle that she could remain on this land only if she entered into an agreement with the council that she would not harbor any more fugitives. It went against Belle's nature, but she felt a strong commitment to the quieter life she intended to lead, so she promised to turn away any of the bad lot among her friends.

Belle Starr did, however, enter into a land rental arrangement with one Edgar A. Watson, a man from Florida who was looking for land to farm. Watson and his wife paid Belle in advance for the use of some of her land, so everything seemed on the up and up until Belle had the opportunity to get to know Mrs. Watson well enough for Mrs. Watson to share confidences with her landlady. Mrs. Watson mentioned to Belle that Edgar was wanted in the state of Florida for murder.

Finding herself duped into giving refuge to a fugitive once again, Belle immediately attempted to refund Watson's money and send him packing. Watson would have none of it, insisting that he had paid for the land and he would continue to farm it through the harvest. In a confrontation that rose to the level of an argument, Belle threatened to contact authorities in Florida to tell them where he was. These were the magic words. Watson took back his money, packed up his wife and belongings, and rode off. Soon they found another farm in the area and rented land there.

Belle believed that she had resolved the matter and went about her business. She and her latest husband, Bill July (also known as Jim Starr), rode to Fort Smith on the morning of Saturday, February 2, 1889, where Bill had to appear in court on a charge of horse stealing, and Belle—so inured to the constant stream of arrests and charges in her life that she took her husband's hearing as nothing more than an errand—planned to do some shopping. They stopped for the night with friends in San Bois about fifteen miles east of their own ranch and split up on Sunday morning as Belle headed for home, planning to stop at a neighbor's home for a regular Sunday afternoon gathering.

Among the visitors was Edgar Watson. There is no record of what words they may have exchanged, but Watson left the neighbor's home shortly after Belle got there. After an afternoon meal, Belle bid her farewells, mounted her horse, and began heading homeward, passing within 150 yards of the land Watson had rented after leaving her property.

Moments later a shot rang out. Belle tumbled from her saddle, and quickly attempted to rise enough to see where she was wounded. Before she could assess her injury, the unseen gunman fired again, striking her in the neck and face. Belle lost consciousness as her frightened horse bolted for home.

When the horse arrived at Belle's house with no rider, Belle's daughter Pearl mounted her own steed and raced up the road to find her. She reached her mother minutes before she perished on the road, her wounds rendering her unable to speak.

Bill July was quick to accuse Watson of his wife's murder, and so many others piled on to call for Watson's arrest that law officers went directly to his cabin and took him into custody. Proving his guilt was quite another matter, however. The *Arkansas Gazette* reported on February 21 that July (referred to as Jim Starr) and Belle's daughter arrived in Fort Smith accompanied by ten witnesses who were ready to implicate Watson in the crime. All that testimony could not satisfy the judge, however. As the *Fort Smith Elevator* reported, "Testimony was taken on Friday and Saturday last [February 22 and 23, 1889] before Commissioner Brizzolara in the case of E. A. Watson, charged with the murder of Belle Starr. The evidence was all circumstancial [*sic*] and rather disconnected.

The commissioner is withholding his decision in the case until more witnesses are produced, and Jim Starr is now out summoning them."

The *Daily Arkansas Gazette* went so far as to speculate, "It looks probably that the circumstances will not warrant the commissioner in binding Watson over, and unless Starr succeeded in strengthening the case very materially the accused will likely go free."

Two weeks later, the press summed up the result in a squib: "A. E. [*sic*] Watson, accused of murdering Belle Starr, has been discharged for want of evidence."

No one else was ever accused of killing Belle, so Watson remained the primary suspect, but in an era before forensic examination of firearms and ammunition, the prosecution could not prove the case.

Seven months later, authorities arrested an E. A. Watson for stealing horses in Crawford County, Arkansas, along with another man, J. R. Dyal. The two thieves did not know that they had been observed by two law officers and two private citizens—perhaps the owners of the two stolen animals—until they stopped at a blacksmith shop to have one of the horses shod. When the officers approached them, Dyal immediately confessed, but Watson attempted to escape, running pell-mell for a nearby woods. The officers took Dyal into custody as the other two men obtained bloodhounds from a local contractor, using them to chase Watson down within a few minutes. Even then, with a full confession in hand from Dyal, Watson continued to proclaim his innocence, saying that the horses were not stolen at all—they were actually his.

When the officer brought Dyal in to repeat his confession in Watson's presence, however, Watson finally capitulated—but he asked for leniency because it was, he said, his first offense.

Was this E. A. Watson in fact E. J. Watson? It seems likely, according to C. S. "Ted" Smallwood, a pioneer and longtime resident of Chokoloskee, Florida, whose story is captured in a marvelous volume of local history, *The Story of Chokoloskee Bay County* by Charles W. Tebeau, published in 1955. Smallwood told the story of an Edgar Watson who lived in Chatham Bend and had a penchant for getting into trouble.

"The first time I saw Watson was on Half Way Creek in 1892 or 1893," Smallwood said. "He got into trouble in Florida and went to

Arkansas. Got in trouble out there with Belle Starr, an outlaw woman, and killed her. Then he came back to Florida."

Indeed, the area south of what is now the Ten Thousand Islands National Wildlife Refuge on the southwest coast of the Florida peninsula, so sparsely populated that an island dweller might not see other human beings for weeks at a time, proved to be the perfect hideout for a man perpetually on the run.

Smallwood had heard quite a number of stories about Watson even before he met him. He noted the farmer's short relationship with C. Quin Bass, a man whom newspapers up and down the nation's east coast reported in late 1893 had broken out of jail in Arcadia, Florida. Bass and an accomplice, James North, had both been convicted of murder, with Bass receiving a life sentence and North scheduled to be hanged. They made a break for it on December 27, 1893, and shortly thereafter, Bass made the acquaintance of Edgar Watson.

"Coming through Arcadia, [Watson] got mixed up with one Quin Bass, another bad actor," Smallwood told author Tebeau. How deeply Watson's relationship went with Bass is anyone's guess, though it certainly progressed to the point at which Watson was present while Bass tortured a victim. "Watson said Bass had a fellow down whittling on him with his knife, and Watson told Bass to stop; he had worked on the man enough. Bass got loose and came towards him, and [Watson] began putting the 38–S. & W. bullets into Bass and shot him down."

If Watson put an end to Bass's life then and there—and this seems likely, according to stories passed down through Chokoloskee Island dwellers to their children and grandchildren—he certainly had an alibi that would acquit him of the murder. While there is no available record of whether Watson was arrested for killing Bass, descendants say that he claimed self-defense, a plausible enough alibi. Watson may even have been lauded by the police for apprehending Bass, as he must have been wanted dead or alive at that point. This is all we know about Watson's encounter with this particular killer, however.

Watson's next nearly deadly confrontation served as a warning sign to his neighbors that this man could become violent with very little provocation.

Watson met John Joseph Brown and William Brown, two residents of the Halfway Creek area, and they told him about a piece of land ten miles down the Chatham Bend River that would soon be for sale. The Louisville and Nashville Railroad owned the land, but the company was very willing to sell forty acres of it to Watson. Later he acquired another tract of land for the scant sum of $250 from a widow in Key West whose husband, a criminal named Will Raymond, had been apprehended and killed by law enforcement. Whether Watson had any involvement in Raymond's crimes is unknown, but at this point Watson seemed intent on living the comparatively quiet life of a farmer and businessman. He settled in with his wife and children and set to work raising healthy crops of potatoes, tomatoes, and syrup boiled from the sugar cane he grew— enough to ship to the New York market. He named his syrup business Island Pride and bought a series of larger and more powerful boats to take his produce northward. As he prospered and gained power in the Everglades community, it seemed possible that his criminal days could be behind him.

"He must have been quite a man," local backcountry guide Frank Stapleton told the *Tampa Bay Times* in 2001, when he took a reporter out to the location of the long-since-destroyed Watson place for a Halloween jaunt. "There was once forty acres of cleared land and a two-story house, the largest one south of Ft. Myers."

One day, however, Watson visited an auction room in Key West and met Adolphus Santini, a resident of Chokoloskee Island. "They had some words," Smallwood said, "and Watson cut Santini's throat. Like to got him."

Luckily for both Watson and Santini, the cut did not kill the man. "They got Watson's knife away from him and got it quieted down," said Smallwood. "I think that scrape cost Watson nine hundred dollars"— perhaps in damages to Santini or to the owner of the auction room, if the struggle had resulted in broken furniture and destruction of property.

The next bit of murderous scuttlebutt tells of Watson buying a parcel of land on Lostman's Key, not far from his Chatham Bend property, from a man known as Winky Atwell. The land apparently already had tenants, a man identified only as Tucker and his nephew whose name has been lost to history. Despite Watson's insistence, Tucker refused to get off the newly acquired land immediately, asking that they be allowed to stay until they could harvest the crops they had already planted that season. "I heard Watson wrote him, and he writes him back a sassy letter saying he would not get off," said Smallwood.

A few days later, Tucker and his unfortunate nephew turned up dead. "They laid it on Watson," Smallwood concluded, though who "they" were in this context is difficult to say, as the local press did not cover this news item. Area residents who knew the Tuckers, including those who discovered the bodies when they washed up out of the river, voiced their insistence that Watson was obviously guilty of killing them. Watson himself pointed to his foreman, Leslie Cox, as the culprit. "None of the locals believed Watson," said the *Coastal Breeze News* in a 2020 recap.

Amidst all of these incidents, a terrible accident at the Watson farm may have precipitated another rumor about its owner: that when payday came around, he murdered his employees rather than handing over their wages.

The *Tampa Tribune* reported on January 14, 1904, that twenty-seven-year-old Bob Daniels, "well known as a 'cow-boy' and generally liked by all," had been working for Watson turning sugar cane into syrup for "some weeks past." While grinding juice from the cane, Daniels leaned in the wrong direction, and his apron became caught in the machinery. As he struggled to free himself, the feeder rollers caught up both his arms and the machine tore his arms right off of his body.

"Daniels was terribly mutilated and died in great agony several hours later," the paper reported.

No one held Watson responsible for this accident, of course, but it added one more body to the growing tally related to his farm and his business. And here's where the story takes a very dark turn.

Smallwood believed that Watson treated his employees well, but many area residents thought otherwise. According to a story in the *Coastal Breeze News*, Watson traveled out of the area to find employees to farm his crops and run his syrup mill: Black men with no particular ties and no family, who would not be missed. They worked the season for him on his remote farm, where they would be sequestered for months at a time, the only way in and out involving a twenty-mile canoe or motor launch trip. When the season ended and payday finally arrived, Watson "would kill them and toss their bodies into the river where the locals of Chokoloskee and Everglades City began to find them," the article said.

How could Watson possibly get away with this? Some say it never happened. A man named Alvin Lederer told writer John O'Connor with the *Oxford American* that he knew a guy who knew a guy. "I talked to a man whose father played fiddle at the Watson place," he said. "He said everybody got along. Nobody ever talked about Watson killing anyone." Watson's hands tended to be drifters who needed room and board, and by the end of the season they usually owed him more than the wages they had earned for the alcohol and tobacco he had provided to keep them happy. They left quietly, no better off than they were when they arrived, but no worse off either. "In all my years of research, I've never found any evidence of murder," Lederer said. As none of these rumored bodies seem to have names, Lederer may very likely be right.

Various longtime residents of Everglades and Chokoloskee have told reporters over the years that some of the locals did travel to Fort Myers to report the arrival of bodies on the shores at the base of their property, but the sheriff there could only tell them that he had no jurisdiction over Chatham Bend. Fort Myers was in Lee County, and the islands well south of there were officially in Monroe County, which encompasses the Florida Keys. Collier County, in which Chatham Bend is now located, was not founded until 1923. A trip to the Keys to report the string of bodies to the Monroe County sheriff may have simply been too difficult for locals whose boats had limited gas capacity . . . or perhaps they knew they had no proof, beyond the decaying bodies, that Watson was killing his own men. In short, no one near enough to Watson's place had any authority over his property or what he did on it. Watson had found himself an oasis of lawlessness, and legend and rumor suggest that he made the most of it.

In 1908, however, it looked like the law had caught up with him at last.

The previous summer, farmer San Tolen was found dead on his property near Lake City in Columbia County up near the Florida-Georgia border. This event did not draw much attention from the media, but when his brother, Mike Tolen, turned up dead by violent means on his own farm on March 23, 1908, law enforcement and the media took swift action. The death appeared to the sheriff to be part of an ongoing conflict between the Tolens and a group of desperados in the area, so they assembled a posse with bloodhounds and began tracking the murderous band. "Certain parties are suspected, and it is believed that arrests will soon be made," the *Gainesville Daily Sun* reported on March 26. "The trouble is the outcome of a family feud." A day later, the *Tampa Tribune* reported that the killer was still on the run: "So far officers have been unable to find the guilty parties."

Find them they did, however, and E. J. Watson appeared to be the ringleader, along with the man he called his foreman, Leslie Cox. Watson came to trial for the crime in Hamilton County, a change of venue requested by the defense. "There is much conflicting testimony and feeling ran high," the newspaper explained, but even in a different county, the jumble of circumstantial evidence resulted in a hung jury—so in December 1908, the second trial of E. J. Watson for the murder of Mike Tolen began in Madison County. By this time, Watson's prominence as a regional businessman had elevated the proceedings to what "promises to become one of the most notable [trials] in the history of Florida," the *Tampa Tribune* noted. Counsel for the defense included Col. Robert W. Davis, a leading defense attorney, assisted by Joseph Stripling of Jacksonville and "a firm of well known lawyers at Madison"—the county in which this second trial took place.

Attorneys presented testimony from more than thirty witnesses over the course of six days, and the jury finally received the case. The following day, on December 19, 1908, jury foreman J. R. Lang announced that they had found E. J. Watson not guilty. Watson was once again a free man.

After racking up yet another close call and serving no prison time, you might think that Watson would have counted his blessings, slunk back to his property in south Florida and kept his nose clean for the rest of his life. That, of course, is not how things went, though the story of Watson's last murder may be the murkiest of the entire lifelong compendium.

It's hard to know which account to believe, but let's start with Ted Smallwood's characterization of the events. Smallwood told Tebeau that he had done business with Watson for years, buying Watson's syrup to sell in his own store on Chokoloskee Island and buying other goods from Watson that Watson received in trade for his syrup in Tampa. "A man named Lesley Cox came down and I got a man to carry him down to Chatham Bend," Smallwood said. "Next day Watson came by and stayed all night on his way back home and we told him about it, and he asked if he looked like a preacher and we told him no. He said he might look like a preacher, but he wasn't."

By this time Watson knew that Leslie Cox, a slight, gray-eyed, twenty-year-old, had been sentenced to life in prison for murder and had escaped from a work camp upstate—so it may not have surprised him at all that the man had chosen to hide out in the Everglades. What he may not have expected, however, was the string of "bad actors" who began showing up at his property. In particular, a man Smallwood named as Duchy Melvin—the newspapers later called him Dutchy Reynolds—arrived several months after Cox. Smallwood said he was from Key West and that "he had killed a policeman and burned a factory or two."

Already working for Watson that season were Hannah Smith (later called Miss Ellen Smith in the news coverage), a woman who stood 6 feet 4 inches tall and who served as a farmhand, and a man referred to only as A. Waller. Some accounts also mention a fifth man, identified only as "the negro" in the press. As is all too often the case in Florida history narratives and newspapers of the early twentieth century, Black citizens were treated as insignificant and interchangeable, not important enough to identify by name. This man gave testimony that served to clarify some points and further obscure others.

Watson made a mid-October 1910 visit to Smallwood's store with Dutchy and his family, leaving Cox, Smith, Waller, and the unnamed worker out at his farm. Later Watson told Sheriff Tippens that he went to Chokoloskee with his family to avoid Cox, "who he knew to be a desperate character." He "had reason to believe" that Cox was preparing to kill everyone on the farm, he told the officer. If someone as tough as

Watson feared Cox, the press noted several weeks later, Cox must have been an especially threatening presence in the Watson home.

Cox apparently used the opportunity presented by Watson's absence—though why he needed an opportunity has never been established—to carry out several murders without Watson's direct involvement. The sequence of events gets cloudy here, but it seems that Watson returned home the next day to discover what had taken place while he was gone. Waller and Smith were dead—and before the day was out, Dutchy had been shot and killed as well. The unnamed Black worker had not been harmed.

On October 16, 1910, a fisherman named Cannon, who owned some land on Possum Key, started up the river in his boat to do some clamming with his young son. As they made their way up the Chatham Bend River, the boy spotted something he had never seen before: a human foot sticking up out of the water. He exclaimed to his father, but Cannon's vision was not as sharp as his son's, so he could not see this grisly find. He told his son to calm down, and they moved on up the river.

On their way back down the river to their property, however, the current had pushed the body until more of it rose above the water level. Now Cannon could see it was indeed the remains of a person—and when he pulled up next to it and saw the size 14 shoe on the foot, he knew it could only be Hannah Smith. As if this find on its own would not have made this day one they would never forget, the Cannons found two more bodies as they passed a shoal area.

"Let's go to Watson's and tell him," Cannon said, preparing to put his naphtha-powered motor into gear.

"No," said the boy, "let's go to the Clam Bar and tell them."

It took barely a second for Cannon to see the wisdom in this. He shifted into high gear and motored to Pavilion Key. Here they found a number of fishermen and told them of their find. "Some of the clam diggers came up Chatham Bend River and drug Hannah out and buried her," said Smallwood. However, according to an account by historian Kirby Storter, who was eight years old and living in the town of Everglades when the bodies were found, the other two bodies had been pulled out and buried by the time the fishermen arrived at the shoal area. The fishermen went on to Chatham Bend to confront Watson, but "apparently, he gave them no satisfaction," said Storter to reporter Nixon Smiley of the *Miami Herald* in October 1968.

Watson instead made his way to see George Storter, Kirby's father, about chartering a boat to take him to Fort Myers so he could report the crimes. "My uncle, Capt. R. B. Storter, ran boats between Everglades and Fort Myers and Key West, but he had refused to take Watson because he disliked and distrusted him," said Kirby Storter. "But my father interceded and my uncle agreed to take Watson as far as Marco."

From Marco, Watson hired a boat to take him to Naples, then engaged a mule team to get him to Estero. From there he took a motor launch to Punta Rassa and a steamer to Fort Myers. Then a hurricane came through the Everglades, raising water levels by as much as six feet, so Watson had to wait out the storm. He pursued this multipart excursion because he intended to bring Sheriff Frank Tippens with him to arrest Cox and prove himself innocent. The sheriff, however, told him what he must have already known: Tippens had no authority at Chatham Bend because it was in Monroe County. The sheriff did offer to go to Chokoloskee in a few days to try to calm the citizens down, but he would not return with Watson—so the farmer knew that he would be coming back to a glut of angry citizens who were sure he was the murderer.

Sure enough, the residents of Chokoloskee confronted him on his arrival there. He did his best to convince them that he had not killed his three workers, as this had all happened while he was not at home. "They ordered Watson to go get Cox, dead or alive," said Kirby Storter. "A fisherman [identified by Smallwood as Jim Demere] agreed to take Watson by motor launch to the mouth of the Chatham Bend River, where he would lend him a skiff to row the rest of the short distance."

Watson went home and came back alone a few days later, towing the skiff to return it to Demere. Anchoring his powered boat in the channel, he came into Chokoloskee in the skiff, near Smallwood's store.

"There was a crowd gathering at my landing and supposed there would be something doing when Watson got there," Smallwood said. "I could hear his boat coming down the pass and I did not want any of it.

Watson had done nothing to me." He left the landing and went to his house nearby, where his wife waited with Mrs. Watson.

Just two residents met Watson—Henry Short and Harry Brown—while a posse waited nearby, every one of them armed and ready to shoot.

Henry Short asked Watson where Cox was.

"I don't have Cox," Watson replied. "I shot him but he fell overboard and I couldn't recover the body. I did bring his hat."

Watson reached into the boat, produced a straw hat, and tossed it onto the shore—revealing a loaded and cocked double-barrel shotgun. Watson took aim at Short and fired ... but nothing happened. "The shells, soaked in the recent hurricane, failed to fire," said Storter.

Smallwood, foreseeing this confrontation, had sold Watson the shells the day before, knowing that they had been underwater during the storm.

What happened next has been artfully obscured by the citizens present, law enforcement, the courts, and a line of historians more than one hundred years long. "Pistols, rifles, and shotguns began to fire and Watson collapsed," Smiley told the *Miami Herald*.

Some accounts say that Henry Short took advantage of his close proximity to Watson and shot first, a clear case of self-defense when Watson pointed his own gun directly at him. A Black man surrounded by a white posse, Short would have been an easy sacrifice for the community, who could have blamed him for Watson's death rather than firing themselves. But the amped-up posse wanted blood, and they each wanted to be part of erasing this scourge of death and destruction that was Edgar J. Watson. Rather than let Short take the fall, they all opened fire at once. Dozens of bullets hit their mark, and Watson went down.

"My God, they have killed Mr. Watson!" his wife cried from Smallwood's kitchen when she heard the gunfire ring out. Mrs. Smallwood took a step toward the door, but Ted grabbed her and kept her from leaving the house until the shots had stopped and the deed was done.

Smallwood let several minutes pass before he stepped outside and made his way to the landing. Watson lay dead, just where the gunmen had felled him. "They carried him out to Rabbit Key and buried him," he said. Days later a party returned to Rabbit Key and retrieved the body, burying it properly in Fort Myers.

Such dramatic events could not simply be laid to rest, of course. A group headed out to the Watson place to be sure that Cox was dead and probably to kill him if he wasn't. Sure enough, they found his body about one hundred yards into the mangroves.

Kenny Brown, whose grandfather witnessed Watson's killing, told O'Connor at the *Oxford American*, "Grandaddy Brown said Cox was in the lookout at the Watson Place when Watson come for him . . . I guess he assumed something wasn't quite right and he started running back through the woods." Perhaps Watson tried to talk him out into the open, or maybe Cox shot first and missed. Whatever the scenario, Cox's body was found where it had dropped, with a bullet through the head. (Peter Matthiessen's masterful novelization of this story leaves Cox at large, but history says he did indeed die at the scene.)

The following day Sheriff Tippens arrived in Chokoloskee and summoned every member of the posse and all of the witnesses to court for a hearing. No motive for the killings at Chatham Bend ever came to light, as the only people who could have known did not live to tell their story.

The unnamed Black worker, who was taken into custody by law enforcement at the Watson place, told conflicting stories of what had happened. He said that he and Cox had been forced to commit the murders by Watson. "He tells of the shooting of the two men, and the desperate struggle the woman made when she was attacked," said the *Weekly Tribune*, the daily paper in Tampa, on October 27, 1910. "When all three had been killed, their bodies were cut open and weights inserted, so that they would sink beneath the waters of the bay. The body of the woman came to the surface, and was discovered by clam diggers." Another story suggested that Hannah Smith happened to be visiting Waller when he began quarreling with Cox, and Cox shot her accidentally when she attempted to intervene between them. Finally, the Black worker said that the whole plan was Cox's idea, but once Cox had killed Waller, Cox forced him (the Black man) to shoot the body as well—perhaps for Cox's concept of sport, or because he intended to pin the crime on a worker he considered expendable.

Whether the unnamed worker served time in prison or not is never mentioned by the press, but at least the story of Edgar J. Watson came to a fairly orderly close. His tale has fascinated novelists and journalists for more than a century, however, resulting in a great deal of speculation about his burial site (Fort Myers), whether or not he haunts the old Watson place at Chatham Bend, how many people he actually killed, and whether he got what was coming to him. No one was punished for his death, just as he was never truly punished for the crimes he committed. Perhaps that is a fitting end for this tangled fishnet of a story, one filled with holes, tall tales, half-truths, speculation, and all manner of unanswerable questions.

———

2

Plumage to Die For

BIRDERS VISITING FLORIDA FOR THE FIRST TIME OFTEN WONDER WHY the only American flamingoes they can find live in captivity, strutting their way across open lawns at Disney resorts or at attractions like Flamingo Gardens in Fort Lauderdale or Busch Gardens in Tampa Bay. Occasionally the appearance of a single wild flamingo on a sand bar in Florida Bay, or farther north in St. Mark's National Wildlife Refuge on the Florida panhandle, attracts resident and visiting birders alike to hike miles along sandy trails in hopes of catching a distant glimpse of the salmon-colored, hook-beaked creature. Otherwise, all of the flamingoes in Florida live under the care of humans.

How did a bird that doesn't live wild in Florida become so closely identified with the state? The answer reveals something darkly murderous that happened to statuesque wading birds throughout the state—and like all stories in this book, it also involves human deaths, though these were for a noble cause.

During the latter half of the nineteenth century, nothing made a woman more recognized for her fashion sense than feathers in her hat. Cleverly designed to incorporate plumes, wings, and even entire birds, these hats were a pricey luxury, but one within reach for women of their own means or those with affluent husbands. Demand boomed for these cunning styles, and with them the market swelled for the opulent feathers of long-legged wading birds of subtropical America.

Plume hunters scoured the southern states to find these birds and shoot them by the hundreds. Herons, egrets, spoonbills, ibises, and flamingoes nest in colonies, making them tragically easy targets because hunters who discovered their rookeries—with typically hundreds of nests—could sit day after day, shooting the nesting birds like targets in a shooting gallery. These hunters used rifles engineered to fire quietly to keep from spooking the surrounding birds, so they could take down an entire rookery in a matter of days—and the rewards were almost irresistible: A single plume from a "snowy heron" (today's snowy egret) might net its hunter as much as ten dollars (nearly $300 in today's currency), making successful hunters very rich in a very short time.

Flamingoes, of course, were especially highly prized for their shocking pink feathers, so they died by the thousands at the hands of these plumage harvesters. By the end of the nineteenth century, these birds had all but disappeared from Florida, mass casualties of human avarice and vanity. They were hardly the only victims, however: The American Ornithologists' Society has estimated that by the late 1800s, plumage hunters were killing as many as five million birds annually. Warblers and vireos became colorful ornaments, fastened whole onto hats; one advertisement from 1901 features a hat with an entire gull sitting atop it as if incubating eggs on the wearer's head.

Horrified by the senselessness of this, one wealthy socialite in Boston, Massachusetts, took action to put a stop to the slaughter of birds for the sake of fashion. Harriet Lawrence Hemenway and her cousin, Minna B. Hall, began to encourage their friends to stop wearing plumes in their hats and to take an interest in the birds themselves instead of the feathers that had been robbed from them. Holding tea party after tea party to plead their case with the fashionable women of Boston, Hemenway and Hall formed the Massachusetts Audubon Society in 1895, recruiting more than nine hundred women to join and inviting area ornithologists to lead the new organization. Mass Audubon's members agreed to boycott the plumed fashion trade, causing demand to plummet for festooned hats. Pennsylvania women followed suit in 1896, and the trend began to spread across the nation. Soon the Audubon Society became a national organization with tens of thousands of members, and a national outcry began to swell in opposition to the plumage trade.

This, however, did not stop the plumage hunters. By this time, they had strafed the southern states and cleared nearly all of the most highly prized wading birds out of their former rookeries—nearly all of them in the Everglades. Worse, by killing the adult birds on their nests, they left the young birds undefended and exposed, making them easy pickings for natural predators and so killing the next generation of plumed birds—which, of course, made the surviving birds even more valuable to the hunters and the fashion trade. In the late 1890s, an ounce of aigrette feathers—the showy breeding plumes of an egret—sold for $65 ($2,150 today), making an ounce of feathers far more valuable than an ounce of gold, which sold for $20.67 in the same period.

Not only was this practice of murdering entire rookeries economically unsustainable, but it also had the potential to wipe out virtually all of the birds in Florida. To prevent this, the nascent Audubon Society held the first meeting of its Florida chapter on March 2, 1900, with officers including New York Governor Theodore Roosevelt, Florida Governor W. D. Bloxham, Frank Chapman of the American Museum of Natural History, two college presidents, and several newspaper editors. This august group worked with the society to convince Congress to pass the Lacey Act, which prohibits trade across state lines of wildlife killed in violation of state law.

At that point, however, there was no state law in Florida that protected birds, so the Lacey Act needed a local boost to give it some teeth. In 1901, Florida Audubon managed to persuade the state legislature to pass what became known as the Model Bird Protection Law, prohibiting the killing of plumaged birds in Florida while allowing the hunting of game birds—turkey, grouse, quail, pheasant, and ducks—to continue.

Overnight all of the plumage hunters in Florida became poachers. Now someone had to enforce this law against the taking of feathers for fashion, so the National Audubon Society hired a former plumage hunter with an intimate knowledge of the Everglades, its birds, and the people who sought them: Guy Bradley, a man who would become "America's first martyr to environmentalism," according to his biographer, Stuart B. McIver.

"Bradley was unusually fitted for the work," said a lengthy piece in the *Morning Post* of Camden, New Jersey, in August 1905. "He was one of the best woodsmen the Audubon Society ever found. He was a crack shot, thoroughly familiar with all the birds in Florida, fair in his treatment of them—a bird lover, in fact." In his early thirties, athletic, and unafraid of spending copious amounts of time in the wilds of the Everglades, he took the year-round position and made his home in Flamingo his base of operations with his wife, Fronie, and two sons, Morrell and Ellis.

For three spring seasons, when the birds came into their most desirable mating plumage, Bradley did his best to keep the hunters in check, and the hunters made it their life's work to elude him. In one encounter, the Roberts gang—fathers, uncles, and sons of a wealthy and well-armed family—had targeted rookeries and shot all of the nesting birds, but when Bradley caught them with piles of dead plume birds in their boats, the gang turned their guns on him and fired—in one case close enough to knock Bradley's glasses off of his face. Arrests in these circumstances became virtually impossible. In spite of this, the diligent warden continued his work to protect the birds, knowing full well that any day on this job might be his last on earth.

He grappled often with other repeat offenders in his territory, one of the most pernicious of whom was Capt. Walter Smith, who "was in the habit of breaking these [game and fish] laws," the Miami *Daily Metropolis* noted in August 1905. Smith had a wife, Rebecca, and five children, and the Roberts gang had gone so far as to shoot up Smith's home with his children inside to intimidate him out of the plumage business. Smith became convinced that Bradley had made some kind of pact with the Roberts gang—one of whom, Gene Roberts, sometimes served as a deputy to Bradley—and that Bradley let them get away with shooting birds and, by extension, with shooting at Smith. So Smith wanted Bradley out of his way for good.

Bradley and Smith locked horns over more than plumage, however. Smith fancied himself a better candidate for the job of game warden than Bradley was, and in the winter of 1905 he openly challenged Bradley for the position. Smith made his play for the job by approaching Monroe County officials who knew him well—but this proved to be futile, because the appointment had to come through the Florida governor's office and the governor took recommendations for the position from the state's Audubon chapter. Even more important, the National Association of Audubon Societies provided the funding for the position. "And," wrote McIver, "Audubon wanted nothing to do with Walter Smith."

Bitterness grew between Bradley and Smith. Smith's oldest son, Tom, who was seventeen, repeatedly flouted the law by shooting birds in the open, leaving Bradley little choice but to arrest him more than once. Walter Smith, furious that Bradley would take Tom's youthful antics so seriously, became angry enough to threaten Bradley's life. "You ever arrest one of my boys again, I'll kill you," he said to the warden, according to McIver.

Bradley had no doubt that this was not an idle threat. When William Dutcher of the New York Audubon Society visited Bradley in Florida in February 1905, Bradley told Dutcher that the plume hunters "had sworn to take revenge on him for breaking up their business," the Star Special News Service reported. "He said his life was in his hands all the time, but that he had no intention of giving up his work."

On the morning of July 8, 1905, Bradley put his life on the line for the last time.

At about 9:00 a.m., Bradley had not yet left his home in Flamingo when he heard "suspicious shots," according to the *Morning Post*. "They came from a rookery in Oyster Keys." This pair of islands about two miles from Bradley's home and across the water from Flamingo hosted a rookery that attracted shooters on a regular basis.

His sailboat was becalmed on this still day, so Bradley took a rowboat and headed toward Oyster Keys alone. Two other game wardens in the area were out of town, so there was no one to contact for backup.

Bradley probably knew what awaited him, McIver suggests. He could see Smith's boat moored off one of the Oyster Keys, clearly lying in wait.

As Bradley approached in his dinghy, Walter Smith fired a single shot into the air, "a signal to his two sons to stop shooting cormorants and return to the schooner," McIver wrote. In full view of the approaching warden, Tom and Dan Smith fired into the rookery, collected two dead cormorants, and got back into their smaller boat to return to the family schooner. Meanwhile, two more boys were below in the schooner's cabin: Alonzo Baker, who had come along with plans to do some turtle hunting, and Frank Eldridge, who lived with the Smith family.

Bradley saw Tom Smith come out of the dense foliage with his dead birds, and he made ready for action. He let the young man board his father's boat, and then pulled up in his skiff alongside Smith's craft—Smith would later claim that he and Tom were "out turtling near Flamingo," according to the *Miami Metropolis*—and demanded that Tom surrender to him.

Smith told the police later that day that he demanded a warrant for his son's arrest, but Bradley didn't have one—he had seen Tom's poaching with his own eyes, eliminating the need for a warrant. Smith didn't care. He wanted a showdown with Bradley, so he accused him of being part of the Roberts gang, even of being "one of the fellows who shot into my house." To emphasize his point, Smith picked up a brand-new .38-caliber Winchester.

He claimed that Bradley then fired a wild shot with his pistol, sending both Tom and Dan sprawling to the deck. The bullet missed both boys and lodged in his boat's mast, Smith said. Smith fired an answering shot down into Bradley's boat—straight into Bradley's right shoulder.

Bradley fell forward into his skiff. "He succeeded in rising sufficiently to level his pistol at Smith but fell back before pulling the trigger," the *Daily Metropolis* said later that day, quoting Smith's account.

Smith knew that he had fired a lethal shot in front of several witnesses—even if they were his own sons—leaving him no choice but to give himself up. At that moment, however, his schooner was grounded in place until the tide came in. He was forced to wait until the water level rose again before he could head into Key West.

In the time he sat grounded, "Smith did not ascertain wether [*sic*] Bradley was dead or only wounded," the *Metropolis* continued, "but came in immediately to the city and gave himself up. He is now in the county jail awaiting investigation."

The *Miami Evening Record* took the implication a step further: "Smith, who did the shooting, quickly got his family together and departed for Key West . . . to escape a lynching at the hands of Bradley's friends."

A headline the following day made another attempt to set the record straight: Guy Bradley had been killed instantly "and then buried," the *Metropolis* said.

But Bradley had not been buried that day. His body remained adrift in his dinghy overnight, "and the murderers made no attempt whatever to care for it and it drifted about the bay until found the next day," the *Record* reported.

When Bradley did not come home that night, it fell to his deputy, Gene Roberts, to go looking for him the following morning. Roberts came upon the little boat drifting some distance from Oyster Keys. Guy Bradley lay dead in the bottom of the boat, his pistol by his side where it had fallen from his hand, a bullet hole straight through his chest, with an exit wound in his back.

Roberts went back for the coroner, Judge Lowe, and others who could help transport the body and build a coffin for it. The judge performed an inquest and discovered that the bullet had crushed two of Bradley's vertebrae on its way out of his back. They dug a grave on East Cape Sable, used some cypress they found there to construct a coffin, and gave Bradley something like a proper burial.

Deputy Sheriff Peter Knight left for Flamingo immediately and came back the following day with the four witnesses to the killing. He had also learned that after Bradley's death, Smith had ordered his employees to burn his own house down and leave the grounds, even though his home contained "some very fine furniture, among which was a piano," the Key West bureau of the *Metropolis* reported. The purpose of this destruction of his own property remains unknown.

Meanwhile in Key West, Smith attempted to hire a defense attorney, Louis Harris—but Harris told Smith he had been a close friend of Bradley's, so he would prefer to prosecute Bradley's killer rather than defend him. This did not stop Smith from telling Harris his side of the story in great detail, even though the attorney informed him that anything he said could be used against him in court. Smith attempted to make it clear that Bradley had shot first and that he had returned fire merely in self-defense.

Once retained by the Audubon Society to prosecute Smith, Harris told the media he didn't buy this story at all. "It is my belief that Smith deliberately sent his boy into the rookery for the purpose of enticing Bradley out and killing him," he said.

The *Morning Post* added more perspective on the plot: "Those shots were fired on that morning with the knowledge and well-founded belief that the warden of the birds would be sure to respond as soon as he heard them, and that they far outnumbered this skillful woodsman and splendid rifleman."

As the story unfolded over the ensuing several days, Audubon chapters across the country reacted with shock and sadness. "The cause of bird protection has its first martyr," the Star Special News Service declared on August 12, 1905, when news of Bradley's death reached the New York press. The news service quoted a statement by Dutcher, president of the National Association of Audubon Societies, who expressed the society's outrage over Bradley's murder.

A home broken up, children left fatherless, a woman widowed and sorrowing, a faithful and devoted warden, who was a young and steady man, cut off in a moment, for what? That a few more plume birds might be secured to adorn heartless women's bonnets. Heretofore the price has been the life of the birds; now is added human blood. Every great movement must have its martyrs, and Guy M. Bradley is the first martyr in the cause of bird protection.

While Smith awaited the empaneling of a grand jury, friends and relatives spoke out to the media about their doubts that Bradley's killing could have happened in self-defense. They noted that Bradley was left-handed, so if he took aim and shot at Smith, Smith's return shot would have hit him in the left shoulder instead of the right. In addition, all of the chambers in Bradley's gun were full, so it appeared that he did not take a shot at Smith at all. "As he [Bradley] was a sure shot, Smith would have been hit had he opened fire upon him," the *New York Herald* reported.

Despite the doubts of an inflamed public, the engagement of a second prosecuting attorney from Miami (Col. J. T. Sanders), and a period of five months to gather evidence, the state "made out a very weak case," the *Miami Metropolis* reported on December 6, 1905. Sanders found himself scrambling to bring witnesses to Key West for the grand jury hearing, as the state had not summoned them to give testimony. Once they arrived, the witnesses gave "testimony of no importance to the State," and all of the witnesses corroborated Smith's story that he had pulled the trigger in self-defense.

Reasonable doubt had clearly been established. The grand jury returned a decision of "no true bill," meaning that the jury had not heard sufficient evidence to believe that Smith had committed a crime and should be prosecuted. Smith was released from jail, where he had been held since Bradley's death pending the grand jury hearing.

No one served time for the murder of Guy Bradley. After his violent death, however, the media took it upon themselves to shame women who continued to wear hats decorated with aigrette plumes. A particularly eloquent accusation appeared in the *Times-Tribune* of Scranton, Pennsylvania, in September 1905.

During past years the sight of any aigrette tip has called to our minds the picture of old birds bleeding and dying with the feathers stripped from their backs during the breeding season and young birds left starving in their nests. This has told a story so plainly that the wearer has invariably been considered either ignorant, thoughtless or cruel. In the future the aigrette tip on a hat will stand not only for the death of beautiful and innocuous birds and the starvation of their young, but will also speak of the assassination of a human being at his post of duty trying to suppress the illegal traffic through which the supposed adornment has been made possible. In regard to imitation tips, it would seem that thoughtful persons would not be willing to imitate any custom or article that tells a story so cruel.

But more human blood was spilled before the plumage trade came to an end. On November 30, 1908, another warden, Columbus G. McLeod, disappeared while protecting rookeries in Charlotte Harbor north of Fort Myers. Much less is known about McLeod and his death than we know about Bradley, but according to a 1909 issue of *Bird Lore*, the Audubon Society's magazine, although McLeod's body never came to light, his patrol boat did, sunk in the harbor with two heavy sandbags "under the thwarts" to keep it underwater. "In the boat was discovered the warden's hat with two long gashes in the crown which had evidently been cut with an axe," the story said. "In the cuts were bits of hair and considerable blood. There was also blood found in the boat."

McLeod's apparently violent death "broke the log jam of opposition to prosecution of plume hunters," wrote Lindsey Williams and U. S. Cleveland in their local history *Our Fascinating Past: Charlotte Harbor, the Early Years*. Laws against killing plumage birds achieved passage across the nation, including the New York State Audubon Plumage Law in May 1910, which banned the sales of the plumes of native birds in the state. Taking the fashionable ladies of New York City out of the plumage trade dramatically reduced the demand for such hats, and in 1911, Parisian haute couture designers declared the feathered hats *déclassé*, killing their popularity for good. Artificial flowers, oversized bows, and other decorations soon became the rage, and fluffy, farm-raised ostrich feathers, removed from the birds painlessly and without killing them, replaced the aigrette. Eventually, fancy hats became impractical for working women and they vanished from store shelves for the long term.

Bradley and McLeod earned permanent places in the world of bird conservation. Everglades National Park named a trail from the Flamingo Visitor Center to Flamingo Campground for Bradley, and it plans to rename its renovated Flamingo Visitor Center for the fallen game warden as well. The National Fish and Wildlife Foundation created the Guy Bradley Award "to recognize achievements in wildlife law enforcement." In Lee County, the Columbus G. McLeod Preserve, a nine-acre island on the Caloosahatchee River, protects large wading birds including white ibis and little blue heron, as well as red-shouldered hawk and other species. The sacrifices Bradley and McLeod made for the cause of bird protection should never have been necessary, but they were not made in vain.

3

The Murderous King of the Everglades

If you could go back to the 1910s and ask any of the Seminoles living in the Everglades about Desoto Tiger, they would all have positive things to say about him. The *Fort Myers News-Press* quoted his countrymen on January 18, 1912, saying that Tiger was "one of the most prosperous and intelligent of the Seminole Indians," a trapper and trader with thriving business connections and a reputation for providing quality merchandise—otter hides in particular—to customers throughout South Florida.

Tiger, the son of Cow Creek chief Tommy Tiger, had been planning to move to Oklahoma in the spring of 1912, perhaps to be closer to family descended from ancestors forced out of Florida during the removal of the 1830s. Unfortunately, an event no one saw coming ruined his plans.

On December 29, 1911, Desoto Tiger made ready to paddle to Miami from a Seminole camp on the shores of Lake Okeechobee with a load of otter pelts from the hunting and trapping endeavors of several members of the tribe. He was just about to push off from the shore when a white man stepped forward and asked to accompany him "as far as the dredge working in the canal," according to the *News-Press*.

That white man was John Ashley, and he was not a stranger to the Seminole. He and his eight siblings were born in Buckingham, near Fort Myers, and made liberal use of the Everglades for hunting, trapping, and fishing as they grew up. In the 1890s when John was still less than ten years old, the family moved to Pompano so his father, Joe Ashley, and his oldest brothers could take jobs building the new railroad under construction on both Florida coasts. In 1911 they moved to West Palm Beach, where John—now a young man in his twenties—became a fixture in the Everglades as he honed his skills for trapping otters and capturing alligators. He knew the value of a good pelt and what made one better than another.

Ashley showed up right around Christmas 1911 at the dredge *Caloosahatchie,* according to the dredge's captain, M. E. Forrey, who provided sheriffs with the most complete description of what may have happened between Ashley and Tiger. Ashley had come from Fort Lauderdale with "several gallons of whisky." Some of the Seminole visited the dredge operation at the time, and on Christmas Day, they partook of the whisky "freely"—so much so that one of them actually fell from the upper to the lower deck of the dredge. He sustained injuries severe enough that he was taken to Fort Lauderdale for treatment.

Meanwhile, six Seminole had been hunting in a nearby woods for several weeks, pitching a camp "between four and five miles back from the dredge." Their work had yielded a total of eighty-four otter hides, which was quite a trove of valuable pelts. Forrey speculated that Ashley brought this party some of the whisky "with the intention of getting the Indians drunk and thus securing the otter skins."

Christmas came and went, but Ashley didn't leave. The Seminole became eager to get rid of him, certain that he was hanging around in hopes of finding an opening to steal their otter hides. Finally, on Friday morning, December 29, the group determined that Desoto Tiger would take the entire supply of hides out to the dredge for safe keeping. "Ashley volunteered to accompany him," Forrey told the sheriffs, "and that was the last the Indians ever saw of either."

Later, Tiger's brother, Naha, told Forrey that not long after Desoto and Ashley left the camp, he heard two gunshots.

When Tiger did not return that night, his uncle, Jimmy Gopher, made the trip out to the dredge the next morning to find him. The captain initiated an investigation, polling the crew to see if they had seen anything suspicious. "Two persons had seen the Indian and white man in the boat together about 8 o'clock Friday morning," he said. "At 10 o'clock that morning the dredge crew saw Ashley go by the dredge in the boat alone." They did not realize the significance of this until Gopher came looking for Tiger.

Just then the Seminole who had taken the injured man to Fort Lauderdale returned and told the others that he "had seen Ashley in the canal near Lauderdale about 4 o'clock Friday afternoon." Ashley had left his own boat at the Seminole camp, so he was still in Tiger's boat. Later that day, Gopher found Tiger's oar stuck in the sawgrass just about two miles from the dredge.

Seeing the evidence against Ashley mounting, Captain Forrey wrote a letter to Sheriff Baker in Fort Lauderdale about his suspicions that Tiger had come to a bad end at Ashley's hands. He sent Gopher to deliver the letter to Baker late Saturday, and early the next morning, December 31, Forrey organized a search of the canal near where the oar was found. It took very little time to locate Tiger's body, which rose to the surface in the wake of the search vessel.

They retrieved the body and performed a thorough examination, determining initially that Tiger had been shot in the back—a coward's shot—and that his boat and his cargo of otter pelts were nowhere to be found. The killing bullet entered the body under the right arm and lodged just above the heart. Forrey had the foresight to remove the bullet before burying Tiger.

The dredge crew buried the body on the banks of the canal between 3:00 and 4:00 p.m., Captain Forrey noted. Desoto Tiger was about twenty years old, and his death widowed his young wife and left his two children, a five-year-old boy and a baby girl just three months old, to grow up without a father.

"Indians at once left by canoes in pursuit of Ashley," the newspapers said. They traced him "to Fort Lauderdale, where he took the train to Miami and disposed of the hides ... the presumption being that the robbery was the cause of the murder."

Canoes can only go so fast, so the Seminole party did not make it to Miami until Ashley had already disposed of the hides, traveling with a man and two women in an automobile. They were shocked to discover that Ashley had actually been arrested in Miami on a petty charge, had paid a fine, and then had been released by police. "At the time of his arrest, the officers did not know of the more serious charge against him, the report of the murder not reaching here until after his release and escape," the *News-Press* explained.

Notably, Ashley no longer had the otter pelts with him when he was arrested. He had sold them to Girtman Brothers for the tidy sum of $584—the equivalent of nearly $17,000 in today's dollars. Girtman produced a record of the purchase of the hides, confirming that it was John Ashley who had offered them for sale.

News coverage already buzzed with Ashley's guilt. "While purely circumstantial, the evidence against Ashley is complete and leaves no room for doubt that he was the perpetrator of the crime," the *News-Press* said. In addition to his appearance at the dredge without Tiger and the receipt for the hides, "the murdered body of Desoto contained two bullet wounds, and the ball which was extracted from the body provided to have been fired from a .38-.55, which caliber of gun was carried by Ashley."

Despite its thorough coverage of the details of Tiger's murder, the *Miami News* felt the need to clarify the veracity of the story. "It is conceded, whatever their shortcomings in other respects, that what a Seminole Indian says is true," the reporter wrote—about as left-handed a vote of confidence as anyone can muster.

Perhaps this makes the newspapers' close attention to Desoto Tiger's death and the ensuing manhunt just that much more of an anomaly at the time. Was it the fact that the murderer had headed straight for areas populated primarily by white people that raised their interest? Or was it the reward that Palm Beach County sheriff Baker offered—just $50, but par for the period—that elevated this story's importance for the general public? Whatever the reason—and we can't rule out genuine sympathy for the young Seminole gunned down in the prime of his life—the media continued to publish every morsel of information they could find about Desoto Tiger, John Ashley, and the heinous crime that had been committed.

The attention could not bring Ashley to the surface, however. On January 16 the *Tampa Times* reported that after his arrest and release in Miami, Ashley had fled the country. Even the arrival of an investigator from Oklahoma, a Sioux tribesman named J. W. Strongheart who served as assistant Indian counselor for the state, could not increase the urgency of finding Ashley and bringing him to justice. Strongheart called for a larger reward to be offered and worked with the Palm Beach commissioners to send a resolution to Tallahassee, asking the governor to allocate state funds for such a reward. (Strongheart was later discredited as something of a con artist and thrown into prison in Key West, but that had little effect on the manhunt.)

As it turned out, Ashley had not left Florida. Instead he disappeared into the Everglades, where he knew the waterways, hummocks, and islands as well as the Seminole did. Here he remained for more than two years with his brother Bob, evading capture as one posse after another attempted to penetrate the wild country and find their way to his camp. "It is said that two deputy sheriffs, at least, came out second best in their efforts to arrest him," the *Herald* reported.

Indeed, two deputies sent by Palm Beach County sheriff George Baker actually found their way to Ashley's camp near Gomez in April 1914, and the encounter did a great deal to build up the legend around this hermit of the Everglades. When the deputies emerged from the surrounding vegetation and stepped into Ashley's camp, it appeared that no one was there. In a moment, however, they heard a male voice say something to the effect of "Stay where you are. Put your guns down. Put up your hands, and step out in the open."

The deputies had two choices. They could hold onto their guns and sacrifice their lives in the next few seconds to a gunman they couldn't even see, or they could lay their guns down on the grass and do as the voice told them. They chose to live.

When they put down their guns and stood up, they saw a campfire burning in a clearing a few feet away. There sat John Ashley and his brother Bob, cooking over the fire. Neither of them even looked in the deputies' direction. John told the two men that he would let them walk out of the camp with their lives if they would deliver a message for him: "Tell Sheriff Baker not to send any more chicken-hearted men with rifles." News reports also suggested that Ashley beat one of the men.

The deputies left, thanking divine Providence for allowing them to escape the confrontation with their lives. Their story only served to solidify the respect that local Floridians had for John Ashley, however—so much so that even those who knew where his camp was, or who knew his whereabouts from day to day, would not give the information to law enforcement. So Ashley continued his sojourn in the Everglades, operating stills and supplying locals with moonshine—and sometimes with money or food when he knew that times were hard for the poorer folks in the area.

Every once in a while an "Ashley sighting" would pop to the public's attention. Roy Chaffin, a civil engineer, told the tale of his trip from Stuart by motorcycle. As he traveled down an open and lonely stretch of road, two men leapt out of the roadside foliage with guns drawn, ready to attack him. They swore at Chaffin, hit him in the face, and fired one shot in his direction, but he soon realized that the men had mistaken him for a deputy sheriff, and in time he convinced them that he was not involved in law enforcement, so they stepped back and let him go on his way. Chaffin asserted that one of the men was John Ashley.

With no arrest of Ashley in sight, the Seminole community's anger and frustration finally boiled all the way up to Washington, DC, where the federal government stepped into the fray. US special officer of the Indian Service Thomas E. Brents received a transfer from a post out west, moving to Florida for the specific purpose of bringing John Ashley to justice.

He began his work with a visit to Kissimmee, where James M. Willson Jr. and his wife, Minnie Moore-Willson, had been working diligently with the Seminole to solve the case. Minnie Willson wrote the respected book *The Seminoles of Florida* in 1896, a second edition of which had just come out in 1910, and the white couple was "known all over the South as the friends of the Seminole, working earnestly in the endeavor to bring justice against the slayer," the *Tampa Tribune* said in April 1914. Their influence changed the timbre of the manhunt: After his interview with the Willsons, Brents "asserted when he left here that he would locate the man if he were still living."

Brents brought his skill in working undercover to the difficult case. He disguised himself as a tramp, a drifter who dodged law enforcement as ardently as did the Ashleys. Befriending Joe Ashley, the brothers' father, he made the man feel so comfortable with him that Joe actually escorted Brents right to his sons' camp deep in the Everglades.

Knowing the location of the camp, Brents then sent two officers he had brought with him from Oklahoma to the camp, where they engaged Ashley in a negotiation. They made it clear that the government would hound him indefinitely and would eventually bring him in dead or alive.

"Ashley, realizing this his only resource to have his life, at any rate temporarily, was to give himself up, asked for three days more time," the *Orlando Sentinel* said. This time "was granted him, and he delivered himself up, in accordance with his agreement, to Sheriff Baker on Monday evening."

So it was that on April 27, 1914, John Ashley gave himself up to authorities. After more than two years on the lam, what well-reasoned argument made him turn himself in? The *Tampa Times* suggested that he was "tired of evading the officers and leading a lonely existence for two years in the Florida Everglades back of West Palm Beach."

With the killer finally in custody, the court in West Palm Beach moved swiftly to bring him to trial in June 1914. Seminoles from up and down the east coast crowded into the courtroom, and the federal government sent US Indian commissioner L. A. Spencer to monitor the proceedings. Seminole witnesses who had moved to Oklahoma received subpoenas, returning to Florida to testify.

Witnesses included a string of people from Miami who had been approached by Ashley in his attempt to sell the otter hides, including Girtman—the only one who could produce an actual receipt for the sale.

But what had seemed like an open-and-shut case did not proceed as smoothly as the eager audience expected. No witness could say that they saw Ashley fire his gun at Tiger. The defense quickly rejected the evidence as circumstantial—even the bullet Forrey had dug out of the victim and its apparent match to the gun Ashley owned. The jury wavered in its ability to commit to one verdict or the other. In the end they could not break their deadlock. The judge had no choice but to dismiss them, ruling the proceedings a mistrial and ordering a second trial to begin in November.

The court moved swiftly to prepare for a second trial. By mid-November 1914, jury selection got underway and John Ashley spent several glum days sitting in the courtroom and listening as the attorneys screened one hundred "talesmen"—people summoned to jury duty when the first pool of potential jurors has been exhausted. So many people had followed Ashley's first trial for this murder that a whole new crop of summons had to be executed just to find people who had not already come to their own conclusion about the verdict. "On Wednesday, November 11, a venire of 100 talesmen was exhausted, without one single juror having been seated," the *Miami Herald* reported. The court brought in another one hundred men, and after two more tedious days, the attorneys managed to select eleven jurors, the *Herald* said.

Ashley scanned the faces of the final panel of jurors and most likely knew that these men would be only too happy to convict him. He left the courtroom in the custody of Deputy Sheriff Bob Baker, but by the time Baker brought him back to the jailhouse, Ashley had determined that his only hope for survival was to bolt.

Baker paused in front of Ashley's cell door for a few seconds, turning his back on the prisoner and fumbling with his keys as he unlocked the door. Ashley saw his opening. He ran, sprinting past the jailor and out the rear door of the jailhouse, clambering up a pile of sand and over a ten-foot fence. In a startling breach of security protocol, Baker had not handcuffed the prisoner.

Deputy Baker drew his gun and fired at Ashley as the fugitive vaulted over the fence. His bullet missed, lodging in the fence. Ashley kept running until he came to another fence, forcing his way through it and turning down the alley beyond. He disappeared into the dark night.

"Sheriff Baker is prostrated over the affair and under a physician's care," the *Herald* reported. "He has offered a reward of $1,000 for Ashley, dead or alive."

Soon law enforcement learned that this escape was not the opportunistic break that it first appeared. A car had been waiting for Ashley beyond the fences. His brothers, who had been by his side in the courtroom throughout the first trial and the jury vetting process, had helped Ashley build a plot to elude the police once again.

"Sheriff Hardie has been notified to be on the lookout for him, as have several others sheriffs and deputies," the *Miami Herald* reassured readers on Sunday, the day after the jailbreak. "A posse has been organized in West Palm Beach and a general man-hunt is on."

The posse immediately headed for Hobe Sound, where Ashley appeared to be headed, but they found no sign of him or any accomplices who might have assisted with the jailbreak. They returned that night empty-handed with a plan to set out again in the morning, when they would have a better chance of finding any clues. Their all-day search the following day yielded nothing, however. "It is generally believed in West Palm Beach that Ashley has made good his escape and that he will never be captured alive," the *Miami Herald* said on Monday, November 16. "Owing to Ashley's remarkable marksmanship, the posse will be careful in their attempt to capture him, as it spells suicide for anybody who gets within range of his rifle." The paper confirmed law enforcement's certainty that Ashley's accomplices had brought him guns and ammunition.

Everyone knew that Ashley and his gang had vanished into the Everglades once again, but the location of his camp remained a mystery. "He is perfectly at home in these practically impassable swamps," said the *Herald*, "and after killing the Indian, lived there for about two years, evading arrest."

With no defendant, the trial could not begin on Monday, November 16 as scheduled. Judge H. P. Branning discharged the jury Monday morning, while Sheriff Baker announced a reward of $500 for Ashley's capture. By November 18—just a few days after Ashley's escape—authorities and the volunteer posse announced that they had abandoned the search. "No further attempt will be made to take up the trail, unless it is done by United States authorities," the *Miami Herald* reported.

This drew outrage from some in the local media. How could a "cold blooded and calculating" murderer be allowed to skate after taking a life for the sole purpose of profiting from the sale of some otter skins? "It might be added that the prediction is freely made that he will never be caught," the *Orlando Evening Star* grumbled. "If the sheriff had been vigilant in the matter it is hardly necessary to say that no such prediction would be made. Such incidents go a long ways toward lessening respect for the law and our system of administering justice."

Bolstered by working as a team to pull off John's escape, the Ashley brothers and their father launched lives of crime that made them some of the most notorious criminals in the country. Rather than lying low for the three months after the jail break, the Ashley gang—Joe, John, and his brother Will, along with accomplices outside the family—went on a robbery spree that signaled their whereabouts to law enforcement time and time again, even as the gang racked up thousands of dollars in stolen cash.

In early February 1915, four masked hoodlums brandishing revolvers attempted to hold up Florida East Coast Train no. 33 as it passed through Stuart. They boarded the train to steal jewelry, cash, and other belongings from passengers in the observation car but were foiled when several women, seeing the gunmen occupied with shaking down the passengers at the front of the car, ran to the next car and told the porter of the robbery in progress. The clever porter locked the door between the pullman and observation cars, preventing the robbers from going forward. This obstruction thwarted the thieves' plans, so they ditched the caper, jumping off the train and running back into the woods.

The week before, the gang had terrorized two hunters from Iowa and their local guide, Claven Myers, at their camp in the woods near a canal. Gang members suddenly appeared on the banks of the canal, their rifles out and ready to shoot. "Build up your fire a bit if you want to see blood," John Ashley called to them. "Business is picking up."

Myers recognized the voice and knew immediately that this was the Ashley gang, quickly surmising that he and the hunters had been mistaken for police or a posse. He had no time to set the record straight, however, because the gang opened fire. Myers felt the searing pain of no less than three bullets connecting with his body. A crack shot himself, Myers could have fired back and probably taken out one or more of the criminals if he'd had a gun in hand—but all the hunting party's guns were on the other side of the campfire, leaving them no way to reach them.

Instead, the hunters ran for the woods, passing their tents as they dove into the darkness. Ashley and his thugs believed that the men had gone into the tents for cover, so he and his men riddled the tents with bullets. "Pots, pans and bedding were pierced, while their big touring car behind the tent was put out of commission, six holes puncturing the radiator," noted the *Orlando Evening Star*.

Finally the gunmen ran off to the north, satisfied that they had wiped out a trio of lawmen. The two men from Iowa realized that Myers had been wounded, so they ran to a nearby farmhouse, borrowed a mule team, and drove to Boynton as fast as the animals could go. Meanwhile the farmer alerted Deputy Sheriff C. E. McIntosh, who came on the double with "several fearless citizens of Delray and Boynton," as per the *Evening Star*. They searched the area and found plenty of empty shotgun shells, while one of the men took Myers to a doctor. Myers survived the ordeal, though one of his hunting dogs sustained a fatal wound.

So on the bright, chilly morning of February 23, 1915, law enforcement up and down the coast were on high alert for the Ashleys' next crime. Soon they heard that the gang had held up a cashier named Wallace at the Bank of Stuart, coming away with about $4,500 in cash. This time law enforcement officials were ready for them. Sheriff Baker and a posse of thirty-three men stuffed themselves into two automobiles and hit the road from West Palm Beach.

They pursued the thieves into the swamp about six miles west of Hobe Sound. This time the posse was hot on the gang's tail, and they would not fail to bring in the man the media called "the Indian slayer" and make him face justice.

They fired shots at the gang—but it was one of Ashley's own men who pulled the trigger that resulted in Ashley's downfall. Ashley himself said later that the gang member "tried to get him out of the way that he might get a bigger share of the booty," the *Fort Myers News-Press* said on February 26. The *Daytona Daily News*, meanwhile, reported that the shot came from an "accidental discharge of a gun in the hands of his brother, who became excited as the gang fled from Stuart in a requisitioned automobile driven by Frank Coventry."

The shot hit Ashley squarely in the jaw and shattered the bone, then exited his head through his eye, draining the fight right out of him and blinding him in that eye forever. He gave himself up to authorities then and there, declaring "that he would rather die a prisoner than in the Everglades," according to the *Daytona Daily News*. "Ashley was rushed to a local physician," the *News-Press* added, no doubt with a substantial police escort.

Sheriffs arrested Joe and Will Ashley as well, but the other two robbers got away with the cash. "Posses have started out again and are determined to capture the two other robbers, but they expect trouble before they are finally taken," the *News-Press* warned.

All three of the Ashleys confessed to the stick-up at the bank, however, perhaps seeing it as clearing the air while John lay on his apparent deathbed. Doctors predicted that he would not recover from his massive head injury.

Ashley did pull through, miraculously, and soon found himself back in jail and under heavy guard as a grand jury reviewed all of his crimes. On March 12, John and Bob Ashley and one of their allies, Kid Lowe, were indicted for robbing the Bank of Stuart. And on March 29, John Ashley finally faced a jury in the court's third attempt to try him for the murder of Desoto Tiger. This time the state's attorney, John C. Gramling, secured a change of venue that allowed both legal teams to select a complete jury, something that had not been possible in Palm Beach County the year before. The trial took place in Miami with another long jury selection process and one hundred talesmen to interview.

Showing signs of fatigue from his slow recovery from the gunshot wound, Ashley sat in the courtroom with a black patch over his right eye and bandages over his jaw and much of his face. Curious onlookers packed the courtroom even for jury selection, and more collected outside as the trial got underway. They all wanted to be present for the big moment when John Ashley himself took the stand and testified in his own defense.

Ashley told the jury that while he and Tiger were in the canoe on their way to the dredge, Ashley had concealed two bottles of whiskey he had brought with him, and the bottles were suddenly revealed as the canoe jostled its way down the canal. "After seeing it he wanted a drink," Ashley said, "and sooner than be unpleasant I gave it to him." Tiger took a drink and almost immediately began berating Ashley for not sharing these bottles with the rest of the hunting party. Ashley put away the bottles, he said, but Tiger continued to insist on another swig—and when Ashley refused to give him one, Tiger stopped poling the canoe so that it grounded against the bank. "He got down in a crouched position something like this," Ashley went on, demonstrating for the jury, "He then said, 'you [expletive], I will kill you,' and I heard his pistol click, so I just grabbed my gun as quick as possible . . . And I started shooting and continued so until he fell."

He then made a hasty escape, losing an oar and poling his way out of the canal and on to Fort Lauderdale, getting there "sometime in the night, and I got right on the train and taken my furs and come to Miami and sold them."

The assertion that the furs were somehow his may have been the detail that sunk Ashley's self-defense for the jury, along with the fact— one he did not deny—that he left Florida and spent months on the run, first traveling to New Orleans and then to San Francisco, Spokane, and Portland, Oregon. He had a well-constructed explanation for this as well: "Just simply because my people didn't have any more money to fight the case any more and I didn't, and they were going to move me to Miami, and I heard the Seminole Indians of Oklahoma had put up $15,000 for my conviction, and I just simply taken it for granted it was my final chance for a trip, and I just made a clear getaway. I got away, all right." He ended this with a smile, and many in the audience smiled back.

Ashley was the only witness for the defense, so the attorneys presented their closing arguments soon after. A. J. Rose, one of Ashley's attorneys, reminded the jury that this trial was about just one of Ashley's crimes, not an indictment of his entire portfolio. "He's charged with one distinct offense—the murder of Desoto Tiger," he reminded the jury. "When one commits premeditated murder, then he is guilty of murder in the first degree. You must decide whether he killed Desoto Tiger in cold-blooded murder. You have not the right to consider what he did subsequently. John Ashley stands before you for the murder of Desoto Tiger; let him be good or let him be bad, this does not enter into the question of whether or not he is guilty of the murder."

He then noted that the bulk of the evidence was circumstantial at best. "Until John Ashley took the stand here, there wasn't a scintilla of evidence to show that Ashley killed the Indian. No man saw John Ashley do it, except John Ashley himself. . . . There has not been shown by the state any circumstances as to how he was killed. Not one bit of evidence has been introduced by the state to show how he met his death."

John Gramling, the attorney for the prosecution, delivered a much shorter summation than Rose's speech. He reviewed the information about the bullet wounds—one piercing Tiger's body under his right arm, while the second penetrated his hand, which was raised to his face. He also emphasized that Tiger's revolver was found at the bottom of the canoe—if Tiger had been about to shoot it, he would obviously have taken it out of the boat. He ended his statement by making a verdict of innocence a matter of patriotism: "A man who would not shoulder a gun if this government should be disrupted, a man who would be a traitor to his country, let that man be the first man to vote John Ashley not guilty." The defense objected strongly to this statement, asking the court to tell the jury to disregard it—and the judge did so, just before declaring a recess until the following morning.

Prosecutor G. A. Worley made a more definitive argument in his closing statement the next day. He picked apart Ashley's testimony, pointing out the inconsistencies and gaps in its sequence of events, and emphasized the testimony of one man, Powers, who actually heard the shots and "saw something fall across the stern of the boat," and then saw Ashley alone in the boat, poling away as fast as he could.

Even more unlikely, Worley said, was Ashley's story that Tiger had hesitated before actually pulling the trigger on Ashley. "Can you believe for an instant that of all men in the world that Indian, with the drop on Ashley, would have sat still and let him kill him? Is it possible? Why, the Indian could have shot him half a dozen times. That statement won't do."

The case finally went to the jury at about 4 p.m. on Monday, April 5, and the following day they returned their verdict. They found Ashley guilty of murder. Four days later, Judge Branning sentenced him to death by hanging.

It looked like Ashley's life of crime had come to an end. He awaited a June 18, 1915, execution, though his attorneys filed a series of appeals that succeeded in delaying the date.

On June 2, John's brother Bob showed up at the jail, guns in hand, and called jailor Wilbur W. Hendrickson to come to the door. Miami Sheriff Hardie had taken extra precautions to prevent any kind of a jail-break attempt, hiring a blacksmith to make extra-heavy chains to secure the doors leading into the jail. The chains would have made a forced entry through the doors impossible . . . but Hendrickson had not fastened the chains that day. He also did not look out a window before he opened the door to Bob Ashley's call and knock.

As soon as he appeared in the doorway, Bob Ashley asked him, "Are you Hendrickson?"

"Yes, I am," said the jailor, and Bob Ashley shot him.

Hearing the shots, Hendrickson's wife came to see what had happened and immediately grabbed a rifle from a stand in a corner of the room. She took aim and fired at the fleeing killer, but the gun just snapped—it wasn't loaded. Her cries brought city police officer J. R. Riblett, Sgt. E. V. Stephens, and another officer, Will Flowers, on the run.

Bob Ashley took off for a city park, "dashing down gravel walks and causing consternation among nurse-girls wheeling infants," news reports said. Several men pursued him as he ran, but when he pointed his gun at these unarmed men, they fell back. Bob found a tree large enough to shield him from bullets and waited for a car to pass, then ran out in front of it and forced the driver, T. F. Duckett, to stop.

"Take me out the county road quick!" he shouted.

Duckett sized up the situation in seconds, realized that police were in hot pursuit of this man, and tried to stall for time by claiming he didn't know the way. Bob Ashley jumped on the car's running board and began making violent threats, scaring Duckett into driving off with him. But at the edge of town, Duckett managed to feign car trouble and pulled over, leaping out and popping the hood open to make a show of attempting to fix it. Officer Riblett pulled up alongside the car, but rather than opening fire immediately, he made a valiant attempt to arrest Ashley. Bob Ashley had no intention of giving himself up. He raised his rifle, but Riblett closed the space between them and grabbed for it. They struggled, and Ashley fired directly into Riblett's jaw at point-blank range. Remarkably, the shot exited through the officer's cheek—a survivable wound—but as Riblett recoiled, Ashley shot him again in the torso.

Riblett went down, but before he fell he managed to fire his own weapon, sending a bullet into Ashley's head. He fired twice more, his second bullet finding its mark near Ashley's heart. Two other policemen with Riblett caught him as he fell.

"Ashley fell prone to the street and lay writhing in a pool of blood, rolling his eyes and frothing at the mouth," reported the *Miami Herald*. Both men were rushed to the city hospital, where Hendrickson's body already lay in the emergency ward. Riblett succumbed to his wounds sometime later that afternoon. Sheriff Hardie, a Miami law enforcement official, made the decision to move Bob Ashley from the hospital to the county jail to protect him from the angry mob that quickly gathered around the city hospital. His caution proved to be unnecessary: Bob died within half an hour of arriving at the lockup.

With Bob Ashley dead, the crowd redirected its outrage to his brother on death row. Some called for an immediate lynching as rumors flowed that more members of the Ashley gang were in town, and another jailbreak attempt could be on the way. Sheriff Hardie questioned John Ashley about this plan and any others in the offing, and the condemned man denied any knowledge of such activities.

In November, as attorneys' appeals dragged on, the jailer and Sheriff Hardie discovered that John had attempted an escape by digging through the dirt floor of his cell with a spoon. He had carried on this activity for five weeks, covering his progress with a rug and coming within three feet of the outside wall and freedom, but Hardie told the press that he had known all along that Ashley was engaged in this activity and he was glad the man had found something to do. If he had actually come close to escape, the police would have taken action, he said. "If he had made a break during the night he would have been killed," he said. "On Monday when we broke up his playhouse, I told him that my business is to keep him in jail, and his business is to get away if he can, and that if he gets away I lose. I dismissed the matter with that statement." Once Ashley's plot was exposed, the sheriff moved him to a new cell, and announced plans to install steel floors in all of the cells. In the meantime, he took away Ashley's spoon.

Eventually, the appeals did their job. A judge reversed the decision in the Tiger case, leading Ashley to plead guilty to the crime in a court hearing and receive a seventeen-year sentence to Railford Prison. He served part of his time as a model prisoner, so much so that prison officials placed him on a road gang, a privilege reserved only for convicts who behave well. This gave Ashley the opportunity to enjoy some fresh air on a regular basis—and to attempt yet another escape. He succeeded, fleeing into the Everglades he knew so well. The Ashley gang continued their lives of crime, robbing as many as forty banks over the course of the next several years, while John Ashley spent three years running stills in the vicinity of Palm Beach.

When Prohibition began in 1920, the gang began running liquor into Florida from British warehouses in Bimini, Bahamas. Two of John's brothers, Ed and Frank Ashley, disappeared one night while making a run from Bimini to Jupiter Inlet, perhaps the victims of rough weather or—more likely—removed by rival members of the gang. Coincidentally or not, three competitors in the smuggling trade vanished at sea on the same route shortly thereafter. Some believe that their deaths were a hit job authorized by John Ashley.

Eventually the cops caught up with Ashley once again. They cornered John while he delivered liquor to customers in Wauchula, seventy miles south of Tampa, and sent him back to prison at Railford—but he repeated the pattern, earning a place on a road gang and escaping yet again.

But no crime spree goes on forever, and the Ashley gang's exploits would not become the exception. On November 1, 1924, deputies of Sheriff R. C. Baker of Palm Beach County received information from an unnamed source that Ashley and three members of the gang—Hanford Mobley, Shorty Lynn, and Bob Middleton—were expected to pass through St. Lucie County that night. At 5:00 p.m. the deputies approached Sheriff Merritt of that county to assist them in apprehending the criminals at long last. Merritt agreed but told them, "I'll do it, with the understanding that [we] work to my plans."

Merritt's plans involved stringing a heavy chain across the Dixie Highway (now Route A1A) at the Sebastian River bridge on the St. Lucie and Brevard County line. The deputies hung a red lantern at the chain's midpoint, hid their cars across the river in Brevard County, and took concealed positions in the mangrove trees along both sides of the bridge.

Here they waited until 10:45 p.m. when a car pulled up to the chain and stopped. Just behind it another car stopped as well—this one containing the four members of the Ashley gang.

"We waited until they stopped, then came up from behind and covered them with our guns," Sheriff Merritt told the *Miami Herald* the following day. "They were caught unawares, being interested in seeing why the automobile ahead had stopped."

Ashley was the first to make out Sheriff Merritt in the darkness. He reached for his rifle, but Merritt shoved his gun in the man's face. "Deputy Wiggins pushed a gun into his ribs at the same time, telling him to throw up his hands," the sheriff said.

The lawmen grabbed the rifles they could see inside the car, and ordered the four gangsters out of the car and in front of the headlights. With the criminals surrounded and seemingly unarmed, Merritt got into the other car—driven by "a young man named Miller," who was part of the sheriff's plan—and rode across the bridge to get his police car. He drove it out of its hiding place and up onto the bridge, shining his headlights at the gang members.

"I got out and went to the side door of my motor car to get the handcuffs," he said. "The first pair I got I did not have a key for. I asked Deputy Wiggins if he had a key to fit them, and was getting more handcuffs out of the pocket of the door when Ashley gave a signal."

All four of the gang members pulled out their six-shooters. Merritt realized then he had not had the men searched, but the deputies surrounding the gangsters were on high alert.

"Right then and there the shooting began," Merritt said. "When the smoke cleared away, all four of the desperadoes lay on the ground dead." Not one of the law enforcement officers was wounded. The deputies loaded the four bodies into their own car and drove to Fort Pierce.

So ended the career and the life of John Ashley, King of the Ever-glades, although the legend of this convicted murderer and multitalented felon continues to this day—and the stories get taller the more often they are told. He and his brothers are buried in their family cemetery in Stuart, if you wish to pay your respects one day. Rumor has it that some fan or other stopped there, dug down into John Ashley's grave and stole the glass eye right out of his skeleton's head. If you believe that one, I have some swampland in Florida to sell you.

4

Hurricanes with No Names: 1926 and 1928

NOWHERE IN AMERICA DID THE 1920S ROAR MORE LOUDLY THAN IN South Florida. A time of rampant prosperity for much of the nation, the 1920s brought a land boom to the state from Miami southward and westward as developers championed the long-awaited drainage of the "abominable pestilence-ridden swamp," as newly elected governor Napoleon Bonaparte Broward called the Everglades in 1905.

Broward's pet project barely got underway during his tenure as governor, but by the century's second decade, canals crisscrossed the region and dry fields had emerged from the once-verdant wetlands. Speculators bought up millions of acres for pennies on the dollar and auctioned them off for ten times what they had paid. The year-round pleasant weather promised by winter billboards on New York's Times Square—proclaiming "It's June in Miami" over swimsuit-clad women on white-sand beaches—drew tourists in their first motor vehicles, driving down from snow-covered cities up north. Once they arrived, they wanted their own piece of paradise, a tiny sliver of land to call a little bit of south Florida their own.

Average folks with savings to spend on a sure thing bought tens of thousands of small lots, some just a quarter of an acre in size, and began building homes with cheap materials. A home in the newly created towns of Coral Gables and Hialeah certainly didn't need the insulation that northern houses required, developers told them, nor was a solid foundation with a basement necessary. In a matter of months these homeowners could move into their new houses in towns like Moore Haven, Belle

Glade, and Clewiston on the shores of Lake Okeechobee, or Opa-locka, Hollywood, and Okeelanta further east.

Amid these largely white landowners, another population moved into the fertile area: Black migrant workers and farmhands looking for steady work in an area where crops were raised year round. As any farm required just one owner but hundreds of workers for planting, tending to crops, and harvests, Black families were far more prevalent than whites throughout the Everglades. Few records were kept of who they were and which farms they worked for, however. "Migrants from the South or the islands came in, worked, got paid, and went back to their families," said Eliot Kleinberg in his masterful 2003 book *Black Cloud: The Great Florida Hurricane of 1928*. "There was no paperwork. Pay was in cash. Many workers were known to their bosses only by a first name. If someone died, it might not be counted if no relative was looking for him."

Amid the furor over newly available land, one word seems entirely absent: *hurricane*. Today the National Hurricane Center can tell us that 159 hurricanes are known to have affected Florida before 1900, and major storms had already taken place in the 1900s when the land boom began. The United States has had an official weather bureau since 1870, but its ability to track storms from their point of origin in the Atlantic Ocean did not begin until the 1940s, when aircraft became part of the operation. If a storm was coming, the weather bureau could only wait for ships at sea to encounter and report it or for warnings to come in from stations on islands in the Caribbean. Florida remained in the dark about most storms until they were nearly upon the peninsula.

Developers certainly did not tell their customers that their homes and livelihoods might be obliterated by a violent storm or that these new residents would receive little to no warning that such an event might be on its way. So in September 1926, Floridians had no idea that a storm measuring category 4 on the modern Saffir-Simpson hurricane wind scale—bringing winds of up to 150 miles per hour—had passed north of the Virgin Islands on Wednesday, September 15, accelerating its pace through the Bahamas on September 16 before focusing its destructive energy on the Miami coastline.

The first storm warning issued to the Florida coast came on Friday, September 17, just hours before the hurricane made landfall. Radio communication and newspaper services worked overtime to disseminate the information to ports and government officials, but for the most part, private citizens received little warning other than a late-edition, city paper notice. The *Palm Beach Post*, for example, printed a page-one alert with the headline "Tropical Storms Moving Up Coast May Strike City," with an additional bulletin.

Weather bureau advices received by Palm Beach Radio station after midnight regarding the Turk Island storm stated: "This is a dangerous storm and every precaution should be taken. The center of the storm has passed Turk Island and is moving west-northwestward attended by dangerous shifting gales.

Some of the new residents had seen big storms before. In the little town of Moore Haven, seventy-five miles northwest of Miami at the southern end of Lake Okeechobee, fishing and agriculture had drawn an extension of the Atlantic Coastline Railroad, which in turn brought in an industrious citizenry of about 1,500 residents. Storms and flooding were just another part of the busy way of life here, the price the townspeople paid for the pleasure of living in the heart of the Everglades. They had seen nuisance floods—water two to three feet deep washing through the town after heavy rains and high winds, wetting down their streets and seeping up through their floorboards. This oncoming storm sounded no worse than usual. They trusted that the dikes constructed by the government at their end of the lake would hold the water in place. So on Friday afternoon when the winds picked up, the townspeople of Moore Haven went about their business as they always did, taking no greater precautions than on any other wet day.

They were probably long asleep by the time the hurricane slammed into the South Florida coast, making landfall about fifteen miles south of downtown Miami, its 145 mph winds scouring an area from the upper Florida Keys north to St. Lucie County.

The huge tropical cyclone wiped out entire neighborhoods as it whirled across the coastline, turning landowners into refugees in minutes and forcing thousands of people to flee for their lives. In Fort Lauderdale just three buildings remained standing after the hurricane passed through, all of them immediately transformed into makeshift hospitals to treat the injured as officials began to count the dead. Governor John Martin moved quickly to declare martial law in Miami, sending troops to organize and close off the area along sixty miles of Miami coastline as medics found and transported the dead, assisted the injured, and assessed the damage in the storm's wake.

As Moore Haven residents rose early Saturday morning, they found themselves in the midst of the most powerful storm they had ever experienced— and it was about to get worse. The maelstrom delivered the town's death blow at about 7:30 a.m. As the siren at the canal locks' power house pierced the howling wind, the gale burst the dikes holding back Lake Okeechobee, releasing all of the lake's water on the town. "In ten minutes the water was six feet deep in the streets and half an hour later it was 12 to 15 feet deep," wrote Travers Green of the *Tampa Tribune*. Added Jack Falconnier of the *Tampa Bay Times*, "Water ran seven to ten feet in the streets of Moore Haven, and waves were rolling eight to ten feet higher."

The flood submerged small houses in minutes. "Scores of families were trapped in their shanty-like houses when the water began to rise with appalling speed," wrote Green, interviewing refugees who managed to survive the deluge. "Dozens escaped by climbing on tables and cutting their way through the roof as the water rose around them."

With flood waters rushing through their doors and windows, many people died trapped in their own homes. Others were swept out by the force of the water and drowned in the fearsome current. Some managed to make it to small boats or grabbed part of a house as it sailed by them on the waves, using it as a raft. Those who survived the initial flood rode out the rest of the storm as best they could, many shivering on their roofs in the 100 mph winds and praying for their lives.

Desperate to save her four children, Mrs. H. H. Howell, the Moore Haven marshal's wife, gathered the children to her and tied them together, then secured the rope to herself to keep the wind from whipping them away from her. The wind took them anyway, plunging them into a deep hole created by opposing currents and dragging her after them. She managed to cut two of her children loose and save them, but the remaining two never came to the surface.

One couple, their names not mentioned in Falconnier's story, climbed to the top of a pine tree to get as high above the water as they could, their five children suspended there with them. They clung to branches and maintained their precarious perch for most of the gale, but as the waves rose, the father made an attempt to carry his children even higher in the tree. He lost his footing and fell into the waves. Soon each of the children—soaked, terrified, and probably numb with cold—ran out of strength to hang onto their branches and dropped into the water as well. Only their mother managed to cling to the tree until the storm finally subsided and a rescue boat could pull up close enough to assist her. No one else in her family survived.

Stories like this one came into newspaper offices all over Florida. "There is one mother in the Great Beyond today whose last thought was of her baby, and if she can look back on this earth she can see the little one playing contentedly on the floor of the hotel here with toys, knowing that her sacrifice was not in vain," Falconnier wrote. "With the last ounce of ebbing strength she tied the little one to an improvised raft, and it rode through the storm until rescued."

Mrs. L. F. Dey described her own experience in the storm to the *Pensacola Journal*. She, her husband, and their three children had moved to Moore Haven just a month before the hurricane hit and had barely acquired furniture for their new home. When the storm started, her husband took her and their baby to Citrus City (now the community of Citrus Center, west of Moore Haven) and then went back for their two sons. "The house the baby and I were staying in was filled with people," she said. "Finally it collapsed, too. When the morning came and my husband did not return, I decided I would go back to Moore Haven after my little boys."

All through the day after the storm, she walked the seven miles from Citrus City to Moore Haven, the water up to her waist. "Even the snakes would not harm me," she said. "They were in danger too and were trying to find some way to get out of it all."

When she reached Moore Haven, she found her new house upside down and completely destroyed. To her great joy, though, she discovered her two sons on top of another house, patiently waiting for rescue. Her husband was already at work with the crews recovering bodies and had found fourteen of the dead himself. "He is in Moorehaven [*sic*] now looking for more," she said. "We dug graves for those all day Monday. There was not enough men, so ten of us women helped. I dug two myself." She added, "I know that more than 100 white person [*sic*] are dead, and at least 75 negroes."

"Virtually all the deaths were due to drowning, not an instance having been reported of anyone being crushed under a falling building," Green reported. "That no persons are believed to have been crushed to death is attributed to the fact that virtually all the houses were of slight construction." Just one row of brick buildings remained standing in Moore Haven by the storm's end, the only structures built to any kind of safe standard.

Out in the middle of Lake Okeechobee, some forty or fifty fishing boats had been plying their trade before the storm despite the signs of bad weather. "Government warnings had been posted, but the hardy men of the lake region attached little importance to them," the *Tampa Tribune* said. Capt. H. E. Smith, his fishing craft thirty-five miles from the nearest shore, saw the surf rise up with sudden fury at about 10 a.m. on Saturday morning as the hurricane moved toward him. He and four other fishing boats in a fleet owned by G. J. Elsmith soon found themselves fighting thirty-foot swells and winds at a "conservative" estimate of 115 miles per hour, he told the Tribune News Service days later. Blown forty miles south of Clewiston by the icy wind, he and his crew "were bleeding from the eyes, nose and mouth when they finally ran ashore," the news service said. Smith's boat lost $7,000 worth of fishing gear—a fraction of the $56,000 in tackle his employer sacrificed to the storm.

But Elsmith's losses were nothing compared with the fatalities other fishing fleets suffered. A number of the boats on Lake Okeechobee went down that morning in the face of the mighty winds, taking their gallant but misguided crews with them.

Meanwhile Smith's father, H. B. Smith, took the storm on in his own way. When he saw many of his Moore Haven neighbors torn from their rooftops and cast into the roiling waters, he jumped into an eighteen-foot rowboat alone and battled the wind and rising waves to reach those closest to him. He managed to get to two men fairly quickly, pulling them out of the water and into the boat, and they both grabbed paddles and started to row as fast as they could to the next head they could see bobbing nearby. Before they were through that day, they had gathered seventeen more people into the boat and hurried them to safety.

When the wind finally abated in the very early morning hours on Sunday, rain and deep water remained. Townspeople still could not see in the pitch blackness of the stormy night, but they could hear one another calling out to missing family members, trying to determine who was nearby and who had survived. They did their best to console each other as they awaited some kind of rescue, clutching pieces of their homes or sitting precariously atop their own roofs. Daylight brought the first positive news: The waters were receding, dropping to about four feet deep in some areas—enough to allow taller people to make their way through the water, muck, and debris hidden below the surface.

"By 9 o'clock the first relief from Sebring arrived on the scene on railroad motor trucks, and the rescue work began," wrote Green. He stood at the station in Sebring as rescue trains pulled in from the town on Monday, September 20, bringing the first bodies of what were estimated to be as many as 350 dead from Moore Haven alone. "The heavens wept copiously later this afternoon," he began his story, watching refugees standing in the pouring rain as seven blanket-wrapped bodies were unloaded and carried to trucks, which in turn took them to hastily constructed emergency morgues. Some of these refugees told stories of working on crews to recover bodies as the waters receded. "One man said the crew he worked with alone has sighted the bodies of 40 white persons and recovered a large number of them," Green wrote.

That number—40 white people, later identified as women and children—became the only figure that the Associated Press (AP) blasted out to newspapers across the country that day. Green went on to quote refugees who said they thought the death toll would reach 400, and that "all reports agree that two thirds of the dead are negroes." The AP, however, did not make that clarification until several days later. The story that the rest of the country received was that just 40 people of any importance had died in Moore Haven, while the real figure was at least six times larger. While local papers were reporting the possibility that as many as 250 people had died in Moore Haven, the *Orlando Sentinel*, taking its figures from the AP, reported just 41 dead there on September 21.

Luckily, the American Red Cross and the Florida department of the American Legion did not take their direction from the AP. By Monday evening, September 20, five relief trains had arrived in Moore Haven, including one that had been stymied by washed-out tracks at Lake Stearns until repair crews came to the train's rescue. The trains were loaded with relief workers, doctors, nurses, civilian volunteers, and supplies to care for the injured and feed and clothe the survivors, as well as tents to shield them from the continuing rain. Some of these trains also brought motor boats to transport Moore Haven refugees to nearby Palmdale, twenty miles north along the Lake Okeechobee shore.

They found what Jack Falconnier described as "a smelling sepulcher of the dead."

"At least 100 are dead," said Dr. J. W. Mitchell to the *Miami Herald* on his brief return to Sebring from Moore Haven, just before he boarded the next rescue train back to the afflicted town. He noted that twenty-three people drowned in the collapse of a two-story frame building, while others had been washed right off the roofs of their own homes. Another article on the same page tallied the known fatalities at 140 and noted that a pilot circling the disaster area reported "many bodies strewn along or near the Atlantic Coast Line railway." (The pilot, Ralph DeVore, told reporters in Avon Park that all of this damage was in Clewiston, not Moore Haven, which set up a panic among people with families and friends there. It took a day or so for newspapers to clarify that Clewiston had survived the storm comparatively unscathed.)

"The drainage dyke built around the city at a cost of hundreds of thousands of dollars is wrecked," Mitchell continued. He also confirmed that bodies of Black citizens were "washed upon the railroad grade on the outskirts of the city."

The Red Cross and other organizations reported that they had located 150 bodies in Moore Haven, though they considered their report to be incomplete. The rushing waters had carried an untold number of bodies deep into the undeveloped Everglades beyond the town limits, from which they would never be retrieved. Much later, the National Oceanic and Atmospheric Administration (NOAA) revised the number of deaths from the 1926 hurricane to 372, making it the tenth deadliest tropical cyclone to hit the mainland United States between 1851 and 2010. About 240 of the lives lost were in Moore Haven, with the rest in and around Miami and several in Mobile as the storm moved westward.

With the deadly deluge receding, the Red Cross and other rescue organizations raised the alarm about another looming crisis: The possibility of a massive outbreak of typhoid—a potentially fatal bacterial infection transmitted in spoiled food and contaminated water. One case had already emerged in Fort Lauderdale with two more suspected, and several sick patients in Davie had nausea, diarrhea, and vomiting, all symptoms that could be related to *Salmonella typhi*, the bacterium that caused typhoid.

The possibility of waterborne illness was not new to Davie. Positioned on the outskirts of the Everglades, its drainage and sanitation systems had not been improved as the town grew during the land boom. Now with every building in town flattened by the hurricane, residents found themselves marooned with nowhere to congregate safely, and help was slow to arrive. "The people were forced to remain in what was left of their homes," said the *Tampa Tribune* four days after the storm had subsided. "Illness and suffering resulted." Many Davie residents refused to evacuate, however, even when "the medical authorities pointed to the gray-green stagnant water which covered the entire area around Davie to a depth of from two to five feet. Bodies of cattle, dogs, cats, and fowl were floating here and there, and decomposing under the rays of the hot sun, and with the aid of insect life of the swamp."

Red Cross national medical director William R. Redden began sounding the alarm on Wednesday, September 22, three days after the hurricane passed, when the problem of polluted water and festering corpses became clear. Bryne C. Anderson, field superintendent of nursing with the Florida State Board of Health (and possibly the highest-ranking woman in the rescue effort), concurred with Dr. Redden's assessment and began working with state officials and teams of nurses to address it.

Dr. Redden ordered the evacuation of all survivors in Moore Haven and Davie, requesting trucks and rail cars to take them to higher ground and cleaner environments as quickly as possible. "All persons remaining or coming in must submit to vaccination," the *Tampa Tribune* reported. Even the most stubborn Davie residents finally succumbed to evacuation, allowing the cleanup effort to move ahead with alacrity. In Moore Haven, where about two hundred residents had escaped death in the flood, the military officer in charge of the rescue mission, Col. S. J. Lowry, ordered the last of them to evacuate despite their objections when the regimental surgeon deemed the area ripe for the spread of bacterial infection.

The quick, decisive action and the aggressive vaccination program averted the predicted epidemic, Dr. Redden announced a few days later. "I believe I am safe in saying that splendid immunization carried on by the doctors constituted one of the finest pieces of preventative work the country has ever seen outside of military forces," he told the *Pensacola Journal* on September 28. "A thorough prosecution of the program already outlined for the prevention of epidemics should give confidence to the communities throughout the whole area."

By this time the AP had reported that 110 bodies had been recovered from Moore Haven, and as many as 200 more lay decomposing throughout the town and the surrounding area. "Further effort to identify later recoveries will be abandoned," the wire service reported, adding, "It is impossible to determine whether the bodies are those of negroes or whites." Once again, keeping a tally of deaths by race seemed important to the AP.

It only took another day or so before the Moore Haven community's shock, bewilderment, and grief inevitably gave way to anger. The focus of their fury was the internal improvement board, the federal organization responsible for keeping Lake Okeechobee from flooding. "Plans are being made in the stricken area for a sweeping investigation," the *Tampa Tribune* reported on September 23. The citizens blamed the state for refusing to open the locks that had been constructed to regulate water levels in the lake under any circumstances, even for a storm of this magnitude. Opening the locks earlier in the storm season would have kept the lake at the state's recommended height of fifteen feet instead of its nineteen-foot height just before the hurricane struck. "The terrific wind swept across the lake, driving the water into the canal at Moore Haven, swelling the water to a 21-foot level," the *Tribune* reported. "In the height of the hurricane the water went to a depth of 20 feet." The subsequent flooding destroyed ten miles of dikes, allowing deep water to inundate the town and the surrounding area for miles around. "If the gates of the locks at Moore Haven had been opened six weeks ago . . . a sufficient amount of water would have passed to the gulf by way of the Caloosahatchee [River], thereby lowering the lake level." The surviving citizens of Moore Haven sent a cable to President Calvin Coolidge detailing their request for a more thorough examination of the issue, before simply rebuilding the dikes that had failed so spectacularly.

As days passed with no immediate action beyond an inspection of the damaged dikes by a handful of officials, Moore Haven residents' calls for an investigation increased in volume and specificity. They began to talk about issuing a coroner's warrant for an investigation into the deaths of the people who drowned in the flood—in other words, an examination that could lead to criminal charges for government officials.

In something of a panic, H. E. Daniel, president of the Sebring relief organization, and Carl Wittrock, chairman of the flood committee, sent telegrams to Governor Martin to pay a visit to Moore Haven posthaste, to reassure the populace that action would be taken to prevent such a complete failure of the water control system from happening again.

Governor Martin stepped up to the challenge. He traveled on October 2 from the state capital in Tallahassee to a military base at Ortona, and from there he rode in a car with a state health officer and others until "the road became so deep in water as to drown out the motor car engine." Their military escort was prepared for this, making a quick transfer of the governor and the rest of his party to high-clearance trucks so that they could complete the eighteen-mile drive to Moore Haven.

From here Martin boarded a large boat and cruised down the canal and into the lake, paralleling the destroyed dike to get as close a view as possible of the damage. He then made a full tour of Moore Haven with Fred C. Elliott, chief engineer of the Everglades Drainage District. After the tour, Martin responded with swift and decisive action. The AP reported that Martin "gave implicit and unrestricted authority and instruction to put this city and its surrounding storm devastated area into such condition as will permit return of residents at the earliest possible date." This gave Elliott the authority to "repair immediately the dikes which are continuing to permit water to sweep in from Lake Okeechobee, and see that the city is rid of its water as quickly as possible."

Just below this spirited account of the governor's tour in the *Miami Herald*, quite another account of Moore Haven's condition appears—this one told by Colonel Lowry of the National Guard, who was leading the rescue and recovery effort still in progress. In Atlanta, Georgia, to ask for more aid, he sought to clarify a misunderstanding in Red Cross headquarters

> *regarding Florida's attitude toward aid ... I wish it to be clearly understood that Florida does need help and needs it badly. I know this because I have seen with my own eyes conditions which were appalling and I know from personal observation that there are sections of Florida which will perish unless conditions are relieved.... While the winds have died down and the water has receded to a degree, conditions in Moore Haven are by no means alleviated. The town now stands under water from three to six feet deep and relief will not come until the level of Lake Okeechobee is lowered or the dam rebuilt.*

He finished, "When you consider that 250 of the 1,000 population were killed, you can get an idea of what the hurricane meant to Moore Haven. The town is ruined and is utterly incapable of helping itself."

Waters in Moore Haven did not recede completely until early November, at which time the Red Cross finally announced that rehabilitation and home reconstruction could begin. Lower sections of the town still had as much as two feet of standing water, but sanitary conditions had been restored, and aid money had begun to flow to families to help them rebuild and restock their homes. About 450 Moore Haven families had spent the last six weeks in Sebring, some as refugees staying with families in private homes, while others waited in a tent city for word that they could return to their property, such as it was.

By November, however, it became clear that the hurricane had brought the land boom in south Florida to a dramatic end. Despite a pretty argument made by nationally known advertising executive Barron Collier in *American Review and Reviews*, the stories of the devastation of Moore Haven and other towns along the state's southeast coast sounded the death knell for land acquisition there.

"It will take more than a wind storm—which, after all, has caused damage in only a small portion of that state—to change my belief or to alter my faith in Florida," Collier said in the article. "The whole state should not be pictured as a victim of calamity because Miami and Moore Haven were unfortunate enough to lie in the path of the storm."

Even in the 1920s, the words of an adman could not stave off the consequences of the storm. Developers saw enough of a loss in business that many of them were plunged into bankruptcy, stuck with land they had bought at inflated prices and now could not sell. Earlier in 1926, the railroads had placed an embargo on the shipment of anything but essential materials into the region, because rail traffic had become so gridlocked by shipments of building supplies and other expansion necessities that the Atlantic Coast Line railroad could not keep up. Banning the shipment of lumber and other materials had already brought developers to their knees. The hurricane swept away their last resource: portrayal of Florida as a carefree paradise.

The state repaired the mud dike around Lake Okeechobee, but they did so in the most expedient way possible, adding no strength or height to the 6.6-foot structure. A plan had been in place for some time for the Everglades Drainage District to construct a more secure and permanent dike around the lake, one 27 feet tall and 20 feet wide at its top, with a nearly impenetrable base of as much as 130 feet at its widest points. This plan stalled, however, when the city of Miami objected to the funding—the proposal called for the city to put up the lion's share of the money, but it would receive only a fraction of whatever profits the new dike would generate. Miami filed a lawsuit that sat in court for years, delaying the construction past its intended 1927 start date.

So Moore Haven and other towns that had seen hurricane damage around the lake—particularly Belle Glade and Clewiston—continued their slow recovery into 1927, in time for the planting season and a good harvest later that year. It seemed then that the survivors could put the worst of the hurricane of 1926 behind them as they enjoyed a second season of planting in 1928, looking ahead to another healthy harvest and the return of the comfortable lives they originally expected here on the shores of Lake Okeechobee.

On the wide flood plain left open and dry around the lake by the system of canals and drainage ditches, farmers and their hands were busy planting their winter vegetables. "Tractors growled through the muck fields like terriers; in seeds stores and supply houses, clerks labored half the night," wrote Ralph Wallace for the *St. Louis Post-Dispatch* in a look-back piece in 1945. Migrant workers crowded tents and makeshift shacks in the lowlands, as many as five thousand field hands and their families living in camps below the height of the lake. None of these camps had telephones or other means of communication; even radios were scarce.

Still the residents hoped that the promised levee around the lake would finally be built. They suffered a particularly discouraging blow in August 1928, however, when a $10 million bond sale for the construction of the levee collapsed and the commissioners of the Everglades Drainage District were dismissed from their posts. "Only enough [were] retained to work the locks in the district and to perform the other necessary upkeep," the *Miami Herald* reported. "Well, these things perhaps will work out. It has been a long, dry spring and summer and people forget much in such weather."

But late summer 1928 proved to be especially rainy. Heavy downpours began on August 8 and lasted well into September, driving Lake Okeechobee's water level up by three feet and filling every canal, stream, and ditch up to the top of its banks.

No one living in Florida in 1928 had ever seen a category 5 hurricane (that classification system had not yet been devised and would not be in use until 1973). After their experience in 1926, many people likely believed that they had seen the worst storm they would ever see. They were wrong.

On September 10, 1928, residents and migrants around Lake Okeechobee did not know that a major storm had been sighted by the *S.S. Comack*, an American freighter off the coast of Barbados. They did not hear about this storm gaining strength and streaking across the island of Guadeloupe, killing 660 people and leaving thousands more homeless. No one could tell them that this hurricane now measured 235 miles across or that it made landfall in Puerto Rico on September 13, taking hundreds of lives and wiping out the homes of 200,000 people. Everglades dwellers did not hear any of this because despite the storm's intensity, it did not appear to be coming in their direction. In fact, on September 14 and 15, it looked like the tropical cyclone would move east of the Bahamas and not come ashore in Florida at all.

So it was that about noon on Sunday, September 16, residents around Lake Okeechobee got their first warnings from the media that the storm had turned and was now heading directly for them. They had only hours to gather up whatever belongings they could and evacuate their homes. "Businessmen of South Bay drove about the countryside, collected 211 men, women and children, and placed them on a big barge in the lake for safety," said Wallace. "Dr. William J. Buck of Belle Glade dispatched trucks to outlying sections to round up everyone who could be induced to leave home." Days later, Buck—the only doctor in the towns on the south and west side of the lake—told the media, "Whites and negroes were brought in alike. It was a time of terror and there was no discrimination. Our effort was to save lives."

Memory can be short, and for some people living around the lake, the perils of the 1926 hurricane seemed to have been forgotten. Some refused to evacuate, preferring to stay and guard their own homes and try to ride out the worst of the storm. For others, however, the last storm remained a fresh wound, so they joined 650 others at the Glades Hotel and the Belle Glade Hotel, filling rooms on the buildings' second floors.

By 6:00 that evening, the strongest wind they had ever seen howled around the buildings. "The huddled groups in the two hotels watched in awe as the wind tipped over automobiles and rolled them down the street," Wallace said. "A huge roof sailed by at treetop height; a farm wagon rose, its wheels gently turning, and disappeared skyward." Soon the wind lashed rain against the windows, whipping horizontally into the sturdy buildings as women shrieked prayers over the din of the storm.

How could Lake Okeechobee, normally just nine feet deep, resist the force of such a hurricane? The lake gave over, the wind scooping up the water down to the lake bed and carrying it over the dikes as if they did not exist. The dikes crumbled like sand before the massive wave. In seconds, Belle Glade was completely underwater.

The wave tossed electrical utility poles, trees, and even buildings across the town, crashing this wall of debris into the Belle Glade Hotel—which, miraculously, held its foundation. Water began to creep into the first floor, sending stragglers scrambling upward to escape the flood. From here they watched houses drift by on the rapid current as people caught in the flood waters reached out their arms to them as they passed. Fifty homes and businesses were scoured off the map in minutes; only the two hotels and one warehouse remained.

Again the Red Cross and other helping organizations poured into the communities along the lake. They made their way through roads blocked by debris, working with crews provided by city and state municipalities to reach storm-isolated towns where bodies lay strewn along streets, covered by parts of ruined dwellings, or carried by raging waters deep into Everglades fields. The death toll mounted in the first few days, rising exponentially as relief workers made more discoveries of multiple bodies.

By Friday, five days after the storm, local Red Cross chairman Howard Selby of Palm Beach declared that the staggering number of bodies presented an unprecedented health hazard, with a typhoid outbreak a near certainty if the bodies were not dealt with immediately. "Unless all bodies are recovered and buried within 24 hours, the territory must be evacuated completely, even by relief workers," he informed the media. At that point, the estimated dead numbered between 700 and 800, he said, with only 404 of the bodies buried. But not all of the dead had been recovered. More still lay beneath sections of houses and fallen trees, and far out in farm fields and swampland.

"We may have to spray whole sections with lime from airplanes," said Selby, citing one of the few known antidotes to the spread of bacteria from decaying bodies.

The same day, the threat of disease mounted as Dr. E. D. Clawson, who headed the medical relief effort, told Selby that he could account for 1,385 dead. Coral Gables Health Department chief Dr. A. F. Allen, on duty at an emergency hospital set up at the Pennsylvania Hotel there, tabulated an even larger figure based on reports from burial crews, ambulance drivers, and others on the front line: 1,800 bodies to date, with more still to be accounted for.

"We have gone over the death situation pretty closely," he told the *Miami News*. "When the final report is written, the general agreement among our doctors is that the total dead will not be far from 2,500."

The search for survivors ended and the effort became a recovery mission, with men from the American Legion taking motorboats into the lake area and burying bodies where they found them. Governor Martin returned to the area on Saturday, September 22 and found it worse than he could have imagined, calling it "the worst sight I have ever seen in my life." He and his party had no choice but to make their way along the highway to Pahokee, the only open road, where corpses could be seen in every direction.

Today in traveling six miles on the road between Pahokee and Belle Glade . . . I counted 27 corpses floating in the water adjacent to the road, or lying by the road. . . . The total number of dead lying on the roadside and not yet buried, but in plank coffins numbered 126. . . . Fifty-seven additional bodies were hauled out today in trucks, and tonight, four truckloads of bodies were brought from adjacent areas by boat, loaded and sent to Palm Beach for burial.

The worst of the nightmare came almost a week after the storm, when Red Cross officials finally reached the town of Pelican Bay—and found that it had disappeared. In its place were the bodies of 450 men, women, and children. Every resident of the community had perished in the floodwaters. "Isolated since last Sunday's storm and the only community on the lake shore not to receive prompt relief because of impassable roads, Pelican Bay, the last death pocket of the Everglades tragedy to give up its secret, was believed by Red Cross officials last night to present the most gruesome picture of the entire storm area," the *Miami News* reported. The remains of two hundred townspeople were found hidden in a five-foot-high pile of debris and mud that covered the road into town, while the rest lay in the town proper, where five feet of water still remained captured in the lowland as if cradled in a spongy basin. The dike on the west side of town and a railroad grade on the east side had formed a veritable sluiceway, funneling the lake's runaway waters into the heart of town. The speed and ferocity of this deluge proved inescapable.

Even as officials reported this gruesome discovery to the media, the *Miami Herald* published a page-one story on September 27 denying that there was even a settlement in the Everglades called Pelican Bay. The story quoted a resident of nearby Pahokee, a W. A. Cuthill who had worked on building the dikes in the area years before, who said that "not more than 125 persons, mostly negroes, lived in quarters along the shores of the bay." Cuthill and a crew of rescuers went into Pelican Bay on September 19 and 20 and found only a few bodies along the dike, and named two people from these settlements whom he knew had survived. This, he told the *Herald*, dispelled the rumor that there were no survivors in Pelican Bay. Cuthill was not there, however, on the day that rescue workers turned over the pile of debris that contained two hundred bodies.

By this time, the situation throughout the Everglades had become so dire that the state resorted to the quickest solution to prevent the spread of bacterial infections: burial of bodies in mass graves and cremation of decaying bodies as they were found. As a result, hundreds of bodies were never identified. Two mass graves were dug in West Palm Beach: one for 69 white bodies in Woodlawn Cemetery and one for 647 Black bodies in a cemetery on Tamarind Avenue. "Some corpses were too deteriorated to determine race, leaving workers with the terrible possibility that a Negro would go into a white grave," wrote Eliot Kleinberg, his tone tinged with sarcasm. "But they toiled on."

On Sunday, September 30 at 3 p.m., the city of Palm Beach held two memorial services simultaneously at the two gravesites about five miles apart, to remember those who had fallen in the storm. Five thousand people attended the ceremony for the white victims at Woodlawn, while between two thousand and three thousand came to Tamarind Avenue for the Black funeral. Hymns were sung, prayers were said, and people—many of whom had lost individual loved ones or entire families—began the overwhelming process of starting to move on.

The Red Cross reported a total of 1,836 deaths attributed to the hurricane and subsequent flooding, but in 2003 the National Weather Service revised that figure to "at least 2,500." There is no list of all of the people who died in the storm, however, because many were buried or cremated before they could be identified. To this day, many families cannot be certain whether they lost an ancestor—or a number of them—in the hurricane of 1928.

In 1930 the federal government appropriated $7 million so that Florida could finally build an appropriate flood control system for Lake Okeechobee and the Caloosahatchee River. The state raised another $2 million, and construction began in 1931, with the first of six dikes completed in August. Budgetary issues, dynamiting that led to additional flooding, and other obstacles slowed progress, but in March 1937, 140 miles of levees and a network of channels and gates went into operation, protecting residents, migrant workers, and crops until an even stronger hurricane came through in 1947. The resulting flooding moved the state to reinforce and enlarge the dike once again in the 1960s, and so far it has not yielded to storms passing directly over the lake, including Hurricane Wilma in 2005, Tropical Storm Ernesto in 2006, and Tropical Storm Fay in 2008.

5

Running Rum: Death of a Police Chief

IF THERE'S ONE THING EVERY CRIMINAL KNOWS—FROM PICKPOCKETS committing petty theft to drug cartels smuggling kilos of cocaine—it's this: Never kill a cop. Nothing will bring the wrath of an entire profession down on you faster than one of their own killed in the line of duty.

So on Christmas Eve 1931, chances are good that the group of rum runners on the edge of the Everglades did not begin their illegal activity with the intention of shooting a police officer—much less the Everglades chief of police. Their attention was on the operation they planned to complete as quickly as possible, transferring sacks of liquor to their car from a boat obscured by tall sawgrass.

J. Harold Davis and Robert Brown intended to transport the liquor to Fort Myers that night, no doubt to a clandestine distributor who would sell it for a significant profit. At the height of Prohibition, the high crime of smuggling liquor could be extraordinarily lucrative for common folks like Davis and Brown. The town of Everglades—what would later become Everglades City—offered the perfect inlet for supplies from the Caribbean. Situated at the northern terminus of the Ten Thousand Islands, a network of waterways, tall sawgrass, mangrove swamps, and hummocks provided all the hiding places smugglers needed to meet the continuous demand for booze.

Prohibition, of course, had done little to tame the nation's craving for demon alcohol. Temperance crusaders applauded the 1919 passage of the 18th Amendment, which banned the "manufacture, sale, or transportation of intoxicating liquors," but they did not foresee the unintended consequences such a law would create. Instead of wiping out alcohol from America's communities, it created an underground industry that continued to produce or procure beer, wine, and liquor from clandestine sources. Scofflaws banded together and standardized their smuggling operations, creating an entirely new kind of delinquency: organized crime. Some of these outfits imported alcohol from the Caribbean where liquor was legal, while others manufactured their own, giving rise to "bathtub gin" and other moonshine-like distillations—some of which contained ingredients that turned out to be lethal.

Temperance advocates thought that all the saloons they saw in immigrant communities would be forced to close down, but many of these simply turned to the crime of making their own booze. They purchased watered-down "near beer" at 0.5 percent alcohol to sell over the counter while their basements and back rooms became speakeasies, where they served the gin they made in hidden stills or real beer brewed behind locked doors. An in-the-know culture of illegal drinking made it fashionable to thumb one's nose at the law by knowing which door to knock on and what password to say to get into the kinds of parties that made the 1920s so festively wild.

By 1931, so many smuggling routes had been established that the Everglades fairly buzzed with illicit activity. No one was more aware of this liquor-transport network than W. F. Hutto, Everglades chief of police and a staunch enforcer of the law. Long before he rose from deputy sheriff to chief, news reports regularly charted his achievements in capturing and destroying alcohol operations in his district: a 50-gallon still on Turner River one day, an 80-gallon still in Naples the next, as well as gallons of mash and moonshine. Some interceptions happened on open roads, like the capture of a Ford filled with whiskey on the Immokalee highway one Friday night in June 1930 (for which the driver was fined a hefty $200).

Hutto often served alongside his commanding officer, Sheriff L. J. Thorp, as they worked to drive the evils of alcohol out of their briskly busy corner of the Florida coast. By the end of July 1930, in his dual capacity as chief of police of Collier County, Hutto was working directly with federal prohibition officers to take custody of stills throughout the

Naples area and further south. One series of raids netted four stills "completely outfitted," according to the *Fort Myers News-Press*, "three of them in operation and the fourth idle on account of high water."

Chief Hutto's record for stripping moonshiners of their equipment and resources spoke for itself, driving lawbreakers deeper into the backcountry to continue to ply their dicey trade. He knew that he had bigger fish to catch, however: the smugglers who operated under cover of the region's darkest nights, gliding between islands on the smooth Everglades waters to bring jugs of liquor to waiting automobiles on boggy shores.

Hutto undoubtedly knew which slim inlets and portable docks in his territory these rum runners frequented. Catching them in the act, however, proved to be tricky. So on the night before Christmas in 1931, when whispers among the townspeople about a shipment coming in that night reached his ears, he set out—on his own, with no backup—to surprise a band of smugglers and bring them to justice.

His evening began at a community Christmas party where he helped give out presents to the town's children, including his own. Leaving these festivities, Hutto arrived on the banks of Barron River and crept closer to the action, watching several men unload sacks of bottles from a boat and place them into a waiting car. When they had filled the car and the driver revved the motor, Hutto leapt out of his hiding place and landed nimbly on the car's running board. "Halt! Police!" he announced at the top of his voice.

The car did not slow, but that was the least of Hutto's problems. Two of the men inside responded by reflex—they pulled their guns and fired. One of the bullets hit Hutto squarely in the chest. He slumped, losing his grip on the car and falling from the running board. He attempted to run after the car for a few yards, but soon dropped to the ground and died. The car sped off and out of sight.

How exactly the news reached the county sheriff's office is not clear, but soon officers from throughout the county were patrolling every road leading out of the town of Everglades. Roadblocks stopped motorists to examine their cars and look for any evidence that might lead to a description of the cop killer or killers. "No description of the automobile or its occupants was available," the *Miami Herald* reported on Christmas day. "Only meager details of the shooting were included in the report."

No law enforcement officer in Collier or the adjoining counties enjoyed Christmas at home with his family that day as the investigation ratcheted into high gear. The manhunt centered on two culprits: J. Harold Davis, whose rap sheet contained a number of liquor smuggling charges, and a Black man, Robert Brown, employed by Davis.

By 4:00 a.m. on Christmas Day, Sheriff Thorp already had information that pointed to Brown as the trigger man. He telephoned the police in Lee County at that early hour and they went directly to Davis's house to question him. He was not there, however, though his family said he would be back shortly. The officers waited until 7:00 a.m. when a visibly upset Davis made his appearance. His jumbled story left out key facts: He did not tell them the route he took back to Fort Myers after the botched liquor pickup, and he refused to answer questions about his involvement with the liquor, saying that his response would be self-incriminating.

At the coroner's inquest on December 26, Davis and Benton Boggess—the driver of the liquor-filled boat—told the jury that they saw Brown, "several sacks believed to contain liquor," and Hutto near town on the bank of the river. Their testimony endeavored to lay all the blame for Hutto's death on Brown, the expendable Black man, and deflect any guilt or even involvement from Davis. Later state attorney Guy Strayhorn observed, "It is plainly evident that if Robert Brown had not been at Everglades on the night before Christmas as the employee of Harold Davis in the liquor running business, that the highly esteemed and well liked officer, W. E. Hutto, would be alive today and his wife would not be a widow and his little children fatherless."

On December 29, Sheriff F. B. Tippins of Lee County told the media that an automobile had been found near Immokalee, and that it appeared to be the one used by Robert Brown on the night Hutto was killed. Later that day, however, Davis said the car was his—though he continued to deny any connection to the shooting.

Brown, meanwhile, was nowhere to be found. Police staked out his home in the Safety Hill area of Fort Myers and several other places they thought he might appear, but they picked up no trail and saw no sign of him.

The search for Brown finally ended shortly before 10:00 p.m. on December 29, when Deputy Roy Larson saw him enter his home. When Larson went to the door, Brown put up no resistance, and he was only too happy to tell his version of events before and after Hutto's slaying. Larson and Sheriff Thorp subjected the suspect to "an hour of severe grilling," according to the *News-Press*, but Brown stuck to his story start to finish. He said that Davis had approached him during the day on Christmas Eve, asking Brown to meet him at Everglades for a job. When Brown got to the meeting place in his old automobile, Davis said, "I know where there's some booze, and I want you to bring it back to Fort Myers."

The two men drove in separate cars to the river bank, where Brown could see "a stack of liquor piled up on the bank. I don't know just how much there was." They pulled their cars in and parked them, but before they could get the liquor into the car, they saw the lights of Hutto's car approaching them.

Davis jumped into his car and raced off, leaving Brown with the liquor. Brown backed up into the sawgrass, he said, and laid down flat on the ground, hoping to hide there while the police took away the liquor. As he lay there and his eyes readjusted to the dark, he realized that there was another car just behind him, sitting silently with its lights off.

Three men jumped out of the car, grabbed Brown and pushed him into the vehicle. As soon as the doors were closed, the driver hit the gas and the car sped off—but Brown heard shots fired. "I thought they shot Davis," he told the officers. He had no idea where they were taking him, except that the car made a lot of turns and drove down some winding roads. When pressed, he guessed that the car was a new Chevrolet.

The car finally stopped at a small office building—although in another round of questioning, Brown said it was a garage—and the men made him go inside. "A tiny crack admitted the only light in the small building," the *News-Press* quoted from the interrogation report, "and he was fed meagerly on crackers and water." Two men stood guard, neither of whom he had ever seen before. The door never opened.

After three days, his captors reappeared, put him in a car and drove him to a spot between Lake Okeechobee and Arcadia, leaving him there by the side of the road. He had no choice but to walk back to Fort Myers from there, a journey that took him the entire day. When he had walked as far as Punta Gorda, he heard for the first time about Hutto's murder and the manhunt in progress. It had not surprised him to find Deputy Larson waiting for him at his home.

Most important, Brown asserted repeatedly that he had not been otherwise involved in shooting Hutto. Larson and Thorp pressured him to confess, but it became clear that he had no intention of doing so. "I know the law's the law," he told them, "and I wouldn't lie to you gentlemen. I wouldn't kill anybody. I know if they catch me with liquor they can send me up for a few years but I would not kill an officer or resist one. I know how serious that is."

Larson and Thorp tried to convince Brown that they had insurmountable evidence against him, but he did not waver from his story. They even went so far as to threaten to jail him in the town of Everglades, where many townspeople would just as soon see him hanged rather than wait for the due process of law. When they could not goad him into a confession, they finally took him out of the county jail in Fort Myers and to an undisclosed location, where he would not be in danger of a spontaneous lynching by an angry mob.

What was this evidence that implicated Brown? Two eye witnesses had come forward, ready to help with the investigation and to testify in court. A Seminole woman, identified only as the wife of Charlie Billie, was walking home to her village with a group of women when they heard gunshots. When she got home, she told her husband she had seen "white man riding on car, saw white man run and fall and no get up." She also was certain that the car from which the shots had been fired was driven by a Black man.

Billie mentioned this to a gas station owner near Everglades the following day, and the station owner called Sheriff Thorp. Despite his best effort, Thorp could not locate the other Seminole women walking with Billie's wife, an issue attributed to language barriers and Thorp's "inability to make himself understood," the *News-Press* said.

The second witness, sitting in the kitchen of resident D. Graham Copeland, heard five gunshots and ran out of the house to see what was happening. He also said he saw Hutto take a few steps in the street and then fall.

In this era before Miranda rights, Sheriff Thorp had forbidden Brown—who was being held in Miami in a Dade County jail—to see an attorney until the officer had finished interrogating him. By the time Brown finally met with attorneys including George J. Baya and R. Percy Jones, Baya had already taken action on Brown's behalf in court. Baya filed a writ of habeas corpus demanding Brown's release, saying there had been no warrant for his original arrest on December 29 (though a warrant for his arrest was issued January 2 after the coroner's inquest). Brown was released, but Dade County deputies then re-charged Brown, taking out a warrant that stated he was a fugitive. Thorp re-arrested Brown, "whisking him out of the jurisdiction of the Dade County Circuit Court before a second habeas corpus action could be instituted," the *News-Press* reported on January 10.

Judge George W. Whitehurst of Collier County announced on January 17, 1932, that he would convene a special term of the grand jury the following week on January 25, bringing a jury together six weeks before its regularly scheduled session beginning March 7. Whitehurst declared the murder of the chief of police "a challenge to law enforcement within the judicial system over which he presides," the *News-Press* reported. The jury would be charged with deliberations on Hutto's murder and the liquor charge against J. Harold Davis, which Whitehurst considered "an outgrowth of the investigation into the murder." This was Davis's second offense on liquor charges, and while by this time he had been released on $2,500 bond, his record made his further conviction a matter for a grand jury.

On the day the grand jury convened, Judge Whitehurst charged them to "spare no effort or expense" in determining whom to bring to trial. He called the murder "a challenge to officers of the law and to every citizen of the country." The grand jury moved ahead with vigor, hearing testimony from a long list of witnesses including Sheriff Tippins and Deputy Roy Larson as well as Stafford Powers, a fisherman who had found the murder car; Mary Brown and Mercy Brown, the grandmother and wife of Robert Brown; and Davis and Boggess. On the second day, the jury heard from the Seminole woman who had seen Hutto fall, "although it was impossible to determine how much credence would be placed in her testimony by the jury," the *News-Press* reporter felt the need to comment. Two other witnesses—Henry Brown and Charlie Jolly, both of whom said they heard three shots fired—completed the lineup.

In the interim between his arrest and his appearance before the grand jury, Davis had appeared before the county judge in Collier County, and that judge had dismissed the charges against Davis in exchange for his cooperation and assistance in finding Hutto's murderer. This came as a complete surprise to state attorney Guy M. Strayhorn, who had been ready to prosecute Davis before the grand jury. "As state's attorney, none of the officers has ever informed me of any voluntary assistance Davis has given them," he told the media on January 25 as the grand jury began its work.

So Davis would not be tried on liquor charges, but the jury handed down the indictment of "Robert Brown, negro," as the newspapers referred to him, for Hutto's murder.

Brown's trial finally began in May after several false starts and legal rows over the jury selection process and other technicalities. Prosecutor Strayhorn, representing the State of Florida, planned to present a long list of circumstantial factors that led to Brown as the most likely trigger man in the case. While Brown stuck to every detail of his story about being kidnapped from the banks of Barron River on the night of the shooting, Strayhorn planned to propose an alternative version of events: Hutto was in the process of arresting Brown and taking him to jail when Brown shot him. Defense attorneys George W. Scofield and E. M. Magaha did not reveal their strategy to the media before the trial, keeping their proverbial cards close to the vest.

During jury selection, Strayhorn made it clear in his remarks to the venire that he intended to seek the death penalty should Brown be found guilty. He asked if any of the panel of jury candidates had a conscientious objection to this, and when several said they did, he excused them from selection.

The prosecution began with J. Harold Davis as the first witness. He told the court that he was on the riverbank with Brown on Christmas Eve to receive "merchandise" and that he told Brown to load the unspecified items into his car. Strayhorn tried his best to force Davis to define what the merchandise was, but Judge Whitehurst allowed the witness's refusal to say what he had received, citing Davis's Fifth Amendment right to refrain from incriminating himself.

With this issue resolved, Davis went on to add a new character to the story: a "blonde man" whom he said was on the riverbank with himself and Brown. As the boatman, Benton Boggess, was not blonde, this person had to be someone else—someone who had never been mentioned in all of the testimony to date, including the questioning of Davis in front of the grand jury. "Davis said he did not know the 'blonde man' and that he 'had never seen him before,'" the *Fort Myers News-Press* reported in its coverage of the trial's first day. "He did say, however, that he believed the 'blonde man' had landed the 'merchandise' from a skiff."

When Davis saw Hutto's headlights coming toward them, he said, he got into his car and drove off toward Fort Myers on the Immokalee road. Brown and the unnamed blonde man remained on the riverbank as he rode away. He made no mention of Boggess at all, intimating that the boatman had nothing to do with the shooting—though Strayhorn quickly produced a transcript of Davis's grand jury testimony in which he had said Boggess was still there when he departed.

Boggess had his chance to testify after Davis. He said that he had come up the river on his boat and spotted Davis and Brown loading "something" into their cars—and that he "thought the stuff was liquor" but could not say for certain. He corroborated the story that Davis had driven away in a hurry when headlights appeared, and added that Brown also jumped into his auto and started to leave but that Hutto blocked the narrow exit with his own car. Boggess, apparently wishing to distance himself from whatever happened next, pushed off from the riverbank and started down river, so he did not see who shot Hutto.

The trial's second day began with an eighteen-year-old Seminole boy's eyewitness testimony, filtered through two interpreters—one for the state, and one for the defense to ensure accuracy and avoid any kind of inherent bias. Frank Billy had begun to cross the street on Christmas Eve night when he heard five gunshots. He stopped and peered down the road, and saw an automobile coming toward him and a man running behind it. As the car passed, he recognized it as a Ford sedan, and the moonlight illuminated the driver: a Black man wearing a light-colored cap. The running man continued for about fifty yards before falling down, clearly collapsing from a wound.

The defense cross-examined Billy aggressively, doing their best to discredit his recollection, but the young man stood firm. "Asked point-blank by defense attorneys if Brown was the negro in the car, Frank Billy asked that the negro be given a light cap to wear and he believed he could identify him," the *News-Press* reported. "The defense did not put the cap on the negro's head, however."

Next the attorneys asserted that the car must have been around a corner when the shots were fired, and therefore out of Billy's view. Billy "refused to be led into an admission that the car was around a corner," the newspaper said. "He maintained it was on the same street which he was crossing and passed him only a moment after he heard the shots." Perhaps most important, he insisted that the five shots came from inside the moving car.

Once Billy had been released from the witness stand, the prosecutor called Dr. M. F. Pender of Everglades to testify. Pender had been the first doctor to reach Hutto's body in the street. He noted that the bullet that killed him went straight through the police chief's heart and into his left lung. Dr. J. William Jones, who had performed the autopsy on Hutto in Fort Myers at the Lawrence A. Powell funeral home, gave the same description of the killing wound.

Sheriff Louis J. Thorp was the next witness for the prosecution, serving as an expert on shooting a bullet through glass. He said that he had performed a number of experiments, shooting his gun through panes of glass like the window of an automobile, and he was certain that the bullet that killed Hutto had been shot from inside the vehicle with the window closed.

On the fourth day of the trial, Robert Brown took the stand as the primary witness for the defense. He proceeded to surprise the jurors and spectators with a whole new narrative of what had happened to him on Christmas Eve.

Instead of his story of being kidnapped and held in a garage for three days, Brown started over from the beginning. He told the court that he and Davis were on the river bank with a third man, LeRoy Orme, when Hutto's headlights appeared down the road. He jumped into the same car as Davis, and the two of them took off—a direct contradiction of Davis's own testimony that he had driven away alone. Brown confirmed that they were loading liquor into the car—something Davis had refused to say—and when he and Davis drove off, Orme remained on the riverbank.

Orme's name had not come up before during this proceeding, but he was a known player to the investigators. They had questioned him in Fort Myers about his whereabouts on Christmas Eve and "he had furnished a satisfactory explanation of his whereabouts at the time of the murder," according to the *News-Press*.

Brown said that he was the driver of the automobile as they bolted, swerving to miss Hutto's car and taking off down the Everglades road. He drove as far as Carnestown and then relinquished the wheel to Davis, who drove to Immokalee for gas and oil. Davis dropped Brown off at the gas station and told him to stay out of sight there for a few days.

So Brown hid in the gas station garage—making part of his original story true—until Davis returned early the following day. He was going to Carnestown, he said, and would come back with food for Brown. When he did come back, however, he did not bring anything to eat, and Brown finally decided to head home on foot. He walked to Fort Myers and hid at a baseball park frequented by the Black community, finally making his way back to his home in Safety Hill on December 29. There he encountered Deputy Larson, who arrested him immediately.

"Why did you tell us that you were kidnapped?" his attorney asked.

"I was afraid if I told the truth, Davis would kill me," he said.

Additional witnesses gave Brown's revised story the ring of truth. Deputy Larson told the court that he had seen Davis in Fort Myers on Christmas morning, once at 6:30 a.m. and again at 11:00 a.m. Two fishermen who had been on the Tamiami Trail north of Carnestown on Christmas Eve said that at about 10:00 p.m. a car had sped past them and slowed down at a temporary bridge. When the driver used a hand signal at the bridge crossing, the arm that appeared was white.

The defense rested its case shortly thereafter. By 4:00 p.m. on Thursday, May 5, Judge Whitehurst assigned the case to the jury ... and seven hours later, at 11:00 p.m., they had not yet reached a decision. "No word of the balloting had come from the jury room and there was nothing to indicate the trend of the voting among the 12 men who will decide the negro's fate," the *News-Press* reported on Friday morning, May 6. The jury reconvened at 8:00 a.m. on Friday, and it turned out that they had indeed reached a verdict the night before just prior to midnight, but the judge had already ordered the jury sequestered for the night.

The unanimous vote stunned the courtroom: The jury had found Brown innocent.

"Out of a maze of contradictory testimony offered before two grand jury sessions and during the trial of the negro, very few actual facts were established," the *News-Press* analysis asserted. Had there been another person in the car whom no one mentioned? Were the police too quick to accept Orme's alibi as fact? Or had Davis been the trigger man?

"In the unsuccessful effort to convict the negro, Brown, of the crime, it was believed likely last night that the door had been closed against possibility of the conviction of anyone for the murder of Chief Hutto," the newspaper concluded. "Guy M. Strayhorn said yesterday he knew of no evidence that would justify indictment of any other person as the slayer of Hutto and that it seemed a sufficient alibi was available to preclude involvement of anyone who might be suspected."

For a time, it seemed like the story had come to an end ... but later that year, another chapter emerged.

On October 13, the AP discovered that Sheriff Thorp and three other men had been indicted two weeks earlier by a federal grand jury. The charge was "conspiracy to violate the national prohibition act" with specific reference to the loading of a boat with liquor on Christmas Eve—a boat that then traveled up Barron River to the spot where Davis, Orme, and Brown picked up the liquor and W. E. Hutto found them. Nine days later, a federal indictment charged that five men "did shoot and kill" Hutto while they unloaded a liquor boat. The men charged included

J. Harold Davis, Benton Boggess, and three names that had not come up in the original trial: Lloyd and Dan House and Hamp Jones. With the exception of Jones, all of the men also were charged with conspiracy against the Prohibition Act, as were several other men who were not associated with the murder.

For a few exciting weeks it looked like a conviction might be in the offing, and that justice might finally be done for Chief Hutto. Federal Judge Halsted L. Ritter, however, had the unpleasant but necessary job of dashing this hope on the day the trial was scheduled to begin. Instead of a trial, Ritter ordered that the Department of Justice begin "a rigid investigation" into "agents that 'bought and perjured' testimony by negroes aided in securing the indictment" of Thorp and the others.

The accusation of perjury came from Bart Riley, defense counsel for Dan House. He said that the witnesses who testified before the grand jury in Tampa had been paid to appear and lie to the jury, providing testimony that would implicate Thorp and ten other men with rum running and Hutto's murder. He told the judge that Louis Bell of Fort Myers had told him that Charlie Williams had "promised witness fees and mileage to him and to other negroes if they would testify before the jury in a manner to be outlined by Williams," according to the AP. Bell had refused the offer, but eight men had accepted.

Williams's specifications for their testimony were that they would name certain white men in the shooting of Hutto, "including a railway conductor and another railroad man, as having assisted in preparing freight cars for loading with liquor." Riley demanded that the eight witnesses be brought into this court for questioning to determine if they had been paid for their false testimony.

Assistant district attorney B. R. Cisco supported Riley's request, referring to rumors in the community that supported the claims of perjury. He added that he had tried to find these eight witnesses, but he could locate only one of them—and that one had insisted he was not the man Cisco said he was. The day closed with Judge Ritter issuing bench warrants for the eight men.

Federal agents never found the men in question. In March 1933, the conspiracy charges against Thorp and the others were dismissed for lack of evidence, and in May, Judge Alexander Ackerman of the U.S. District Court in Miami dropped the murder charge.

No other suspect ever emerged, leaving the murder of Chief Hutto unsolved. With no murder weapon to examine, no fingerprints to match, and no eyewitnesses who could identify a shooter, investigators were left with a cold case that remains open to this day.

6

Unintended Consequences: Deaths on the Tamiami Trail

MIAMI HERALD STAFF WRITER WILLIAM STUART HILL LOVED TO TELL the story of a day in 1914 when he paid a visit to Dade County tax assessor Capt. James F. Jaudon, just after the assessor had returned from a drive to Fort Myers.

"It is a shame we people down here have to drive to New Smyrna, cross the state, motor down the west coast, a distance altogether of 550 miles to reach a point 150 miles from Miami," Jaudon said.

Hill immediately urged Jaudon to advocate for building a road across the Everglades from Miami to Naples and Fort Myers. "I will write a boosting story stressing the need for the road, and quote you," Hill said. "Tomorrow I will interview some prominent citizen as to his opinion of your plan, and the following day publish another story from some other individual." Hill would keep at it, he promised, while Jaudon worked to get "influential backing" that would pressure state and county commissioners to consider building the road.

Jaudon agreed to give the plan a try, and Hill set to work finding one person after another to endorse the idea. The two men were far from the first people to wish for a shorter route across the southern portion of the peninsula, though they may have been the first to take definitive action on the concept.

Coming together in pieces with many stops and starts, the difficult process of actually building a road down the west coast of Florida and across the Everglades revealed itself over time. Bedrock beneath the river of grass turned out to be much harder than expected, requiring a reported 2.6 million sticks of dynamite to blast away. Funding for the east–west portion of the 284-mile road ran out in 1919, so Jaudon called on his own company, the Chevelier Corporation, to provide the necessary funds—but only if the road could be rerouted through the company's own holdings in Monroe County. This resulted in the segment now known as the Loop Road, extending into Naples through Big Cypress National Preserve.

When the 275-mile Tamiami Trail opened on April 26, 1928, its construction cost had soared to $8 million—roughly $129.3 million today. The ability to drive across the peninsula in hours instead of days, however, so delighted residents and tourists that the expense seemed well justified. "Today as thousands of automobiles roll along the smooth surface of the most talked about road in America toward their goal on the shores of Biscayne Bay, the west coast is linked with the east," Hill wrote in the *Herald* on the opening day of the road he helped create. The people of the state's west coast, he enthused, "are stretching out their hands for the warm handclasp of the people of the metropolis of the east coast."

Jubilant drivers enjoying the sunlight, fair weather, and long, straight, two-lane blacktop, however, could not help but press down harder than they should have on the accelerator. On January 19, 1929, the *Fort Myers News-Press* reported what may have been the first fatality on the new road. Thirty-eight-year-old patrol officer William Irwin, a member of the Collier County Mounted Police stationed at Trail's Patrol System Camp in Monroe County, was making his way by motorcycle through heavy fog at about 8:00 a.m. when he apparently veered a little too far to his left. He may never have seen the oncoming vehicle driven by N. G. Brennan of Birmingham, Alabama, with his wife and two sons, P. W. and John. Irwin's front wheel collided with the Brennan's front tire and the car flipped over, continued to roll, and came to a stop in an upright position. Irwin was not so lucky—his motorcycle threw him off and skidded to the side of the road. Irwin suffered a skull fracture that killed him at the scene. The Brennans escaped with cuts and bruises.

Today's readers of this account have no doubt already started to tick off the safety precautions available to us today that would have prevented anyone from serious injury in this crash. We can assume, for example, that Irwin did not wear a helmet, as Florida did not require one then (and, in fact, still does not require motorcyclists to wear one). Seat belts, the staples of every vehicle today, did not become standard equipment until 1964. Even in dense fog, drivers may not have turned on their headlights—and those of us who often drive in fog know that headlights do not always make it easier to see through all that billowing vapor. Guardrails might have stopped the car from rolling, though they probably would not have kept Irwin from hitting his head on the pavement. Even speed limits may not have been established in the road's early years.

To drivers in 1929, this fatality seemed like an unfortunate one-time accident and not an indictment of the new road's overall safety. The same could have been said when, on March 23 of that year, Mrs. Harold K. Hallan, a tourist from Chicago, drove her car into the side of a bridge between Naples and Everglades City. The car rolled and burst into flames, and Mrs. Hallan became trapped inside. She died in the fire, while her passengers—her son Jerry, who suffered severe cuts and bruises, and a Mrs. Goodlong—both survived the ordeal. The three tourists had just returned from a visit to Cuba and were on their way back to Chicago via Fort Myers.

The next death on this road on June 7, 1929, involved a Miami resident, Waddie A. McCreary, who was twenty-nine at the time. A manager in Miami for R. G. Dun & Company, the predecessor to corporate watchdog Dun & Bradstreet, he served as a member of the American Legion post in Tampa, held memberships in the Biscayne Bay Masonic Lodge and the Miami Acacia Club, and had just hosted a visit from his mother the previous week when she came from Evergreen, Alabama, to see him.

Edith Blackburn, a twenty-eight-year-old stenographer from Tampa who had been visiting Miami, was driving her coupe at about 6:00 p.m. when a tire blew out, sending her car veering off the pavement and onto what little shoulder the road provided. Blackburn held onto the wheel and worked to bring the car back under control, but as she tried to straighten out, she hit an oncoming car and lost her grip on the wheel. The coupe flipped over and landed on its roof in the middle of the road, while the other vehicle, a sedan driven by Jim Springer of Tampa with McCreary as a passenger, slid sideways. The cars themselves did not take on much damage, but McCreary died immediately from a compound skull fracture, and Blackburn sustained extensive but not fatal injuries. Springer, who found himself bruised but not seriously hurt, quickly escorted Blackburn to his car and drove her to Lee Memorial hospital in Fort Myers. The coroner, investigating the accident and interviewing the survivors, decided the next day that the crash had been "unavoidable."

By this time, questions had begun to arise about the haphazard condition of the cross-country road. The road's surface, constructed long before the innovations of America's interstate highway system, had been laid over an uneven structure of dirt and rock dug up to create the canal that paralleled the road all the way across the Everglades. Just two lanes wide—one lane in either direction—it lacked stable shoulders, making its edges treacherous and any oncoming traffic potentially dangerous. While traffic officials considered the road safe if drivers maintained a speed of less than 50 mph, there may have been no road signs to this effect.

By 1937, fatal accidents on the Tamiami Trail numbered as many as ten annually. Each tended to be an isolated incident with reasonable explanations for its causes, however, and the numbers were not out of line with the high rate of traffic fatalities across the country. Mass travel by automobile was still in its infancy in America, with many of the laws that keep modern roads safer still barely a conception in the minds of city planners and engineers. Ten deaths per year did not raise enough red flags to suggest that something about this fairly new road might be unduly hazardous.

Then came what Florida State Railroad Commission member Eugene S. Matthews would call "the greatest disaster to my knowledge in Florida transportation history."

On January 25, 1937, twenty-nine tourists, a porter, and the driver of an aging but streamlined bus owned by Tamiami Trail Tours set off at 8:00 a.m. to cross the Everglades from Miami on the tour company's namesake road, continuing to Tampa. Passenger Vincent Rogers, visiting from Walla Walla, Washington, told the *Miami Herald* later that day that he and his wife, Elizabeth, were at the bus terminal at 7:00 a.m. so they could get what he considered to be the best seats on the bus. When they boarded the bus, however, they found that another passenger, a woman, had draped her coat across the front seat, the very place that Rogers wanted to sit.

"I grabbed the coat and tossed it onto another seat," he said, "and I told the porter, when he tried to interfere, that there were no reserved seats in the bus, because I had been told there wasn't." When the female passenger who owned the coat returned to her intended seat, she could see at a glance that there was no point in arguing with Rogers for it. She picked up her coat, he told the *Herald*, and moved to the back of the bus.

Another of the passengers, Frederick Gilliland, noticed that the bus driver, twenty-three-year-old Bill Hammond, "got down on his knees and looked under the rear end of the bus when he stopped to take on a passenger in Coral Gables," the *Miami Herald* reported. Gilliland told reporter Henry O. Reno, "I remarked to my wife afterwards that the rear end didn't sound just right to me."

The rear end, it turned out, was the least of the bus's problems. Hammond had simply performed a routine check on the back wheels, as his job required him to do at every stop, and he had seen nothing amiss.

Twenty-three-year-old porter Robert Singleton, whose duties included acting as a tour guide, had just sat down after telling the passengers about the Everglades, the construction of the road, and the trail's unusual features. Sitting next to Hammond, he later told the AP that the bus was traveling at a normal speed—about 50 mph—when "suddenly something happened."

Hammond added, "Either the steering gear broke or the right front wheel collapsed."

At 9:05 a.m., about twenty-seven miles west of Miami in the heart of the Everglades, the bus lurched hard to the right. "I think it was the collapse of the right front wheel," Singleton told the reporter. Later he told the *Fort Myers News-Press*, "The driver was fighting the wheel and I just hung on." He elaborated for the *Miami Herald* the following day, "Something popped, and then the front end seemed to fall to the ground."

Hammond had the fight of his life on his hands. After the initial swerve, he managed to swing the bus back onto the pavement, but the right front wheel veered off once again as it contacted the uneven, pothole-strewn surface. The bus zigzagged along the edge of the road, wrenching control of the steering away from the driver until both front wheels were on the shoulder.

The bus careened toward the canal that paralleled the road, gaining momentum as it vaulted through and over the large, jagged coral boulders positioned between the pavement and the canal—the only barrier between land and water. Later, AP photographer B. F. Glander reported seeing a long scraped-up area in the dirt next to the road, "indicating the bus had slid along on its side before falling into the water." Police measurements of the long skid found it three hundred feet long.

"The driver must have fought desperately to hold the bus in the road," Chief D. E. Sox of Coral Gables said to the *Fort Myers News-Press*.

The impact tore the entire front wheel assembly out of the bus—the front wheels, axle, and spring—leaving the vehicle essentially unsteerable. The bus flipped, rolled into the twelve-foot-deep canal, righted itself, and sank its wheels deep into the mud.

"I saw the water come up over the window," Singleton said. We can only imagine the bedlam that ensued inside the bus as its passengers found themselves trapped in a metal can rapidly filling with water. "Women screamed and men shouted," the porter said. "I lashed out with my left fist and broke the glass and crawled out," holding up a hand still covered in his own blood. "I came up to the surface and started for shore."

With his head just out of the water, Singleton looked back over his shoulder to see how many others had escaped and saw just one man splash to the surface. "Then I realized that all of those folks were trapped inside."

Singleton turned around and swam back, diving down at the doorway and reaching inside. He pulled out Hammond, whom he saw was injured. "I dragged him to shore," he said. He went back twice more, pulling out two men who were able to swim for the surface. "I was out of breath but I went back again and I got one more," he said. By this time, other people had arrived on the scene and were in the water, working to free others. "One white man pulled out six persons but four of them were drowned," he said. "It was all awful and no time to think."

Hammond, injured but alive, told the AP he thought he should have gone back down and broken the windows to help others get out, but that motorists who had gathered by the side of the road "thought air might still be in the bus and people might still be alive."

James I. Woolsey of Atlanta, Georgia, was driving his own car behind the bus on the Tamiami Trail when the bus suddenly went into the ditch about a mile ahead of him. When he saw the bus roll into the water, he hit the gas and drove up to it, leapt out of his car and started to remove his shoes to wade into the canal.

"Two people were sitting on top of the bus," he told the *Fort Myers News-Press*. "Heads of two others appeared. Other cars started to drive up and stop."

The two on top of the bus turned out to be Mr. and Mrs. Frederick Gilliland, who had clambered up there after releasing the bus's emergency exit door. They had taken the rearmost seat on the bus by the emergency door, and happened to be chatting about how to release the door when the bus suddenly jolted and began to skid. "When we went into the canal and the water began pouring in, I shoved the door open and shouted, 'Swim, don't mind me,' to my wife," Frederick told the AP. "Then I pushed her out. I followed her. She is a good swimmer, but I can only swim a few strokes."

He swam well enough to save his own life, popping up on the canal bank on the opposite side from the road, but thick vegetation there prevented him from getting out of the water. His wife had surfaced as well and found some kind of handhold on the side of the bus. She called to him to swim toward her. "I managed to clamber up on the bus and helped her on it," he said. "I was afraid it would turn over in the water, but we managed to pull two or three out of the water as they were swimming around and I told them to hang on until help came." Several people got a grip on the luggage rack on top of the bus and held on for dear life. "I told my wife if the bus rolled over, to save herself, so one of us would be left living."

The Gillilands' quick thinking in opening the emergency door also saved F. L. Matthews, who was sitting near them in the back of the bus.

"I got out very soon after the bus struck the water and I managed to grab hold of somebody to rescue them, but I am not a good swimmer," he told the AP reporter.

Rogers, visiting from Walla Walla, Washington, freed himself as well and then spotted a man's foot sticking out a window. "I went down again and managed to get his other foot through the window and so got him unfastened until he could get out," he said. Rogers's own wife, however, was not so fortunate; she remained trapped inside the bus and drowned.

Winifred Williams of Binghamton, New York, was likely one of the people whose head appeared above the water's surface just as Woolsey pulled up on the canal bank. Williams considered herself a veteran of bus travel: She had ridden buses across the United States five times for a total of more than forty thousand miles. Before she had taken to travel, she served for eighteen months in France during World War I, an experience she credited with her ability to think under pressure while making her escape from the submerged bus. From her room at a Miami hospital, she told the *Miami Herald* about her escape.

"I don't believe I was thrown from my seat," she said. "I saw it going, but I thought the driver could right the bus. There was lots of space on the canal edge, but it struck the rocks and turned over and over like a child's toy bus. I knocked the glass out of the window. It was dark under the water. I put my hands out and went out." Looking at a bruised knuckle on her left hand, she added. "I guess I hurt my hand when I broke the glass. I swam out from under the water and grabbed the bus top which was the only part above water. A moment later somebody offered to throw me a rope but I could swim so I told them to throw the rope to a man struggling in the water who seemed badly injured. It looked like he had been struck on the head by luggage."

Gaining perspective, she added, "It was terrible. The woman seated beside me was drowned. The man sitting in back of me, I heard him say he was from Detroit, he's gone. And there was a darling little boy. I'm afraid he didn't get out."

As heads appeared above the water and more and more drivers pulled over to help, Woolsey, removing his shoes on the bank, heard someone shout that he should drive back to Miami and alert authorities. This seemed like the most constructive contribution he could make, so he gathered his shoes, jumped into his car, and drove "like mad" to get to the first nearby settlement and spread the word. "All the way in, the picture of those people trapped like rats inside the bus was in my mind," he said. "I drove faster than ever before in my life."

Every time he saw a cluster of houses or a little store, he pulled over and told them what had happened. Many of the people he saw went to their vehicles and started for the accident scene. "I finally got to a hotel and had them telephone for help," he said. "I had a drink to calm my nerves and started back."

When he returned to the scene, a crowd had gathered, and bodies had begun to appear on the bank. "I will never forget seeing those people in the bus and wishing I knew how to save them," he said.

A Coast Guard truck soon arrived with a professional diver and a full diving rig, as well as an auto wrecking truck that also brought a diver and helmet. Police with rescue equipment and ambulances also rushed to the scene. "Police authorities attempted to set up short wave radio communication with the remote spot, but it was too far for their set," the AP reported.

By this time, everyone knew the grim truth: The operation was one of recovery, not rescue. Divers brought body after body up to the surface. "About 75 people were lined up beside the canal," Glander told the wire service's reporter. "There were three men stripped to the waist working desperately above and below the water line trying to get inside of the bus."

Hundreds of onlookers watched as every five minutes or so one or more of the rescuers brought a body to the surface, where waiting crews threw them a rope to tie around the body. The spectators became a problem in their own right, crowding close for the best possible view of the proceedings. "Time and time again police pushed the crowds back from the wreckers," the *Miami Herald* reported. "One section finally was roped off."

The crews on the banks dragged each body out of the water and onto the canal bank to be loaded into waiting "ambulances" (what we now call hearses) sent by every funeral home in Miami. Hearse drivers even worked alongside the divers—one of them, Art Woods, worked so hard to bring bodies up to the surface that he collapsed from the effort. The morticians quickly came up with a system to hasten progress with the recovery crews: They lined up their cots near the diving equipment, and the recovery workers gave a shout each time a body came up from the canal's depths. Whichever cot was next in line took the body, and the waiting mortician stepped forward and waited as Lt. J. O. Barker of the Miami Police Identification Bureau blocked the corpse from public view with a sheet. Barker took photos of the body for identification and then stepped back so the mortician could transport it to the ambulance.

Seventeen of the passengers had drowned inside the bus, their bodies floating to the ceiling as they gave up their battle for life. Eight others suffered serious injuries, but managed to escape with their lives. Singleton and five others were relatively unhurt.

Rogers sat grieving on the canal bank, his back covered in blood from the cuts he had sustained working his way out of a broken window. He waited while divers brought up one body after another, watching for the one he knew would be his wife, Elizabeth Rogers, who was fifty-four. "I'm not leaving until they take her out," he told emergency medical personnel who insisted he needed medical attention. Spectators tried to console him while every newspaper covering the scene snapped photos of the openly weeping man. He reflected briefly on the woman whose coat he had moved to take her seat in the front of the bus. "Poor soul," he said, "I think she is down in there dead now, but I don't feel as though I'm responsible. I lost my wife, you know."

Two men from the P&A Garage in Miami—Bill Bailey and B. R. Curry—recovered eight bodies between them. Equipped with goggles that allowed him to see well underwater, Bailey had the dubious privilege of seeing inside the submerged bus better than anyone else.

"The bodies were all up to the top and they all seemed to be in about the middle of the bus," he told the *Herald*. "I got three of them by going inside the bus and three others I pulled through the open door."

"No attempt was made to identify the victims at the scene," the AP reported. The first bodies raised by the divers were brought to a private mortuary in Miami, where the undertaker maintained strict rules that they not be "disturbed" by family members until the police had examined all of the bodies.

To recover the last of the victims, however, the bus had to be raised out of the canal. The sheriff's office in Miami sent out auto wrecking crews to do this, but the canal bottom held the vehicle fast in its muddy grip. Almost completely submerged with only "a small corner of the rear end" showing above the surface, the bus refused to give up its place in the twelve-foot-deep water.

The sheriff's office obtained two big trucks from Southern Bell Telephone & Telegraph, as well as "three regular wreckers and three derrick equipped trucks," to pry the bus out of the muck and bring it to the surface. Spectators had a long wait as mechanics connected all of the cables, winches, and chains from the trucks to the bus, and then "with one combined tug the trucks and wreckers budged the bus from the bottom of the canal, and by 3 p.m. the bus had been pulled to the bank," the *Herald* said—but not without further incident. A cable on a wrecking truck overloaded as it pulled on the bus and snapped, sending a U-bolt flying through the air and hitting a fireman from Miami, James Singleton. The bolt lacerated his scalp, removing him from recovery duty for the rest of that day.

"Thousands of spectators" showed up to watch the crews work to pull out the bus, the *News-Press* said. "State patrolmen had to rope off a section so normal traffic could proceed, unhampered with their grim task."

When the severely damaged bus finally stood on dry land, the process of towing it twenty-seven miles to Miami became "long and tedious," the *Herald* reported. "The big truck equipped with a derrick which towed it, ran out of gasoline on the way," the paper said. "Fortunately, [it happened] near a filling station on the Trail."

The state railroad commission, which was in charge of bus lines, impounded the bus at P & A Garage until an inquest could be held and an inspector could investigate and determine the cause of the accident. In the meantime, Tamiami Trail Tours was quick to make a statement to the media. "In 16 years of operation over the Tamiami Trail, this is the first catastrophe we have suffered," said Burton H. Schoepf, bus company vice president and general manager. "Trouble with wheels or tires is always extremely dangerous, and we have escaped such disasters with the exception of one other instance when tragedy was averted just as a bus came to a stop at the edge of the Tamiami Trail canal. We are making every effort to ascertain the true facts as quickly as possible."

Capt. Henry Gleason of the Miami Fire Department led the team of mechanics who made the first examination of the ill-fated bus. He told the *News-Press* that they discovered that the left front tire had blown out, and they cataloged the massive damage to the front wheel assembly. Gleason said they could not be sure whether the tire blew before the bus left the pavement or if it ruptured when it hit the boulders along the edge of the road—though some of the mechanics thought the nearly bald tire's explosion could have caused the accident. They also speculated that the impact of the boulders also disabled the air brakes, making it impossible for Hammond to stop the bus. Soon a six-person coroner's jury arrived, its members selected from the spectators at the accident site, followed by state officials, insurance company experts, and representatives of the Tamiami Trail Tours bus company.

Meanwhile, identification of the bodies began. The bus line had no passenger roster, so the identifications had to be made using personal effects collected from the bus.

Edgar H. Whitney, 77, from Winthrop, Massachusetts, was traveling to St. Petersburg after visiting his twin brother in Coral Gables to celebrate their mutual birthday. Robert H. Halpenny, 38 years old and an accountant for Collier hotels, was on his way home to Everglades City after spending the weekend in Miami. Emily Best of Wyncoate, Pennsylvania, a forty-two-year-old wife and mother of two, had been visiting her mother in Miami for ten days and was then planning to pay a short visit to Sarasota. Louis Frank Sergent, 41, a cable splicer for Florida Power & Light Company, had bought a ticket on the bus to go to Punta Gorda to repair a cable there. Gladys C. Wood, a thirty-eight-year-old writer from Binghamton, New York, had traveled from the north to Miami on January 10 and was on her way to visit her parents in Orlando.

Helen B. Watters, 29, of New Rochelle, New York, and her three-year-old son, Thomas Jr., had moved to Miami three months earlier with her husband, Thomas, and had bought a ticket on this bus to visit her mother in Bellaire while the family waited for the completion of their new house. Her husband, a construction engineer from New Rochelle, New York, spent a terrible day going from one funeral home to another until he found the body of his son at one mortuary and his wife's remains at another.

The victims also included C. O. Towles, 60, of St. Louis, Missouri; Sarah House, 53, from Detroit; Betty Heidt, 67, of High Springs, Florida; Mr. and Mrs. W. P. Heinrich, 65 and 60, of Chicago; Clara Young, 64, of New Castle, Pennsylvania; and Sarah Lisk, 56, of Matawan, New Jersey.

The last to be identified were two retired schoolteachers, Mabell Black, 59, and Cora Lindburg, 55—both from New Jersey—who had written to the manager of the Friendly Service Travel Agency in St. Petersburg that they would arrive there by bus from Miami on Monday afternoon, January 25 at 4:30 p.m. for a six-week stay. "The letter explained the two women had intended to make the trip Friday, but later changed their plans and would not leave until Monday," the *Tampa Bay Times* reported. "This last-minute change cost both their lives."

Two of the survivors, Morris Senkoff of Wildwood, New Jersey, and Milton Fishbein of Brooklyn, New Jersey, were photographed by the *Tampa Times* smiling and shaking hands from their hospital beds a day after the accident, celebrating their good fortune in escaping death. Fishbein nearly slept through the crash, awakening just as the bus slipped into the water. He found his way to an open window and made it out of the bus. Later he noted that his watch had stopped at exactly 9:00 a.m., just as the accident took place.

Senkoff said he also was seated over one of the rear wheels when the bus began to swerve. When it slid into the water, "the bus was filled with water in less than two seconds," he said. "I held my nose with one hand and tried to break a window with the other. When this did not work, I found one that was open and swam out. It seemed that I was under the water for five or six minutes."

Senkoff climbed to the top of the bus and caught his breath, then managed to get to shore soon after. Once he stood on dry land, he spotted a man bringing an elderly woman out of the water, and Senkoff thought she "showed a faint spark of life." He went to her side and began giving her artificial respiration. Half an hour's work did not revive her, however, and he finally had to acknowledge that she had not survived the ordeal.

Morris Evans, 50, of Red Oak, Iowa, nearly gave himself up for lost as he searched in the rising water inside the bus for an open window. By chance, he found "a small pocket in the top of the bus" that the water had not reached, and he hovered there, suitcases floating past him and bumping his head, until he got his bearings and spotted an open window nearby. He squeezed through the opening, losing his wallet with $166 and his watch in the process—but making it to the surface made these losses seem trivial in comparison to staying alive.

In addition to those already mentioned, survivors included Edward Lisk of Matewan, who was hospitalized with a fractured neck; Callie Riddle of East Palestine, Ohio, who was admitted for shock; Phillip Ahsler of Miami, who suffered multiple bruises; Edgewood Price, 65, of Enterprise, Alabama, admitted to the hospital for observation; and Alphonse Adelcoster of Naples, who was uninjured.

The shock, horror, and grief of this accident were still very much in evidence two days later when Everett Clemons, investigator for the state railroad commission, told the AP that this tragedy needed to result in "legislation to govern trail traffic."

First on his list of recommended improvements was a series of emergency stations with telephones along the road, closing the current twenty-mile distance between that week's accident site and the nearest phone line. He also proposed steel guard rails along the highway between the road and the canal, replacing the big boulders that compounded the bus's mechanical failure. "Investigators agreed that the coral boulders placed in piles along the Trail highway are a menace to cars forced off the highway," the *Herald* reported the day after the accident. Were there no boulders there, "the driver might have had a chance to recover his control."

The *Herald*'s finger-pointing at the boulders came too soon, however. One week after the accident, the coroner's jury returned a verdict in their inquest: Tamiami Trail Tours was to blame for the deaths. "Negligence of the bus company for failure to maintain the bus in a safe condition" had caused the crash, they said, specifying a broken right spring as the direct cause of the accident. The three mechanics who inspected the salvaged bus found that six leaves of the spring were broken, "four of them for some time before the accident," based on rust where the breaks occurred.

Captain Gleason described what happened when the bus hit a bump in the road, causing the spring to break free. The bus "did not bounce back into its regular position, causing the right front wheel to be pulled back several inches out of position. . . . When the driver attempted to pull the bus back into position, it snapped the steering knob of the radius rod. For the short time that the driver was fighting to control the bus, the right wheel being out of line caused the left wheel to be forced around." The wheels skidded back and forth across the road, "tearing away from the air tubes, leaving the driver helpless." The air tubes connected to the brakes, so the brakes failed—even the emergency brake, which the driver pulled as soon as the bus started to skid.

They completed their deliberations by making a statement.

We the jury urge more rigid inspection of common carriers on the highways of the state of Florida in order that there might be material lessening in the number of yearly deaths caused by defective equipment, and we further urge closer supervision by the state railroad commission.

The jury also noted that the driver's speed may have exceeded recommended limits for a vehicle the size of a bus, but critics of this inference quickly took a stand on this. If the bus truly were going too fast—between 60 and 70 mph, according to the jury—"that fact alone cannot be set down as the major cause of trouble," an editor at the *Miami Herald* argued in an opinion piece:

The only answer is safer highways. We know of no main road in the state so surrounded with artificial dangers as that part of the Tamiami Trail in Dade county [sic]. The same considerations that dictated a two-lane highway leading north through this country should have warned the state road department years ago that the Tamiami Trail also needed attention, not only to place a safe guard rail along the canal bank, but also to smooth over the rough surface.

As road commissions debated the finer points of road improvements and government budget offices bemoaned the lack of funding for the recommended safety measures, accidents continued to happen on the Tamiami Trail. Particularly tragic was the loss of three of the four people riding in a car on March 27, 1938, when the car left the road and plunged into the canal. The victims included Ralph Banks, the fifteen-month-old child of Vincent and Leona Banks; Leona Banks, who was twenty-seven and died of pneumonia—the result of breathing in water while she was submerged in the canal; and a third passenger, Samuel A. Malone, who also died of pneumonia. Vincent Banks managed to survive the accident.

But even the death of a baby did not sway commissioners to spend the required money on the road. While a few minor improvements near Fort Myers took place in 1939, major changes did not receive approval until 1940, when it became clear that a major war loomed on the horizon and Florida would be an important player in national defense. A conference in the summer of 1940 involving both state and federal officials "found that the government's military requirements in Florida will be extensive and will necessitate a large number of highway improvements," the *Fort Myers News-Press* reported on August 2.

Among those mentioned were the bridges on the Tamiami Trail, many of them wooden structures inadequate for war equipment traffic. It was estimated that some $10,000,000 would be needed for the bridges alone, and Florida officials felt that if the bridges were rebuilt, a considerable amount of road construction would go along with it. . . . It appears certain that Florida *roads will get a big boost in the national defense program, and that it will be of permanent benefit.*

Sure enough, the 1940s saw a series of timber bridges and other improvements along the road, making the road safer and reducing the number of accidents that ended with cars in the canal. By the 1950s, however, the construction of I-75 as part of the national interstate highway system focused most of the cross-peninsula traffic on this far more sophisticated road system, making the Tamiami Trail a secondary conveyance from Miami to Fort Myers and Naples.

Today Everglades National Park is working on the Tamiami Trail: Next Steps project with the goal of raising U.S. Route 41 about thirteen feet above the land's surface "to restore more natural water flow to Everglades National Park and Florida Bay," according to the National Park Service website. This effort will bring back the "ecological connectivity" that makes the Everglades a critically important water feature in south Florida, while improving habitat for the wading birds that draw hundreds of thousands of birders to the region every year. The Tamiami Trail continues to serve as a convenient road across south Florida from Miami to Naples, but it no longer poses the threat to life that it did—instead, it provides a direct route to airboat rides, Everglades Safari Park, the national park's Shark Valley unit, a Miccosukee Indian Village, and the "real" Everglades: hundreds of miles of open, largely untouched wilderness.

7

Murder of a Moonshiner

FISHING CAN BE EXTRAORDINARY IN THE EVERGLADES, AS ANY LOCAL angler can attest, especially in the desolate backcountry where the noise and crush of tourists never disturb the peace. That's why a pair of fishermen from Lake Worth, Fred L. Costlow and Carl Brown, made their way from Twenty Mile Bend on State Route 80 on November 7, 1958, to Canal C-7, a spot about five miles south of one of the Everglades pumping stations, piloting their boat down a canal that rarely sees a visitor.

No one made a record of what their catch might have been like, but when the boat's propeller struck something metal underwater, everyone took notice—from a young wife in Macclenny, west of Jacksonville, to the state sheriffs and the FBI.

Costlow and Brown reached into the water to free their propeller and discovered a long chain with a heavy weight on one end. Peering into the murky depths, they spotted clothing, skin, and handcuffs—enough to know that they had happened upon a dead body.

The fishermen dragged the body out of the canal, shielding it from a nearby alligator that seemed to be taking an interest, and rushed to the nearest phone to notify the Broward County sheriff. Police arrived quickly and retrieved the body. They determined that the murder victim had been a young man who had come to a bad end: A towel stuffed in his mouth and held there with adhesive tape must have kept him from crying out when the murderer shot him, execution-style, with a .32-20 caliber bullet through the back of the skull. The victim's hands were handcuffed, and heavy, two-inch-wide tape strapped his legs together, making it impossible for him to run. A large, concrete building block bound to his thighs weighted the body in the water, keeping it submerged until the boat's wake disturbed it—in fact, had it not been for a couple of fishermen on a day out, the gangland murder might never have come to light.

"Police theorized he was a rum-runner, 'rubbed out' by hired killers when suspected of being a stool pigeon," the *Miami Herald* noted. A few weeks earlier, local law enforcement had completed a successful bust of illegal moonshine operations, so it seemed possible that this killing might be connected with that.

The FBI took over the process of identifying the body using fingerprints on file. Sure enough, the mystery man turned out to be someone the police had encountered before: Lew Gene Harvey, a twenty-one-year-old moonshiner who had been one of forty-one people charged in the September raid, ending a moonshine operation that stretched from Jacksonville to Miami. Harvey had been released on $500 bond shortly after his arrest and had kept out of view of the police until his body turned up in the canal.

This discovery led the investigation to Harvey's wife—the young woman in Macclenny mentioned earlier—who told police that her husband had left home with another man on November 3 and "her fearful husband gave her the license number of the car in which he was leaving . . . supposedly on an air-conditioning installation job," the *Herald* said. "That was the last he was seen alive."

To the inexperienced eye, this all may have looked like just another gang-on-gang violent episode, removing a bad apple from an ever-rotting bushel. To Broward County police, however, the circumstances clanged like an alarm in a firehouse. The moonshine connection, the single-shot slaying that suggested a professional killer, and the body trussed up and weighted to vanish beneath the water's surface . . . all of these clues harkened back to a cold case from 1955, when Circuit Court Judge Curtis E. Chillingworth of West Palm Beach and his wife, Marjorie, disappeared without a trace.

Chillingworth, described by the *Miami Herald* as "scholarly" and "refined," had knowledge of this moonshine ring back in 1955 as well as its connection to a gambling numbers game called *bolita*. He may have known who the high rollers were in the game and even who led the entire racket, as well as the heads of moonshine production and transport. Whatever he knew, the "brain trust" involved in the crimes may have believed that the judge was about to crack down on the whole operation.

When the judge and his "charming, devoted" wife vanished, the only physical clues discovered by police were a few drops of blood on a board-walk leading to the beach from their home and a full roll and a partial roll of two-inch adhesive tape on the beach, "something professional mobsters might well take with them on a killing," said the *Miami Herald*. The same kind of adhesive tape had been used to bind Harvey.

Since the judge's disappearance, two full-time investigators had worked on the case. Everyone on Chillingworth's court staff worked with police to "comb dusty registries and files of closed cases," according to the *Herald*, looking for a contentious decision that might have sparked an attorney's ire or incited a criminal to revenge. Nothing came to light until Lew Harvey's body rose to the surface of a remote canal.

Harvey's foresight in giving his wife the license plate number rapidly narrowed the search for his killer. Palm Beach Sheriff John F. Kirk and Deputy Sheriff John A. McCants traced the car to a Dade County man by the name of John F. Lynch—but they knew that "Lynch" was the alias of a man who was already well known to local law enforcement: Floyd A. "Lucky" Holzapfel.

Already an ex-convict, thirty-six-year-old Holzapfel had a multifac-eted past as a hero and a criminal. Originally from Oklahoma, he served as a paratrooper in World War II and had been wounded at Bastogne. After the war, he became a law officer with the Oklahoma City Police Department. His model citizenry fell apart, however, when he was con-victed of bookmaking in Los Angeles and armed robbery in Oklahoma, for which he served four years in prison. Holzapfel's record also included charges of attempted rape.

He relocated to Miami after he was released and took a job as house detective at the Deauville Hotel in Miami under his John Lynch alias. He helped organize the West Palm Beach Young Republicans Club and even led a Boy Scout troop. None of this meant that he was "going straight," however, as his growing list of crimes indicated: He had beaten a rap in

December 1956 when he was charged with conspiring to murder Harold Gray, a West Palm Beach attorney.

Holzapfel had been hired by a West Palm lawyer and former city judge named Joseph A. Peel Jr. to wait behind a sketchy tavern downtown as Peel drove Gray, his law partner, to the bar. When Gray got out of the car, Holzapfel jumped him and beat him senseless, leaving him for dead—with Peel as the beneficiary of his $100,000 life insurance policy. Gray survived the beating, much to Peel's chagrin, and Peel and Holzapfel were arrested for the crime. In the end, however, the court could not prove Holzapfel had done it and accepted Peel's resignation from the Florida bar as punishment enough.

The real consequence of this crime, however, was the launch of Holzapfel's side hustle as a hired killer.

Holzapfel continued to expand his resume of crimes. He had been connected to two thefts at the Miami Beach hotel where he had served as the security police chief under the name of John Lynch, stealing cash and jewels with a combined total value of $175,000. In both cases, he had an accomplice: a man named James W. Yenzer. The hotel fired Holzapfel when they learned his true identity, but he was not tried for the crimes.

Why Holzapfel would be involved in the execution of a moonshiner remained to be seen, but the investigative team began to see the pieces come together. "Harvey, they believe, was murdered and dropped into the canal because the bootleg ring with which authorities identified him believed he had turned stool pigeon and given information that resulted in widespread arrests of bootleggers by federal agents in September," reported West Palm Beach bureau chief Ed Pfister of the *Miami Herald*. The fact that the body came to light in an "almost inaccessible" canal, and the added weight of heavy chains and concrete, indicated that the professional killer had no intention that Harvey's remains would ever be found. "Officials believed the killers ... thought alligators would finish their work," the *Palm Beach Post* added on November 15, 1958.

With Holzapfel in his sights, Kirk made the startling decision to request assistance from the Florida Sheriff's Criminal Bureau of Investigation in Tallahassee. This alerted the media that something larger than a single murder might be connected to this case.

Word soon leaked out that Holzapfel was the prime suspect in the Harvey killing as officers from West Palm Beach traveled to Miami Beach to search for him. They located Holzapfel there but encountered obstacle after obstacle in taking him into custody: First, they could not arrest him immediately because they did not have a warrant. Pfister reported that the officers asked Dade County law enforcement to keep an eye on the man so they would know exactly where to find him when they came back with a court order to arrest him.

A week later the men returned with two warrants—one for Harvey's murder, and another on an unrelated forgery charge—and they went directly to the state attorney's office to get an additional warrant to enter and search Holzapfel's home. "But when they reached the Tatum Waterway [Drive] home of the suspect, they learned he wasn't there—in fact, Holzapfel hadn't been there for almost three weeks," Pfister wrote. "The investigators are still asking what happened."

The wanted man had wasted no time in getting out of south Florida. Kirk issued an alert that triggered a nationwide manhunt for Holzapfel, even though evidence connecting the man with the crime remained thin and circumstantial. Reports came in that the suspect had been spotted in Augusta, Georgia, and in Mexico City, but no one made an arrest.

Then on December 28, 1958, the *Miami Herald* revealed an "unconfirmed report" that Holzapfel might turn himself in to authorities. The *Herald* had heard that he "has been in touch with local friends, has made arrangements for bond, and intended to surrender" right after New Year's Day. While authorities did not endorse the report, they did seem to confirm that they had heard the same rumors—and there was some established precedent: In December 1956, Holzapfel had surrendered immediately when he learned he was a suspect in the nightclub beating and attempted murder of Harold Gray.

"Those who know Holzapfel best claim he won't wait to be tracked down and arrested," the *Herald* speculated.

Those who knew him best were right. Holzapfel walked into the Dade County Jail on January 5, 1959, and surrendered himself—not for the Harvey murder, but on the much lesser charge of forging a local bondsman's name on a $4,800 check. This forced the court to set his bail at $5,000, an appropriate amount for a crime at this level, instead of holding him indefinitely on suspicion of murder.

They had him in custody, however, so police finally had the opportunity to question Holzapfel at length about Harvey. Holzapfel had nothing to say. He would not tell them where he had been since the first arrest warrant was issued, nor would he admit to knowing anything about Lew Gene Harvey's killing. In the end, police had no option but to release him on his own recognizance just two hours after he had posted bond.

For the next year the police continued to work to link Holzapfel with the much greater crime of assassinating Judge and Mrs. Chillingworth. What they needed most was an eyewitness account of what had happened to the judge and his wife, and they knew that Holzapfel could provide it if they could devise a way to extract it from him. So they came up with a clever plan to get him to spill the beans—or, in this case, the whisky.

They traced Holzapfel to Titusville, where he had a circle of shady friends with shady credentials. One night on his return from an extended lam in Rio de Janiero, he met two of these friends—Jim Yenzer, his former accomplice, and P. O. "Jim" Wilbur, a bail bondsman—in a motel room, where they all enjoyed several drinks before Yenzer and Wilbur told Holzapfel that Peel had hired them to murder him.

This rattled Holzapfel to his core. Angry, shocked, and good and drunk, he took his revenge on Peel by telling Yenzer and Wilbur that Peel had hired him to kill Judge Chillingworth.

Holzapfel said that he and George David "Bobby" Lincoln (described by most of the media only as "a Negro accomplice") had been promised $10,000 by Peel for getting rid of the judge. They arrived at the victim's home at Manalapan the night of June 15, 1955, and rang the doorbell. When the judge came to the door, they announced that it was a stick-up. The judge reacted with such calm that they changed their story, informing him that it was really a kidnapping for a ransom.

Then Marjorie Chillingworth joined her husband at the door, and she recognized Holzapfel—a fatal error, as this made it necessary to kill her as well. Holzapfel said he and Lincoln walked the Chillingworths to a boat they had secured on the beach, where the judge offered them

$200,000 to let them go. Whether they did not believe they would ever see the money or they felt some special affinity for the man who had hired them, they refused the sum even though it was twenty times larger than the one they were being paid. They forced the Chillingworths into the boat and trussed them up with adhesive tape and chains.

Shortly after they had started the motor and pointed the bow out to sea, the "death boat," as the media called it, began to sputter and stall. It bobbed in the gentle waves for more than an hour before Holzapfel could get it started again. "It was the judge himself who advised the killers how to get the motor started," the *Palm Beach Post* said in its retelling of Holzapfel's story.

When they finally reached a point well offshore, they fastened thirty-pound divers' weights around Marjorie's waist. Holzapfel, murmuring "Ladies first," pushed Mrs. Chillingworth overboard.

As she began to sink into the ocean, Judge Chillingworth said to his wife, "Honey, remember I love you."

"I love you, too," she replied, and the water closed over her head.

A moment later, before the two murderers could apply the weights and dump the judge into the water, Chillingworth leapt out of the boat in an attempt to escape. He struggled against his bonds and had nearly managed to free himself when Holzapfel hit him in the head with the butt of his shotgun. Chillingworth sank into the ocean.

"It would appear . . . that the swift Gulf Stream would have scattered the remains," Ernie Hutter of the *Palm Beach Post* speculated.

Not until days after this confession in the motel did Holzapfel discover he had been duped. Yenzer and Wilbur had been working undercover for the cops, and the entire conversation had been tape recorded by police technicians in the next room. The cops finally had the information they needed to arrest him.

On October 3, 1960, detectives Henry Lovern and Ross Anderson of the Florida Sheriff's Bureau and two police deputies knocked on the door of Holzapfel's motel room and found Holzapfel "lying on a bed in a half-drunken stupor," according to a step-by-step chronology by *Tampa Tribune* writer Paul Wilder. With four guns pointed in his face, Holzapfel had little choice but to surrender. Hours later, they arrested Peel and his current mortgage business partner, Donald Miles, and charged them with conspiring to murder Holzapfel. The two men were held in the Brevard County Jail on $50,000 bond each, an astronomical sum for the time, until the judge there halved their bond and released them.

It soon became public knowledge that Miles had pled guilty to the conspiracy, agreeing to turn state's evidence to avoid a prison term.

Holzapfel gave Chief Criminal Investigator Ralph E. Clark, Lovern, and Anderson no trouble as they took him to jail, but later that day he attempted suicide in his cell, using a razor blade he had somehow obtained. When he was seen during his transfer from Titusville to Miami the following day, reporters noted the bandage on his left wrist, as well as the handcuffs and leg irons visible under the sport coat flung over his head and shoulders to shield him from the media.

The court arraigned Holzapfel on the charge of killing Lew Gene Harvey, a first-degree murder charge that allowed them to hold him without bail, then began the process of wearing him down until he confessed to the Chillingworth murders. Sheriff Kirk and State Attorney Phil O'Connell knew that it would be hard to make their case that Holzapfel had killed the Chillingworths, because the tape itself could not be admitted as evidence. For a tape to be used in court, Florida law requires that all parties on the tape be aware that they are being recorded. Sheriff Kirk told the media that he had never planned that the tapes be admitted as evidence—he intended to play them back for the three men involved in the murder conspiracy, making them more likely to confess in writing in hopes of avoiding the death penalty.

This, it turned out, worked exactly as planned with Holzapfel. He did not hear the tapes themselves, but once he was told what was on them, he confessed on the record, admitting to the Chillingworth murders as well as the murder of Harvey. He also implicated Peel for hiring him to do the job.

Once he arrived in the Dade County jail, however, Holzapfel gave an interview to Gene Miller at the *Miami Herald* and denied everything he had said on the tapes.

"It'll be a damn dirty shame if they execute me for the Chillingworths," he said. "They might come home in the next week . . . I never saw Chillingworth. I didn't kill him. I wouldn't know him if he walked in the door."

He decried the way he had been fooled into saying the things he did. "It is a sorry commentary on American justice when two men who have admitted numerous crimes previously can get a man drunk and keep him drunk for 2½ days consuming over six bottles of alcohol and use unsupported wire recordings to execute a man."

To emphasize how the agents had taken advantage of him, he ticked off the liquor they had consumed: two bottles of Johnnie Walker Black Scotch, one bottle of J & B Blended Scotch, one bottle of Seagram's 7 Crown whisky, as well as two bottles of vodka. Claiming that the two agents had lured him back to Florida by saying that two other, comparatively minor charges against him had been dismissed, he tried to appeal to readers' sympathies: "I figured I could straighten them out in court. And then I could go out and start living like a human being again, instead of a dog." He insisted that the two men he thought were his friends only "wanted that reward money ($100,000). That's why they lie and connive . . . They kept asking how the Chillingworth thing could have been done. *Could* have been."

The lack of physical evidence also complicated the case. The Chillingworths' bodies had never been found, and it seemed clear that the ocean had long since devoured them. The *Fort Lauderdale News* reported on October 6, 1960, that Coast Guard vessels had searched the ocean near the Chillingworth home at length in hopes of recovering chains or weights used in the murder but never found any trace of the crime committed five years before.

During the months between the arrests and the trial, the detectives continued to build their case. They determined that the blood spots found on the boardwalk that led from the judge's home to the beach came from a wound on Marjorie Chillingworth's head, where one of the killers had struck her "when she became hysterical," according to the press. With more certainty of Peel's involvement, they made the connection between the judge and a public reprimand Peel had received from Chillingworth in court in July 1953, when Peel had mishandled a divorce suit. In that case, Peel's client was a woman who could not get a divorce from her husband because he was overseas. She claimed in court that Peel had told her that her divorce had become final, so she married another man. Now she was guilty of bigamy and still unable to complete her divorce from her first husband. Peel denied that he had ever told his client that her divorce was final, but he feared that he would be disbarred anyway.

In early November, police finally charged Holzapfel and Peel with the murders of Curtis and Marjorie Chillingworth. The case went to court in late March 1961, and the defendants began unraveling their convoluted claims to bewildered jurors.

Holzapfel was among the first to come to the stand. He told the court that he and Joe Peel were close friends—"closer . . . than I have been to any other human," he claimed as Peel stared at him from across the defense table. "He told me he was going to be governor of Florida and we would be partners for life." They had known each other for many years, with Peel serving as Holzapfel's attorney in several cases until Holzapfel became his agent in the bolita racket—attempting to "raise money among the Negroes in the West Palm Beach area with promises of protection." As a municipal judge, Peel had the power to issue search warrants, so Holzapfel would warn people of upcoming searches if they paid a monthly fee for this service. This is how he met Bobby Lincoln— after police raided Lincoln's home and found contraband in his attic. Lincoln sought out Holzapfel and paid for his protection from then on, and joined him in the bolita business as a courier.

Holzapfel confirmed why Peel might want Chillingworth "out of the way," Peel fearing that the judge would attempt to disbar him for his mishandling of the 1953 divorce case. Staring directly at Peel across the courtroom, Holzapfel said, "He reminded me of personal aspects of my own life he knew about, and told me I was his best friend, the best friend he had in the world."

Peel, unblinking, met his gaze until Holzapfel looked away.

Holzapfel went on, describing several trips that he, Peel, and Lincoln had made to Manalapan to case the property. On one of these trips, Holzapfel took a .38 special snubnose pistol Peel had brought for him, and walked up to the brightly lit house. "I got scared, and walked back," he said. After so many visits to the scene, however, Peel became impatient. He "suggested that Judge Chillingworth could be taken away in a boat and dumped at sea. Joe Peel said there would never be any body, no crime, and nobody will ever be arrested."

So Holzapfel bought a boat, two pairs of gloves, two rolls of adhesive tape, two packages of clothesline, Army surplus cartridge belts, lead weights, a flashlight, and an extra anchor. He said that Peel had given him a wad of $1 bills to fund the enterprise.

While Lincoln waited in the bushes, Holzapfel went up to the front door and knocked. The judge came to the door in faded pink pajamas.

Holzapfel asked, "Are you Judge Chillingworth?"

"He said, 'Yes, I am,'" Holzapfel continued. "I drew my snubnose pistol from under my blue sport shirt and said, 'This is a holdup—stand real still.'"

Then Marjorie Chillingworth joined her husband at the door in a nightgown, and Holzapfel knew he had his hands full. He whistled for Bobby to join him. "Bobby used the tape first to tie the hands of Mrs. Chillingworth, then the judge," he said. "Then he put tape across the mouth . . . At that time, we told them it was a kidnap."

They forced the two victims to walk with them to a narrow road between their house and the shore. As they reached it, Holzapfel said, "Mrs. Chillingworth rared [sic] back into me. She screamed. I had a pistol in my hand. Both of us started falling at the same time. I swung the pistol, striking her behind the left ear." Acknowledging that she was bleeding, he added, "I was petrified, but I jumped up and picked up Mrs. Chillingworth."

The two men put the victims into the boat, then struggled with engine trouble for several minutes. Holzapfel turned off the engine, let it cool, and started it again, motoring out east of Manalapan until it seemed far enough that the bodies would never be found.

Holzapfel said that he and Lincoln fastened the belts full of lead weights around both Chillingworths. "We throw Mrs. Chillingworth over first," he said. "She disappeared. Then we put Judge Chillingworth in, but he came right up. Bobby started to shoot him with a pistol. I said, 'No, Bobby, the sound of the shot will carry across this water.'"

Instead, they chased Chillingworth, who had started to swim clumsily away. "Bobby grabbed up the shotgun and struck the judge over the head," Holzapfel said. "Then Bobby held the judge against the side of the boat while I tied a slip knot in the rope and put it around the neck of Chillingworth." The other end of the rope held the anchor. "I let go of the anchor and he went right down."

The killers motored back to the docks at Riviera Beach, and Holzapfel called Peel to tell him the deed was done. He also asked his friend to bring him a clean shirt. "I can't go home with this one with blood on it," he said. Peel arrived soon after, excited and full of questions about the murders. "I was sick and disgusted," Holzapfel said. "I said it's done and all I want to do now is go home."

Defense attorney Carlton Welch's cross-examination attempted to discredit Holzapfel's detailed testimony,, but Holzapfel remained firm.

"Do you mean to tell the jury that Peel is responsible for wrecking your life?" Welch asked.

Holzapfel responded, "No, sir. I'm responsible."

Even with this self-deprecating response, wrote columnist Jim Bishop of King Features, Holzapfel clearly came to court to eviscerate Joe Peel. "Floyd came to hang a friend," Bishop wrote. "He hung him high and buried him. The jurors, he hopes, will serve as pallbearers. In gleeful, grinning venom, Floyd A. Holzapfel threw the murders of Judge and Mrs. Curtis E. Chillingworth into the pale handsome face of his pal, Judge Joseph Peel."

Jim Yenzer—who, it turned out, had been an undercover agent for the Florida State Sheriff's Bureau all along—received his day in court to tell what he knew about Peel's involvement in the murders. He said that Peel had paid him $5,300 to kill Holzapfel, with a first payment of $500 in January 1960. Yenzer said he kept raising his price, stringing Peel along in hopes of getting him to confess to his role in the Chillingworth case. A stringent cross-examination did not shake Yenzer's story one bit, *Tampa Tribune* reporter Paul Wilder noted in his coverage the following day.

Bobby Lincoln took the stand later on the same day. He was already serving three years in prison for moonshining, but he had been granted immunity for both the Harvey and Chillingworth murders in exchange for testimony that would implicate Peel. "On direct examination, he sang like a mechanical canary wound too tight," wrote Bishop. "One question from O'Connell and Bobby Lincoln was warbling for eight minutes."

The accomplice provided more information about Peel's use of his position as judge to run a protection operation, making all of the moonshiners pay him a monthly fee throughout 1954 and 1955, collected by Holzapfel. One night, Peel and Holzapfel picked up Lincoln and drove out to Singer's Island, where Peel told him, "There's a man trying to mess our business up and everything we've worked for and we're going to kill him."

That man was Judge Chillingworth. Later that night, Peel and Holzapfel took Lincoln out to the Chillingworth house with the intention of ringing the doorbell and shooting the judge when he answered. The Chillingworths were not home, however, foiling this plan.

When Lincoln and Holzapfel finally completed the crime for which they had been hired, Peel was not with them, Lincoln told the court. Holzapfel called him that day and said, "I want you to go with me some place and I'll pick you up at your house."

Lincoln got his gun out of his truck's glove box and waited for Holzapfel. They went to a boat Holzapfel had just purchased, and he noticed a burlap sack in the bottom of the boat. "Where we going, Floyd?" Lincoln asked.

"We're going to do a little job for Joe," he replied. "All you gotta do is stay with the boat, and I'll take care of it."

When they arrived at the right place on the beach, Holzapfel pulled a pair of gloves and a roll of adhesive tape out of the bag and gave them to Lincoln. He then headed up to the house alone, leaving Lincoln in the boat with the motor running.

"I went up to the house but I didn't want to go in with the light on the porch," Lincoln said. "It was shining real bright so the whole back of the house was lit up. So I knocked the light out with a gun. When I went in [the house], Floyd handed me his gun to hold for him and this lady was coming out of the bedroom. I asked him, 'What you going to do, Floyd?'"

He said that Holzapfel told him to tie up the judge. "He took sort of a lanyard and put it around his neck and then pulled it down between his legs sort of. Then Floyd put the man's hands behind him and pulled out the roll of adhesive tape and started tying his wrists together. He told me to finish wrapping the tape around this man's hands, then he started to wrap tape around the lady."

They walked the two bound victims out the door and toward the boat, and Chillingworth began to attempt to bargain with the criminals. "Boy, if you'll take care of us this time, you'll never have to work again," he said to them.

Mrs. Chillingworth began to scream, he said, and Holzapfel hit her twice with his gun until she fell, pulling Holzapfel with her. She stopped screaming and got into the boat when he pushed her toward it.

When they were out on the water, "I looked around and I saw Floyd messing with the lady," Lincoln told the court. "I said, 'Floyd, what are you doing?' He had the lady under his arm. Then he looked at me a long time, like he was kind of astonished, and throwed the lady over the side of the boat."

Chillingworth had worked his feet free, Lincoln said, and he leaned over the side of the boat and managed to launch himself into the water. He floated there as Holzapfel started yelling, 'Hit 'im, hit 'im, hit 'im!" Lincoln fumbled with the shotgun, which had been disassembled, until Holzapfel grabbed the gun from him and hit the judge with the butt, striking the judge so hard that he broke the stock off.

"I caught the man by the shoulders and helped him back in the boat," said Lincoln. "Floyd picked up the anchor and cut off a portion of the rope and tied it around the man's neck. Then he pushed him out of my arms with the ball of his foot."

This time the judge sank. They then disposed of all the evidence—the guns, the rope from the anchor—by dropping it into the deep water, and finished by washing the blood off the side of the boat.

While Lincoln's version of events differed from Holzapfel's and he repeatedly emphasized that he did not know or understand what Holzapfel planned to do with the judge and his wife, neither man denied committing the crime—and both implicated Peel as the instigator and funder of the plot.

At last, Joe Peel himself came to the stand. He spent five and a half hours on the witness stand in his own defense, insisting that he had had no role in the murders for which he was accused. He had, however, willingly entered into a plot to kill Holzapfel, whom he called "a raving maniac" who had threatened his life.

Holzapfel wanted him dead, he said, because he feared that Peel would inform on him for the murder of Lew Harvey. Peel then proceeded to do exactly that, describing Holzapfel's visit to Peel's place of business—a construction firm in Lake City—to ask for his advice.

The visit, Peel told the court, took place on the day that the media reported the discovery of Harvey's body in the Everglades canal. "He came down but said he didn't want to come into the office and asked if I would step out to his car," Peel said, according to the court transcript. "We stepped out to the automobile and [Holzapfel] discussed with me the finding of this body in the Palm Beach County Canal . . . He wanted some advice. I listened to what he had to say about it . . . Holzapfel made some admission about his participation in the job on the body in the Palm Beach Canal."

At this point, the court interrupted Peel's testimony to discuss whether attorney-client privilege prevented Peel from sharing what Holzapfel had said to him. Eventually and after considerable discussion—some in public and some in the judge's chambers—the judge and attorneys determined that Peel could talk about what Holzapfel had said to him, but not whether or not he admitted to Harvey's murder.

This line of questioning and response proved nearly impossible for Peel and defense attorney Welch. Despite repeated objections and attempts to keep him from saying so, Peel could not describe the conversation without revealing what had been said. "He advised me that he and Bobby Lincoln," he began, but state attorney Phil O'Connell immediately objected.

"The court has already ruled how far he can go in that," O'Connell said.

Peel just kept talking. "He told me in effect, he and Lincoln were responsible."

O'Connell leaped to object again. "Your honor, something is going to have to be done," he said.

"Do you want me to say he made admission against Lincoln?" Peel asked the judge.

"You may," the judge replied.

Now Peel was the one to object. "That wasn't the whole truth," he said. "It involved someone else. He made statements about he and Bobby Lincoln concerning the boy in the canal. I told him, 'You better go get a lawyer and a good one at that.'"

Peel then deftly introduced another motive for Holzapfel's accusations of him: Holzapfel thought Peel was sleeping with his wife, Peggy. Peel did not admit to this on the stand in so many words, but he did describe meetings with Peggy "for a few days" in New York City in February 1960 and again in Miami in July of the same year—both while Holzapfel was on the run in Rio de Janeiro. "I talked with her at length about the Harvey and Chillingworth murders," he told the court.

One day in August, Peggy called Peel to warn him that her husband knew they had been seeing each other. Twenty minutes later, Holzapfel called Peel and told him that he had "received word" that Peel and Peggy had been living together in a motel, "which was not the truth," Peel quickly added. When Peel denied any affair with Peggy, Holzapfel called him a liar.

"I want to put it on the record now, whether or not you have ever had any improper relations with Peggy Holzapfel?" Welch asked.

Peel sat up straight and responded clearly, "I have . . ." pausing for emphasis, "not!"

It soon came out in P. O. Wilbur's testimony that the story of the affair was simply a ruse perpetrated by Wilbur and Yenzer to draw Holzapfel out of Rio and back to Florida, so they could find a way to wangle a confession from him for the Chillingworth murders.

The threat to Peel's life, however, was real enough that Peel and an accomplice, Don Miles, hired Yenzer to kill Holzapfel for them.

Essentially, they hoped to beat Holzapfel to the punch, killing him before he carried out his rumored plot to kill them. They paid Yenzer $5,300 for this task. Yenzer, described by reporter Jim Bishop as "slender, well-dressed, a man with a black mole on his cheek and a mouth which curves up like a waning moon," was only too happy to describe this murder plot—which he'd had not the least intention of carrying out—during his time on the witness stand.

Perhaps the most significant piece of Yenzer's testimony came at the end. He said that he and Peel had met at the Cocoa Beach Motel at the end of September 1960, and that a nervous Peel spent most of his time looking behind and under things in the room for hidden microphones. When Yenzer told him that there was now a $10,000 reward for the recovery of the Chillingworths' remains, Peel said that "if a man was to take a boat and sail it from the center of the Chillingworth front porch due east, about 100 yards beyond the southbound steamer track, he would find the bodies . . . or what was left of them."

After all this damning testimony, noted reporter Jim Bishop, defense attorney Welch looked "fretful, grim, shaken. He appeared to put very little fight into his cross-examination."

As the case went to the jury on March 30, O'Connell asked them to consider the death penalty for the man who ordered the murder of another man of the bench. The jury spent five hours and twenty-four minutes deliberating, and returned with a guilty verdict for Peel—but they rejected the electric chair, choosing instead a sentence of life in prison for the thirty-seven-year-old former judge. He remained in prison for thirty-one years until 1992, when he managed to get a reprieve because of ill health, and died just nine days after his release.

Floyd Holzapfel was not so fortunate. As he himself predicted in a pre-sentencing interview, he received a death sentence, with execution to take place by electric chair.

"You and your cohorts participated in a crime, or crimes, which were gruesome, vicious, cold-blooded, premeditated and designed—the likes of which this state has never seen," said Judge Russell O. Morrow before pronouncing the sentence. "May God the father of us all have mercy on your soul."

Mercy actually came from an appeals court, which commuted the sentence to life in prison later in the 1960s. When Holzapfel last came to public consciousness in 1996, he'd suffered a stroke that had put him in a wheelchair four years earlier and was petitioning the court to be released to live with a daughter in Tennessee. The petition was denied, and he died in prison later that year.

Bobby Lincoln, who made the best deal of anyone involved, left Florida soon after the trial and moved to Chicago, where he became a Muslim and changed his name to David A. Kareem. He lived in quiet obscurity until his death on May 14, 2004, nearly fifty years after the deaths of Curtis and Marjorie Chillingworth.

"Cracking the case cost the Sheriff's Bureau $60,000—one-tenth of its budget for two years," Wilder wrote in the *Tampa Tribune*. "Travel expenses, equipment, salaries, everything, nearly broke the bureau. But the job was done, and it's doubtful whether another killer will dare to try to do away with another Florida judge."

8

Commercial Airline Disasters

Nothing in the Everglades grabs planes out of the sky, but the region has seen more than its fair share of both major and minor plane crashes. Its proximity to Miami International Airport simply makes the river of grass the nearest open expanse that planes encounter right after takeoff from or just before landing at the airport. Many private planes have gone down here as well—my research unearthed eighteen separate incidents that ended in deaths, while many more small plane crashes destroyed the aircraft but allowed the pilot and passengers to emerge with their lives.

I chose to focus on four commercial passenger flights that went down in this remote backcountry, all of which resulted in significant fatalities. From these, readers can see the avoidable errors that ended lives, and perhaps keep these in mind should you pilot your own aircraft over the South Florida wilderness.

MIDAIR EXPLOSION: BRANIFF FLIGHT 971

At midnight on the morning of March 25, 1958, a Douglas DC-7C passenger aircraft flown by Braniff International Airways was already a full day late.

Flight 971 had been scheduled to take off for Panama City and Rio de Janeiro exactly twenty-four hours earlier, but mechanical problems on a plane from Rio grounded it. The Rio flight contained an "almost full load which was to have left on the return trip," according to an unnamed

Braniff spokesperson quoted in the *Miami Herald*. It would have departed Miami for the return flight early in the morning on March 24, but that plane never arrived so Braniff flew a replacement plane in from Dallas at 7:15 p.m. on March 25. Captains George W. Hogan and Donald Showman flew the replacement DC-7C in and would then ride as passengers on the same plane as it took off for Panama City.

When the plane arrived from Dallas that evening, a former airline mechanic who happened to be at the airport—T. C. Sokel of Coral Gables—saw "an unusual blue sparking from the no. 4, outboard engine," as he told the *Herald* later that day. "The pilots apparently noticed the trouble, [and] two mechanics worked on the engine for some time, but on the opposite side from which I'd noticed the magneto flashing."

Twenty-four people, including five working crew, boarded the aircraft in Miami, and when the plane took off, Sokel said, he assumed that the mechanics on duty felt they had resolved the issue. If they assumed so, they were wrong.

Checklists indicated that the plane was operating within normal parameters, but two minutes after takeoff, copilot John C. Winthrop declared a fire in the no. 3 engine, the one closest to the cabin on the right side. The pilot, Capt. Thomas D. George, cut power to that engine and feathered the propeller—turning it so air did not pass through it—then triggered the engine's fire extinguisher.

For a few seconds it seemed like this had done the trick. The fire died down and George began the procedure to return to Miami airport. He began to radio the Miami control tower for permission to land. "This is Braniff 971 . . ."

At that instant a blinding, orange-yellow flash and a burst of crackling and tearing wracked the plane. "There was a shudder over the whole plane, and then an explosion before the cabin cracked in two right behind the wing," said Emilio Ganut of Sao Paulo, one of the passengers seated in the rear of the plane. "The flames swept into the cabin."

The plane ripped into two pieces, its forward section pointed down and rocketing toward the ground, while the tail section, severed just behind the wing, propelled backward into the air by the blast. It "just floated free from the remainder of the plane," said Ganut.

Both pieces fell into swampland six miles west of Miami, the forward section breaking into two pieces as it hit the ground. A third piece, part of the rear fuselage, split from the tail and "whirled over and over for about a quarter of a mile," the *Miami News* reported later that day. The forward section shattered on impact, its aluminum hull splitting and bouncing across the ground and scattering passengers through the swamp.

Copilot-engineer Charles "Chuck" Fink found himself thrown forward from his position behind the two pilots. "The captain yelled, 'Jesus Christ!'" Fink told Civil Aeronautics Board (CAB) officials Frank Taylor and Reed Tait from his hospital bed nearly a week later. "I remember the impact . . . the dirt hitting the windshield . . . then it's a complete blank."

Miami Herald reporter Bob Swift, in Fink's hospital room for the interview, described the copilot's condition, "his head cross hatched with stiches and his right leg in a cast." Captain George and copilot Winthrop were "still in no shape to give their stories," the newspaper added.

"The great column of fire was seen as far away as South Miami," the *Herald* reported. The *Miami News* added, "Witnesses . . . said the airliner seemed to drop almost straight down from its altitude of between 1,500 and 2,000 feet."

Luckily for the passengers in the rear of the plane, the aircraft broke up at a fairly low altitude. The tail section fell into thick, high marsh grass, a softer landing than the headlong nosedive the cockpit and the rest of the cabin experienced. Ganut and the others in that section—Hilton Soares of Rio de Janeiro; Madeline Campion, a stewardess from Lima, Peru; and Pietro Vinga of Coral Gables—all survived with relatively minor injuries. Campion climbed out of the wreckage and immediately began helping others despite severe cuts on her own legs.

Nine others lost their lives on impact, including Hogan and Showman, who had flown this very plane in from Dallas a few hours earlier. Other Braniff pilots, Captains Royal H. King and Davis S. Leake, also died in the crash, as did Paul A. Reed of Paducah, Kentucky; Rosario Rodriguez of Panama City; Adrienne Ducas of New York City; Ricardo Salcedo of Lima, Peru; and Vera D. Rex of Minneapolis.

Bob Grant, a Yellow Cab driver, saw flames flash along the right wing of the plane and then saw the plane list violently to the right just before it crashed. He called his dispatcher and told him, "A big one is crashing." He said to the *Miami News* later, "A big ball of fire went up when the plane hit the ground and I headed toward the wreck. I took a short cut, and I guess I was one of the first to get on the scene."

The wreckage was still burning when he got there. "I helped a Brazilian guy out of the plane," he said. "The guy was in a daze and kept saying he had to call his mother, who has a heart condition . . . I guided him to the road where an ambulance was waiting."

He found one passenger crying because he had tried to retrieve a young girl from the wreckage and had found her dead, and a husband and wife sitting in the mud and clinging to one another, thanking God that they had survived. "The whole thing was awful," Grant said. "It's three or four hours since it happened and I'm still shaking."

It took more than four hours to find the last of the dead. Knowing that one man remained lost as the rescue operation stretched through the night, police organized a line of people to hold hands and wade through the sawgrass and shallow water, hoping to come across a living person dazed from the crash. The body came to light near dawn, pinned under the plane's right wing and out of sight in the darkness.

All fifteen of the surviving passengers and crew came away with injuries that ranged from fairly minor to very serious. Emergency crews at Mercy and Jackson Memorial Hospitals in Miami received credit for their orderly, rapid response, mobilizing as soon as they received word of the crash, flying doctors and nurses to the scene in helicopters and reaching the site west of Milam Dairy Road and NW 58th Street in about twenty minutes. They showed great foresight in using helicopters rather than ambulances to reach the scene, as police found themselves struggling to keep roads clear with thousands of gawkers and would-be rescuers flocking to the site.

Worse, police soon discovered that looters were stealing whatever they could from the luggage scattered for hundreds of yards around the destroyed plane. Tall sawgrass, most of it reaching more than seven feet high, hid these opportunists as they picked through open suitcases and purses and pried open locked bags. Police did succeed in arresting two Miami teens as the night dragged on. James Phelps and Thomas M. San

Cartier were both charged with petty larceny and forced to give back the cameras and coats they had attempted to pilfer. They spent three days in jail until bond could be met, and received a suspended sentence in exchange for their confession.

Despite severe injuries, most of the passengers and crew were released from the hospital within days of the crash. Capt. Thomas George suffered head injuries that kept him in the hospital for weeks, and included a complete memory blackout that extended to at least twenty-four hours before the plane went down.

The investigation into what may have caused the explosion and subsequent wreck went on for some time, with as many as twenty-six experts sifting through the bits at the crash scene and logging their observations in notebooks. The CAB retrieved the largest pieces of the plane by helicopter and transported them to an open field at the end of NW 58th Street in Miami, where they reassembled the plane to examine it more thoroughly.

At a CAB hearing on May 7, five weeks after the crash, Kenneth I. Swinger, CAA supervisor of airway tower operations at Miami airport from 4:00 p.m. to midnight on the night of the accident, said that as the plane approached from Dallas to land in Miami shortly after 7:00 p.m., he saw a bright orange light in engine no. 3. He cleared the plane for landing but scanned it with binoculars in the waning evening light and spotted a light trail emanating from the right inboard engine. "I asked the flight, 'Is your number 3 engine smoking a little bit?' Someone on the crew replied, 'Well, I hope not.'"

Once the plane landed, however, nothing appeared to be amiss. No smoke appeared from that engine on the runway, and "no torching or other discrepancy was apparent."

Another air traffic controller, Carroll D. Bright, relieved Swinger at 11:59 p.m. and was on duty five minutes later as Flight 971 took off.

"I was two or three steps down the stairs when a shout in the tower directed my attention to a bright orange light west of the airport," he said. "I immediately returned to the control cab."

All the controllers heard just one transmission, "Braniff 971 ..." before the aircraft exploded.

Despite considerable testimony saying otherwise, including eyewitness accounts from passengers who said the plane came apart in the air, the CAB concluded that the plane did not break up until it hit the Everglades. Engineers testified at the hearing that the fire in the no. 3 engine did not impair the wing, so there was "no evidence of any structural breakup of the plane or explosion prior to the ground impact," according to Isaac Hoover, an aeronautics engineer from Washington, DC.

The record filed with the Aviation Safety Network, a service of the Flight Safety Foundation, lists the CAB's final determination of the cause: "The failure of the captain to maintain altitude during an emergency return to the airport due to his undue preoccupation with an engine fire following takeoff."

FIRE IN THE SKY: NORTHWEST ORIENT 705

Nothing seemed amiss as Capt. Roy W. Almquist of Northwest Flight 705 asked the ground controller for a recommended departure route to avoid a squall, before beginning a scheduled flight from Miami International to Chicago O'Hare on February 12, 1963. The three-year-old Boeing 720B he would be flying carried thirty-five passengers and eight crew members, barely one-quarter its total 165 capacity. Thunderstorms in the area created some turbulence, but this was a familiar affair for any pilot who flew into or out of Miami in the winter. The departure controller provided instructions to depart "either through a southwest climb or a southeast climb and then back over the top of [the squall]," just as another flight had done moments before.

So Northwest Orient 705 left Miami at 1:35 p.m. with an IFR (instrument flight rules) clearance, meaning that the pilot and copilot would use the plane's instruments, rather than visual cues, to navigate through the cloud cover and expected turbulence. The flight made a left turn after takeoff and used "circuitous routing . . . in conjunction with radar vectors from Miami Departure Control," as these systems helped guide the plane around the turbulence.

When the plane reached 5,000 feet, Flight 705's crew requested clearance to climb higher. This required a discussion with the radar departure controller about the storms, and coordination with the Miami

Air Route Traffic Control Center (ARTCC). Even before these plans could be completed, however, the crew radioed air traffic control to say, "We're in the clear now. We can see it out ahead . . . Looks pretty bad."

The flight received its clearance to climb higher at 1:43 p.m., and responded, "OK, ahh, we'll make a left turn about thirty degrees here and climb." Departure control asked about their climb-out heading and agreed on coordinates that would take the plane "out in the open again."

The crew then informed departure control they were running into fairly heavy turbulence, and said, "You better run the rest of them off the other way then."

A minute later, departure control terminated radar service with Flight 705 and handed the flight over to the Miami ARTCC. This should have been a perfectly normal, routine transfer, but one minute went by and then another without the flight crew confirming the handoff.

Departure control stepped back in and repeated the hand over, this time receiving an acknowledgment from the crew. Breathing a sigh of relief, the departure controller listened as ARTCC requested the flight's position and altitude. "We're just out of seventeen-five," the crew replied.

At 1:47 p.m. Flight 705 began increasing its altitude at a rate that eventually reached 9,000 feet per minute, peaking at 19,285 feet in altitude. Captain Almquist requested clearance to climb to 25,000 feet.

A moment later and seven minutes after takeoff, Flight 705 exploded.

Witnesses as far as seven miles away turned toward the sound of "an explosion which had no echo" to see "an orange ball of flame in the edge of a cloud," according to a report in the Bureau of Aircraft Accidents Archives. The ball of flames plummeted straight down from the clouds to the earth, a streak of bright orange followed by billowing smoke.

At Miami International, loss of radio contact was not enough to trigger a search. Normal procedure dictated that a search did not begin "until the known fuel supply is exhausted," CAB accident coordinator Charles Collar told the *Miami News* the following day. "In this instance, fuel would have been exhausted around 6:30 p.m."

Miami ARTCC, however, decided to jump the gun. It notified Coast Guard Search and Rescue at 2:48 p.m., an hour and six minutes after flight 705 made its last contact, even though a disruption in radio contact could be due to electronic or mechanical problems that would not affect the flight's safety.

So just over an hour after Miami International lost radio contact with the plane, the Civil Air Patrol, Air Force, and Coast Guard had planes and helicopters in the air looking for the jetliner. When fishermen began calling in reports of "fire in the sky," the search focused its efforts on the Everglades west of the airport.

"Suddenly there was a ball of fire within a cloud," said Gordon Swann of Naples, who was fishing in Rookery Creek in Everglades National Park that afternoon with his wife and two other couples. "A rain of fire descended all the way to the rim of mangrove trees on our horizon." He contacted a park ranger, and the ranger called the Coast Guard to report "a red-streaked ball of fire blazing up inside a thunderhead, then dripping fire and smoke, followed by a distant, muffled explosion," the *Miami News* reported the next day.

Even with this solid hint at the wreck's location fourteen miles from the closest highway, it took six and a half hours for a Coast Guard helicopter to find the downed plane. The crew finally spotted three small fires burning close together, and landed on a raised hammock between the separated fuselage and tail.

"The fuselage was all busted up and consumed by fire," Coast Guard Lt. Cdr. James Dillian told the AP. Dillian and Lt. Cdr. W. C. Wallace were the first to find the plane and land on the spongy ground to look for survivors. "It lay smack in the middle of a swamp. All around us were little pieces of wreckage and a lot of luggage."

The crew realized immediately that there were no survivors—not a single track appeared in the mud and tangled vegetation. "Lt. Wallace said it looked as if all the bodies were intact," Dillon continued. "All he had was a flashlight and he couldn't see too much. The tail was broken off." He noted that it looked like the pilot had put up a fight, trying to bring the plane to the ground safely in the midst of some kind of chaos.

Not certain of their position, the Coast Guard crew lifted off and radioed Tamiami control tower to get a fix on their location. With coordinates finally in hand, recovery and investigation teams mobilized immediately. The first members of the recovery operation—personnel from the U.S. Fish and Game Commission—reached the site at around midnight and "radioed that [they] found the plane burning," the AP reported.

The swamp, the AP continued, consisted of impassable undergrowth that "only swamp buggies and weasel vehicles could penetrate." Even so, one of the first things recovered was the plane's flight recorder box, which contained instruments that charted the plane's altitude and speed, the operation of its various systems, stress on the fuselage, and other data that might provide clues to the plane's sudden, catastrophic end. Officials lost no time in shipping the black box to Washington, DC, for examination.

The reality of the crash site could not have been more gruesome. Twisted, mangled wreckage spread across two miles of swampy grassland, the scattered bodies of forty-three people among the contorted rubble.

Searchers discovered the largest piece of the plane, a section of the fuselage, some two hundred yards from the distorted remains of the nose. They found pieces of a wing another four hundred yards away, but these represented less than a third of the whole wing. The fragments made it clear that the pilot had not attempted an emergency landing—in fact, he may not have had any indication that his craft was about to explode.

"One engine lay in the weeds nearly a city block away, and beside it was a metal food hamper with its lid gaping open," wrote Miami reporter Miller Davis from the crash site. "To see the scene in your mind's eye, pretend you're looking at a peaceful field of wheat, and then someone comes along and throws a junkyard of steel in its center, and then douses it with gasoline and lights a match."

National park rangers joined the FBI and Florida Highway Patrol as the body recovery operations and investigation began. "From the air, bodies cold be seen sprawled around the wreckage with yellow markers placed by each," the AP reported.

Officials recruited the assistance of resident Seminoles to find a place nearby where military personnel, tasked with the most grisly part of the operation, could bring the bodies as they were retrieved. They used amphibious vehicles to traverse the swamp wilderness and bring out the dead passengers and crew. Officials requested the use of a nearby

Miccosukee school as a temporary morgue for the bodies, but the tribal chairman, William Buffalo Tiger, refused. Seminoles believe that the passage into death is sacred, and the living should not interfere with the site at which death takes place—making it taboo to spend time around dead bodies. "They [the tribe] would have had to burn the building down. They couldn't go back in there," explained Miccosukee police chief Anthony Zecca years later. "You can't ask the tribe to do certain things."

So a temporary morgue and CAB base of operations were established elsewhere, headed by Charles Collar of Miami as technicians worked to determine what could have befallen the aircraft.

By the end of the day after the crash, searchers had recovered thirty-nine of the bodies, and medical professionals from the Armed Forces Pathology Institute were hard at work trying to identify them as quickly as possible. They were under particular pressure to determine if Dr. Herman E. Wells, a dual resident of Delray Beach and Chicago, was among the dead. Wells had been expected to appear in court that day on abortion charges, and his name was on the passenger manifest. While agents had made only eleven positive identifications by Thursday afternoon, February 14, they soon identified Wells's body, putting that concern to rest.

Stories of other passengers began to emerge. Edwin North, president of the National Lock Company in Rockford, Illinois, and Christine North, his granddaughter, died in the crash exactly ten years to the day after his daughter Marilyn and her fiancé, Robert G. Barnes, died in a plane crash on a National Airlines jet flying from Tampa to New Orleans. North was on his way home to the Chicago area from Florida.

Four of the five members of an Illinois family—Mr. and Mrs. Walter Orzula, their daughter Jerilyn , 20, and their son, 18-year-old Walter Jr.—all perished in the crash. Their other daughter, Joyce, usually vacationed with them, but this year she had stayed home with her husband in Fort Riley, Kansas.

Connie Blank, a stewardess on the flight, was engaged to be married that summer. After this flight, she had planned to change planes in Chicago and continue to Spokane to visit her mother.

Fanny Lebedow of Lincolnwood, Illinois, was coming home from a Florida vacation as her daughter, Shirley Linn, waited for her at O'Hare

International Airport in Chicago. Her nine-year-old grandson Larry told a UPI reporter, "I think planes are the most dangerous things in the world."

Twenty-year-old Fred Olson III of Rockford, his fifteen-year-old sister Joan and two friends, Susan Schwendener and Christine Rever, had all spent a long weekend in Miami with Olson's parents at the Bahama Hotel. The young people all boarded flight 705 to head back home so they would not miss classes the following day. Olson's father, Fred Jr., told Bill Bondurant of the *Fort Lauderdale News*, "It was a special trip for them because they were given extra days off from school for Lincoln's birthday. I drove all of them to school every morning for years. Now they are gone."

The most chilling story, though, involved two couples, Anton and Sally Smigiel and Joseph and Rose Srodulski. They had all vacationed together in Florida, and Anton and Joseph had booked a separate flight to Chicago "just in case one of the planes would crash." Rose and Sally boarded flight 705 and flew off. The men waited two additional hours in Miami because their flight was delayed for repairs, but they finally reached O'Hare, expecting their wives to be waiting for them. Instead, they were ushered into a small waiting area where they found the Smigiels' daughter, Judy, and her fiancé, who gave them the news that flight 705 was missing. Hours later they received official word that the plane had crashed, and it took another four hours before they knew that everyone on board had died.

"There was a tremendous storm," said Anton Smigiel, "but we didn't think anything would go wrong." They never expected their abundance of caution to prove so bitterly wise.

The mystery remained: What made the plane crash? Reports collected from other aircraft leaving Miami around the same time were of light to moderate rain, "medium" turbulence, and a frontal squall 250 miles long northwest of the airport. An advisory that included extreme turbulence was issued at 1:15 p.m., but the crew of Flight 705 had already left the operations office with an earlier report and its turbulence forecast of "moderate." Still, a flight crew that flies daily from Miami to Chicago knows what kind of dangerous turbulence they may encounter.

The flight recorder offered some insights: For seven seconds after its last transmission, the plane lost altitude rapidly. When it passed 10,000 feet, "mean failures in both wings and horizontal stabilizers were in a downward direction, and virtually symmetrical," the Aviation Safety Network report read. "The forward fuselage broke upward and the vertical stabilizer failed to the left. All four engines generally separated upward and outboard"—as dry a description as one could wish of a catastrophic crash.

What did become clear from the flight recorder data turned out to be some comfort to the search crews, who had not been able to locate the jetliner for hours after it crashed. By the time the plane lost radio contact, it was already beyond help, and it exploded seconds later. "Even if they had been in the air seconds after that final report, it would have been too late," the *Miami News* reported.

In its search for answers, CAB used the collected bits and pieces of the destroyed aircraft to rebuild it in an airplane hangar at Opa-locka Airport, creating "the most complete [reconstruction] in the history of aviation," the *Miami Herald* reported in May 1963. Days of testimony and months of continued investigation followed. The flight recorder said that the flight's speed dropped from 270 to 217 knots in five seconds in "a sharp updraft" when it hit severe turbulence at 20,000 feet—a dangerous loss of speed in conditions where 236 knots was recommended.

"If the turbulence was severe enough, the pilot would fully stall his airplane," said FAA test pilot Richard S. Sliff at a CAB hearing in Miami on June 20.

Another theory proffered in the testimony suggested that Captain Almquist had held the nose of the jetliner down as the plane shot upward, causing the plane to stall and essentially fall out of the sky, "disintegrat[ing] in a gyrating, twisting, upside-down plunge to earth."

In the end, no firm conclusion was ever reached. The lengthy investigation looked carefully at the factors involved and determined that the most likely cause of this accident was "the unfavorable interaction of severe vertical air drafts and large longitudinal control displacements, resulting in a longitudinal 'upset' from which a successful recovery was not made."

This may not be a satisfying conclusion, but it closed the book on this tragedy, and no other Boeing 720B went down in such a manner again.

DISTRACTED DRIVING: EASTERN AIRLINES FLIGHT 401

By December 1972, commercial airliners had grown larger and were better equipped to provide answers should one of them go down. The Lockheed L-1011-385-1 Tristar 1 Airbus flown by Eastern Airlines on December 29, 1972, featured 226 seats and such quiet operation that Eastern had tagged the model a "Whisperliner." In addition to all sorts of comfort features, it sported the latest recording equipment: a bright orange box that contained a flight data recorder (FDR) with sixty-four value inputs monitoring speed, altitude, and heading, with the added capability to record the position of the plane's nose, the plane's roll and number of degrees difference from level, the position of the horizontal stabilizers, the G-forces acting on the plane's hull, and much more. Reading the data of older FDRs, like the one on the unfortunate 1963 Northwest Orient flight, required "precision measuring instruments and powerful magnifying glasses," according to writer James H. Hammond of the *Boston Globe*. The new recorders collected their information in computer language on magnetic tape, which could be read by computers at the manufacturer (in this case, Lockheed Martin).

The FDR also provided a time code that could be matched with another new recording device, the cockpit voice recorder (CVR), which captured everything said in the cockpit within a given period during the flight. Having these sources of information helped investigators determine what the crew might know about any malfunction of the aircraft in flight, what they were doing to try to correct it, and what mechanical or electronic issues were in progress when the problem took place.

With this wealth of information, it seemed that there would be no more mystery plane crashes—everything the CAB needed to know would be recorded during every flight. If a critical system shut down during descent, its defects would become obvious through the FDR. If a weather event threw the plane into a dive, instruments would tell exactly when and how this happened and how much force the squall or front administered to the craft.

And if the flight crew made an error, investigators would know—whether or not the crew survived.

Eastern Airlines Flight 401 left New York's John F. Kennedy International Airport at 9:20 p.m. on December 29, 1972, en route to Miami. Thirteen crew members and 164 passengers enjoyed a smooth flight south with warmer weather on their minds, planning New Year's Eve celebrations or time with friends and relatives.

As the plane approached Miami International, however, the crew lowered the landing gear, but the nose gear light did not come on to indicate "the nose gear was down and locked in position." The crew raised the gear and tried again, but the light still did not illuminate.

The crew called Miami International at 11:34 p.m. and reported the problem. "Climb to 2,000 feet and hold," the Miami controller advised them. They did so, and while they remained in a holding pattern circling the airport, Capt. Robert Loft, a thirty-two-year veteran of Eastern Airlines, told his first officer, Albert J. Stockstill, to engage the autopilot while they worked to resolve the problem. Loft then told his second officer, Donald L. Repo, to go into the forward electronics bay to check the alignment of the nose gear. Repo went forward as the crew continued to recycle the landing gear, attempting to correct the problem mechanically. When Repo returned, he told the captain that he could not see the position of the nose landing gear from the electronics bay.

The captain sent Repo back into the electronics bay at 11:38 p.m., and he continued to talk with Stockstill about what might be wrong, with Loft believing that the indicator light lens assembly might have been inserted incorrectly.

But during the recycling of the gear and the attempt to fix the indicator light, one of the pilots jostled the autopilot control yoke, disengaging the part of the autopilot that maintained altitude. This allowed the plane to begin a slow, steady descent on its own.

Two minutes later, a ground proximity warning sounded in the cockpit. The plane had descended at least 250 feet while the crew was focused on the indicator light, and the plane was now around 1,750 feet above the ground. The ground proximity system attempted to warn the crew, but according to the CVR, no one took notice of the chime or thought to check why it had sounded. Instead, another member of the crew—a maintenance specialist—left his seat in the cockpit and went into the electronics bay to help the second officer.

And the plane continue to descend. At 11:41 p.m., Miami controller Charles Johnson noted that the flight seemed to have begun a descent and asked, "How are you coming along out there?"

"OK," said one of the pilots. "We'd like to turn around now and come back in."

Johnson instructed the crew to make a left turn and head back 180 degrees for a second pass at the runway. By this time, the plane had dropped to an altitude of about 900 feet.

Twenty seconds later and too late to react, Stockstill discovered that they were no more than 300 feet from the ground. "Hey, what's happening here?" one of the pilots exclaimed.

They made impact seven seconds later.

Flight 401's no. 1 engine hit the ground at a 28-degree angle and sheared off as the plane skidded on its belly for 1,520 feet. The force of the crash shattered the plane into hundreds of pieces, leaving nothing intact but a fragment of the fuselage near the wing and a piece of the tail. Chunks of the plane pinwheeled through the air as far as 1,600 feet from the crash point, scattering bits of the hull and bodies across Everglades National Park's vast, muddy, swampy backcountry.

In the Miami air traffic control tower, the radar blip that had been Flight 401 vanished from the screen. The controller knew immediately that this meant the plane had dropped below 300 feet. "We have lost you on radar," the controller said. "Please advise your altitude."

No one responded.

Somewhere in the wet, marshy darkness, Gerry Solomon, a twenty-four-year-old salesman onboard the plane, unbuckled his seatbelt and shoved his way through a hole in the side of the hull, emerging into Everglades sawgrass and muck. He stood dazed and in disbelief, amazed that the plane had crashed and that he had somehow had the good fortune to survive.

In seconds survivors began to scream. Some were injured, perhaps mortally. Some had managed to escape major wounds but were overcome by fear. Some of the living turned to those next to them and tried to help. Many lay motionless in pools of their own blood, their clothing and even their watches and rings torn away by the impact.

Becky J. Raposa, a twenty-five-year-old stewardess, found herself bruised but not seriously hurt. She had been thrown back and forth across the rear rows of the plane as it collided with the earth, but when the noise and motion stopped, her emergency training held sway over her fear. She glanced around and saw jet fuel everywhere. "Nobody light a match!" she called to everyone around her.

Struggling to her feet, she tried to move through the shattered cabin, but realized that this was essentially impossible with so many stunned, injured, or dead people around her. With no first aid kit within reach, she did the only thing she had within her power: She started to sing.

"I started leading them in Christmas carols to keep up morale while we awaited rescue," she told Jay Maeder of the *Miami Herald*. "We sang 'Jingle Bells,' 'Rudolph, the Red-Nosed Reindeer,' 'Sleigh Bells,' and 'Frosty the Snowman.' We didn't do too well on Frosty because no one could remember the words."

She helped them face the surprisingly cold night by talking of the hot food and warm blankets they would receive once they were rescued. Raposa helped stave off the surviving passengers' panic for the half an hour it took before they began to hear helicopters approaching. Later she told Maeder she believed that so many passengers in the back of the plane had survived because they were wearing their seat belts in anticipation of landing, so they had not been thrown from their seats in the crash.

Perhaps ten miles away, area residents Robert L. Marquis and Ray Dickens paused as they hunted frogs after dark. Marquis happened to glance out over the water from their airboat at 11:42 p.m. just in time to see "a flash and a red glow, a real reddish orange," he told Gene Miller of the *Miami Herald*. "It just stretched out, maybe for a thousand yards. It couldn't have lasted more than five or seven seconds."

It could only be one thing, he decided, and he fired up the airboat's motor and set off across the expanse at 35 to 40 miles per hour. In about fifteen minutes, he shut off his engine and listened. "That's when I heard the people. They were just yelling and screaming." He guessed that he was within one-quarter mile of the wreckage, and he and Dickens began shining the hunting lights they wore strapped to their heads to try to find the sources of the cries.

Determining a direction, Marquis motored more slowly toward the sounds and ran aground. He jumped out and shoved the boat back into the water, then motored forward again, stopping soon to listen. "I heard someone yelling, 'Hey! Hey! Hey! Hey!'" he said. "They had seen the light and they were trying to let me know where they were."

He shone his light in their direction again and saw the wreckage. In a moment he could make out some people nearby. "Everyone was in a state of hysteria," he said. "I think I was, too . . . I felt so helpless. So many people hollering from so many directions. I didn't know which way to turn."

Then he and Dickens spotted two helicopters in the distance, and they began waving their lights at them. "I think they saw me right away," Marquis said, still relieved by this. In the meantime, he helped several relatively unhurt people out of the water and into the boat. "There were dead people everywhere," he said. "I don't know how many people drowned."

At Miami International, protocol had changed since the deadly 1963 crash that killed everyone on Northwest Orient flight 705. Instead of waiting hours before declaring the plane missing, air traffic control didn't waste a moment after Eastern 401 disappeared from the radar but called the plane "down" immediately. They notified airport authorities, and soon the Federal Aviation Administration (FAA) had called the Coast Guard and helicopters had left the airport to find the jet and begin rescue operations.

Coast Guard lieutenant Mike McCormack was the first to be airborne, departing the airport at 11:55 p.m. as the Coast Guard mobilized its Rescue Coordination Center (RCC) in downtown Miami. What he saw he would never unsee: "Beneath him, limbs protruded from the blackness; some survivors screamed in agony, some sang Christmas carols." As he hovered above them, however, "they saw McCormack and cheered," wrote Mike Baxter of the *Miami Herald*.

The crash site was eighteen miles northwest of Miami International and eight miles north of the Tamiami Trail, the closest highway. A flood control dike crossed the Everglades within a few hundred feet of the crash site, though, giving emergency vehicles the ability to get fairly close to the wreckage and transport people out over a bumpy and uneven road—but better than crossing miles of water.

The RCC ordered medical teams from St. Petersburg and the McArthur Causeway Coast Guard Base, as well as doctors from the local public health service to head eighteen miles into the Everglades. "By telephone and by teletype, a quickly growing and stunningly unchaotic rescue armada had been mobilized and dispatched within the first half hour after the disaster," noted Baxter, his admiration undisguised in his lengthy account of the operation.

Thirteen area hospitals stood ready to take in the injured, with as many as two hundred doctors poised to treat them. Another one hundred doctors stood by on call, ready to come in if the casualties threatened to overwhelm available emergency and operating rooms. Others rushed supplies to the Coast Guard helipad, including plenty of morphine for injured passengers. The Florida Highway Patrol hit the road to block traffic on State Highway 27 where it joined the Tamiami Trail, keeping the lanes open for ambulances and other rescue vehicles and diverting the inevitable flood of spectators.

A veritable fleet of airboats, called to action by airboat club operators, took to the waterways leading to the crash site, knowing that they might be the only craft that could reach a downed jetliner in the backcountry. They turned their motors up full and sped to the site where more than a dozen aircraft had already gathered, making it easy to see where the plane went down. Helicopters and fixed-wing aircraft all instantly accepted the coordination of a Coast Guard amphibious plane—an HU-16E—no matter what organization they represented, one of the many cooperative efforts for the common good that facilitated the rescue operation throughout the night.

"It was disaster itself that forged the bonds uniting nearly 200 rescue workers from a dozen agencies as they carried survivors through the swamp blackness of the Everglades," said Baxter. Without a defined chain of command or a designated leader of the rescue operation, they worked to save as many people as possible and to connect them with the care they needed to survive.

The midnight crash in the heart of a desolate wetland did not make it easy. While the water, mud, and vegetation cushioned the plane's violent, belly-flop landing enough to produce 77 survivors of the 176 people aboard, the total darkness and the lack of dry land close to the wreck made it nearly impossible for would-be rescue aircraft to land. Private citizens showing up in their swamp boats provided flashlights and floodlights for the first rescuers who arrived, and they remained to assist in finding all of the passengers and crew, living or dead, in and around the wreckage. Coast Guard helicopters and Air Force aircraft remained overhead with emergency floodlights blazing, providing the illumination rescuers needed to find everyone they could.

"Some were screaming but we could hardly hear them because of the helicopters," said William C. Lane, a Florida game warden who arrived in an airboat and made six trips to and from the crash site to transport survivors and bodies. "The worst part was running over the dead people to get the live ones out."

Helicopters lifted out the most badly injured survivors and whisked them to hospitals until a system could be worked out to bring victims to the levee road a few hundred yards away. Airboats then took over transport duty, streaking across the wettest areas to reach the potholed road. From here, people formed a human chain to lift victims strapped to litters from the airboats to the top of the levee, where ambulance crews loaded them into vehicles and drove them along levees to the smooth road beyond.

By 2:00 a.m., nearly everyone who had survived the crash had been found and transported away from the site. "Eventually, there was one sure way to tell the dead from the living," said Dr. Eugene Nagel of the Jackson Memorial Hospital Medical Disaster Team. "The dead were under water. The living weren't."

The remaining rescue crews quietly switched their mission to body recovery, and remained at the site until every victim had been found. Technicians marked the locations of the bodies as they were discovered, information that would be important in the National Transportation Safety Board (NTSB) investigation to come. They then moved the bodies out of the Everglades and to the Dade County morgue, as well as to refrigerated trucks that served as a morgue annex.

Of the cockpit crew, only Donald L. Repo survived the crash. He remained in Hialeah Hospital in serious condition, "undergoing surgery for a crushed back, broken arm, broken leg and broken ribs," the *Miami Herald* reported on December 31. Repo died later that day without ever speaking with investigators.

The *Herald* confirmed on January 5 that this crash "produced the second highest death toll of any single airplane commercial accident in this country's history," according to the Air Transport Association in Washington, DC. Dade County Medical Examiner Joseph Davis broke down the causes of death: Almost all of the victims died of "impact injuries" sustained when the plane hit the ground at 200 mph. None had died in the small fires that broke out around the plane's wreckage. Fewer than a dozen had drowned in the swampland. "Had the ground been rocky and hard, I don't think there would have been any survivors," he told the media at a press conference on January 2.

The process of piecing together what had happened began with the FDR and CVR recordings and continued with interviews with air traffic controllers and others. Questions from the media about Captain Loft's eyesight (he wore glasses) and a benign brain tumor discovered in his autopsy attempted to center blame on him, but Eastern officials resisted these explanations in favor of the data from the two recorders. Over the days of hearings that took place during the spring of 1973, a story of pilot error came to light, a series of events that would have haunted this flight crew for the rest of their lives had they not perished in the cockpit on that chilly December night, just a few miles from the safe landing they had made many times before.

DEADLY INCOMPETENCE: VALUJET FLIGHT 592

Nothing illustrates the worst the Everglades can do to a downed aircraft more vividly than the crash of ValuJet Flight 592, a DC-9 jetliner scheduled to carry 105 passengers and five crew from Miami to Atlanta on May 11, 1996.

The twenty-seven-year-old aircraft, purchased by ValuJet in well-used but good condition, already had a record of maintenance issues that had forced a return to airports seven times in the previous two years. Lost cabin pressure, overheating of a constant speed drive, and a door stuck ajar had all led pilots to return to their point of departure, but these were all easily corrected, and the plane continued to transport passengers nearly daily. None of these issues, in fact, contributed to the disaster that came for this plane on a clear, sunny afternoon in the middle of spring.

To understand what happened to this ill-fated flight, we need a bit of technical information. The NTSB's final report on the crash, delivered in August 1997, does its best to explain exactly what happened in fairly clear language, so I will share this chronology with you.

Flight 592 carried five boxes that had no business being on the aircraft. They happened to be on racks near the plane's loading area along with a selection of airplane parts. These boxes were labeled "Oxy Cannisters [*sic*]—Empty."

The five boxes contained chemical oxygen generators, the components of a plane's emergency oxygen system that generate the oxygen for passengers if cabin pressure should be lost. Full, working generators are installed behind panels above passengers in the cabin of every plane, and are attached to masks that drop down in front of the passengers in an emergency situation.

The oxygen generators are connected to the mask by a thin, white cord, which in turn is connected to a pin that prevents the oxygen from flowing until a passenger pulls on the cord to start the flow. (The process for starting that flow is what flight attendants demonstrate to passengers as the plane pulls away from the gate. This is why you need to pull down firmly on the mask when it falls out of the compartment over your head.) When the passenger pulls the cord, an "initiation mechanism" strikes a small cap that sets off a tiny explosion at the end of the oxygen generator, which in turn creates a chemical reaction that starts the oxygen flowing. New, unused generators are shipped with a safety cap that prevents inadvertent ignition and the resulting chemical reaction.

The five boxes on ValuJet 592 contained used generators—but not empty ones, despite how the boxes were labeled—so their safety caps had long since been removed. ValuJet had specific guidelines for any contractors who might be preparing used canisters for transport. Step 2 of its seven-step process could not have been more clear: "If generator has not been expended, install shipping cap on firing pin."

Here's the thing about this chemical reaction: It creates heat, which heats the outside of the generator to as high as 547 degrees Fahrenheit. The NTSB, in looking at other airlines' rules for the safe handling of these generators, found that other airlines defined these canisters as hazardous waste and required that all canisters be discharged completely before shipping or disposal. Alaska Airlines went so far as to require that the canisters be held at the location where they had been removed from a plane's oxygen system, becoming the responsibility of an environmental affairs manager, who would presumably know how potentially dangerous they were.

In March 1996, a maintenance contractor called SabreTech began removing old oxygen generators from planes and replacing the expired ones with new generators. Many of these old canisters had never been used, but the contractor simply labeled them "Repairable" and placed them in cardboard boxes, which then went to a rack in a hangar near the planes. The mechanic who packed the old generators said that he laid them on their side in the boxes, with each white lanyard cord wrapped around its cylinder.

The new generators the mechanics installed had warning labels on them.

WARNING
THIS UNIT GETS HOT!
WHEN REMOVING UNIT INSTALL
SAFETY CAP OVER PRIMER
DO NOT PULL LANYARD
IF ACTIVATED PLACE ON SURFACE THAT WON'T BURN.

How the boxes ended up on Flight 592—and why they were labeled "Empty" when most of the canisters were fully charged—is a story of clerical negligence and incompetence that spans several departments, and one that would appall (but might not surprise) anyone who has worked in a warehouse, whether or not they've ever handled hazardous materials. Suffice to say that the boxes of generators were loaded on ValueJet 592 as if they were nothing more dangerous than miscellaneous mechanical parts, along with three airplane tires in a bin with passenger luggage and sixty-two pounds of U.S. mail. The canisters received no special handling as hazardous waste and were stacked on top of the three tires so the canisters clinked together audibly as the ramp agents placed them in the front of the cargo hold.

"The ramp agent said the cargo was not secure, and that the cargo compartment had no means for securing the cargo," the NTSB report said.

So it was that thirty-six-year-old pilot Capt. Candalyn "Candi" Kubeck took her seat on Flight 592 with her first officer, Richard Hazen, and began preparing for a routine flight with no knowledge of the dangerous cargo. After several short ground delays and a pause while a passenger used a restroom, the plane finally left the ground at about 2:03 p.m.

Seven minutes later one of the pilots asked, "What was that?" A strange sound from outside the cockpit registered on the CVR as a "chirp." In seconds a cockpit officer said, "We got some electrical problem." The other agreed, and then the first voice said, "We're losing everything."

The departure controller bid them a routine "So long" as he handed the flight off to Miami Center, but Captain Kubeck cut him off.

"We need to go back to Miami," she said. Behind her, in the passenger cabin, a shout went up.

"Fire, fire, fire, fire," the flight attendants called out. "We're on fire. We're on fire."

A three-second tone sounded, and Captain Kubeck repeated, "To Miami."

A third voice in the cockpit said, "Okay, we need oxygen, we can't get oxygen back there."

Chimes sounded. Horns went off. A voice yelled, "Completely on fire!"

"Smoke in the cockpit, smoke in the cabin," said a male voice—First Officer Hazen.

The departure controller did his best to guide the distressed plane back to Miami. "Critter five ninety two, when able to turn left heading two five zero. Descend and maintain five thousand."

A sound of loud rushing air filled the microphones in the cockpit. Another voice from air traffic control advised the flight to head to "closest airport available." The captain and crew did not respond. The recording broke up several times and finally went silent.

On the ground below, Sam Nelson and Chris Osceola, fishing in a boat deep in the Everglades, looked up when the low-flying jet came into view, trailing smoke from an engine and banking steeply to the right. They watched open-mouthed as the plane's nose dropped, upending the aircraft until it plunged almost perfectly vertically toward the earth. The plane hit the ground and exploded, shaking the terrain with the strength of an earthquake. A column of smoke, water, and muck shot up into the air as the plane disappeared, the force of its descent driving the plane's nose through the water and mud and into the limestone bedrock below.

"The landing gear was up," one of the fishermen said in the NTSB report. "All the airplane's parts seemed to be intact, and . . . aside from the engine smoke, no signs of fire were visible."

Two sightseers passing over the Everglades in a private plane—Daniel Muelhaupt and Rick DeLisle—saw the impact as well. "It was like a fireball of dirt and debris," said Muelhaupt to a writer from Knight-Ridder News Service.

"Like a mushroom cloud," DeLisle added.

Muelhaupt called for help on his single-engine plane's radio and then circled, searching for the plane and any survivors. They saw nothing until he swooped down to 200 feet. Still they did not see a jet aircraft—all they could see was "part of an engine, paper, and other debris," according to the NTSB final report on the incident. The plane had simply vanished.

"The wreckage was like if you take your garbage and just throw it on the ground; it looked like that," said Muelhaupt.

Jesse Kennon, one of the first people to arrive at the site with emergency rescue crews, confirmed what the witnesses had seen. "It looks like it almost went straight down, and from the impact it was almost crushed like a soda can . . . just like taking a soda can and stepping on it."

The crash, about twenty miles northwest of Miami International between canals L67A and L67C, doused whatever flames had been raging when the plane went down. The water and mud simply swallowed the plane while the limestone bedrock stopped its downward progression and crumpled the plane like a sheet of newsprint.

When the magnitude of the challenge became clear to recovery teams, a call went out for specialists who knew how to sift through this kind of rubble to find human remains. Federal workers arrived who had spent much of the previous spring combing through the wreckage of the Alfred P. Murrah Federal Building bombing in Oklahoma City the year before. "No survivors. No bodies either," confirmed R. D. Paulison, director of the Metro-Dade Fire Department, to reporter Jim Greenhill of the *Fort Myers News-Press*. "We have found nothing. No bodies, nothing."

Nothing, that is, except the first personal effects to be discovered at the site: a photo album with pictures of a mother and baby and a few items of baby clothes.

For the first couple of days, searchers picked their way around slicks of highly flammable jet fuel floating atop standing water, waiting for the heat—which was in the 90s every day—to evaporate the fuel and allow them to begin to dig deeper. As the fuel evaporated, the fumes overpowered some of the recovery crew, making it almost impossible to breathe. The exposed fuel also made the use of airboats especially hazardous, as the slightest spark had the potential to set the entire area ablaze.

The soil in this area—known as Conservation Area 3B—was particularly soft, Kennon told Greenhill of the *News-Press*. The plane, hitting the ground at a 75-degree angle, might have pierced the soil as much as eighteen feet down before striking limestone. Some sources said the mud could be thirty feet deep there. It lay under chest-deep water, making the wreckage even less accessible to recovery teams.

By the day after the crash, the NTSB had already predicted it could be six months to a year before the buried plane and its doomed passengers and crew were unearthed completely and before investigators could determine exactly what had caused the crash. For the moment, crews had found just two areas of scattered debris, and trucks towing trailers filled with high-intensity lighting had arrived to aid in the round-the-clock work ahead. State troopers stood guard along all of the roads leading into the area, turning away would-be rescuers in airboats and other watercraft. They already knew that there were no lives to be saved.

Authorities established a central area to which recovery workers could bring whatever human remains they found. Facing the most ghastly endeavor of their careers, they collected small body parts like fingers, hands, feet, fragments of tissue, and in one case, a section of skin with a tattoo. The need to work quickly before bacterial decay, vultures, and alligators devoured pieces that could be identified through DNA analysis spurred them to work through the night and into the next day.

Searchers spent almost thirty minutes just getting dressed for the job, putting on bodysuits and waders to protect their limbs from the remaining jet fuel and all manner of contaminants living in Everglades water and donning masks to combat the stench of decomposition in the waters around them. This made working in the Florida heat and humidity a struggle, so much so that most of them had to pause every twenty to forty minutes to rest and cool off in an air-conditioned tent or bus. More than two hundred people participated in the effort, including doctors, counselors, and even a chiropractor to help rescue workers cope with the physical and mental effort.

"Everybody is getting tired, but no one is stopping," said Lt. John Reed of the Florida Game and Fresh Water Fish Commission to Ardy Friedberg, staff writer for the *South Florida Sun-Sentinel*, on the operation's fourth day.

Two weeks into the effort, technicians had identified the remains of only eight passengers through dental records, fingerprints, or the above-mentioned tattoo. Rather than finding torsos, arms or legs, technicians working with Dade County Medical Examiner Roger Mittleman had to analyze bits of flesh and tissue, trying to match them with victims' medical records. Divers skirted descriptions of the kinds of remains they had seen come out of the crash site, but they did tell Reuters News Service that the largest body part recovered to date was a single knee.

Families, already knowing the outcome but waiting for word that their loved ones were indeed gone, became increasingly frustrated as the process continued.

"They were saying, 'What do you mean, you are not finding any bodies? What's going on? Get more people,'" said Victoria Cummock, a Miami neighbor who had lost her husband in the Pan Am Flight 103 bombing over Lockerbie, Scotland years before. "They didn't understand what the Everglades is about."

The media, it turned out, did not help matters. Restricted to an area near the Tamiami Trail, a good eight miles from the crash site, they pointed their cameras at blue sky, waving tall grasses, calm waters . . . and then panned to alligators, which lounged by the side of the road entirely undisturbed by the activity around them. This increased the public's certainty that alligators—as well as venomous snakes, and perhaps quicksand—were devouring bodies before recovery efforts could find them.

This wasn't the case in reality. Quicksand is not found in the Everglades, though soft mud can suck in shoes and ankles as if it means to keep them. While witnesses have seen alligators eating decomposed bodies in Everglades canals (and sometimes even farther north), University of Florida researcher Frank Mazzotti told the *Sun-Sentinel* that alligators and other wildlife would be repelled by the jet fuel and hydraulic fluid in the water and would keep their distance from the crash site.

"Everybody's raising this kind of scary swamp thing," he said. "This is a real, serious tragedy. We need to deal with that and not raise specters of things that are not true to make this scarier."

Nonetheless, Metro-Dade Florida State Police stationed sharpshooters around the crash site to keep an eye out for approaching alligators, driving them off when necessary. Human body parts are generally too large for snakes to consume, though the guards around the site protected the searchers themselves by watching for water moccasins.

One class of cargo did not suffer from decomposition, however: the more than one hundred oxygen generator canisters. Investigators zeroed in on these and their volatile ignition mechanism as the most likely cause of the crash. On May 22, the U.S. Department of Transportation banned the transport of these canisters on airlines until a full investigation of their role in the crash could be completed.

Reuters News Service reported on May 25, two weeks after the crash, that the plane's engines, another twenty-five percent of the plane in fragments, and the FDR had been recovered so far. The following day the CVR surfaced, found by Metro-Dade Police Detective Felix Jimenez. Officials rushed the devices to Washington, DC, where the devices' recording could be analyzed. The CVR transcript, released three days later, identified the loud "chirp" heard in the cockpit—the one that made the captain ask, "What was that?"—as a tire exploding, most likely from the heat of an oxygen canister's activation.

From here, things began to fall apart for ValuJet. One month after the crash, the FAA released its own report, including a long list of problems it had found with the way the discount airline conducted its safety operations. Among other things, the report included many violations of maintenance procedures and basic flight operations. Five days later, the airline shut down. It overhauled its procedures and reopened on September 30, 1996, with a limited number of deeply discounted flights. In 1997, ValuJet bought AirTran Airways and changed its own name to AirTran Airlines, managing to keep its aging planes in the air until it was purchased by Southwest Airlines in 2011.

As for SabreTech, the company whose employee mislabeled the boxes of oxygen canisters as empty, it fired the two employees involved in packing and shipping the canisters. This satisfied no one, and on August 7 more than fifty FBI agents raided the company's maintenance facility at Miami airport, seizing boxes of employment and maintenance records.

Hearings in November detailed exactly what kind of destruction the oxygen canisters wrought on Flight 592 and held ValuJet responsible for not checking that safety caps had been placed on the canisters before loading them into the plane. The FAA admitted to lax practices in monitoring ValuJet and SabreTech, citing "mountains of paperwork and too few inspectors." The agency also revealed that it had prepared a report in February 1996, three months before the crash, stating that ValuJet had extensive maintenance problems and should be shut down. The report did not come to FAA top officials' attention until four days after the crash.

In January 1997, SabreTech closed its Miami International Airport facilities and surrendered its operating license to authorities. Days later, the FAA revealed that the company had falsified records by "signing off on work that was not actually performed."

When the NTSB's final report came out in August, NTSB laid the blame for the crash squarely at the feet of SabreTech. It did not spare

ValuJet or the FAA either, but the cargo handling and maintenance company's incompetence led the list of agencies at fault.

It took until July 1999 before criminal charges were brought against SabreTech and three of its employees for 110 counts of third-degree murder and manslaughter, as well as unlawful transportation of hazardous waste, conspiracy, and falsifying records. While prosecutors could not make the charges of murder and manslaughter stick, the court found SabreTech guilty of eight criminal counts of recklessly causing hazardous materials to be transported and one count of failing to train employees in the correct handling of those materials. The judge sentenced the company to pay $11 million in fines and restitution.

Two of the three SabreTech employees named in the case were arrested on charges of conspiracy and lying on repair records, but their defense attorney argued that they had disposed of the canisters as trash. A ValuJet employee, he said, actually loaded the boxes onto the plane. A jury believed this argument and acquitted the two men.

A third employee, Maurio Ociel Valenzuela-Reyes, is suspected of being the one who mislabeled the oxygen generators as "empty" and packed them in the cardboard boxes without placing safety caps on them. He was charged in the U.S. District Court for the Southern District of Florida with conspiracy to make false statements to the FAA and the U.S. Department of Transportation and "causing the transportation of hazardous material." Valenzuela-Reyes fled the country, however, and is now believed to be living in South America as a fugitive under one of several assumed names. The FBI continues to search for him.

The NTSB's final report of the accident tells us that sixty-eight of the 109 people aboard Flight 592 were identified from remains found at the site, but no fragments were ever matched with the other forty-one. Closure becomes a myth in such circumstances. The families of these people know that their loved ones were on the plane, but they will never have conclusive proof.

There may be some comfort in knowing that everyone aboard the plane met death in a split second. "The only blessing about this," said Joe Davis, retired Dade County medical examiner, to the *South Florida Sun-Sentinel* on May 14, 1996, "is the instant obliteration."

.

9

The Worst Highway Tragedy
and What It Revealed

Poor Boy Slim's Bus, a converted school bus operated by driver Edgar Lee Anderson, regularly took Black migrant workers and their children to vegetable fields near Belle Glade to pick crops for truck farms. On a good day, with weather conducive to gathering crops, Anderson's bus might carry as many as forty-two people—adults, children considered to be of working age, and additional children too young to leave at home alone but not old enough to work legally.

On Saturday, May 18, 1963, the bus trundled down Brown's Farm Road, designated State Route 827, a rutted road with one lane in each direction. Riding on the bus were migrant workers coming home from twelve hours in the bean fields—a grueling day's work that a UPI reporter had the audacity to call "a gay Saturday afternoon bean-picking outing." The laden school bus moved at a slower speed than the trucks that whizzed past filled with harvested vegetables, making its way over potholes, cracks, and rocks embedded in the worn tar-and-shell pavement.

Ernest D. Howell—"Ernest D" to his friends—twelve years old and exhausted from working in the fields all day, fell asleep in the seat he shared with two other children, one of them his seven-year-old brother Harvey. They sat three seats from the back of the bus, Ernest D told the *Tampa Tribune* later that day, on the right-hand side.

In the waning light around 8:30 p.m., a pickup truck pulled out from behind the bus and moved into the left lane to pass. The driver, dragline operator James Tully Sconyers, hit the gas and sped up to roar past the bus. When he believed he was clear, he began to move back into the right lane, but he cut the lane change too close. His right rear bumper locked behind the bus's left front bumper.

For at least 100 yards the two vehicles were stuck fast as they veered left and right to try to pull free. The bus finally came loose, but now it was out of control. It slid off the road ten feet and down the embankment into fifty-foot-wide Hillsborough Canal. In seconds it was sinking in twenty-five feet of water.

Sconyers slammed on his brakes and brought his truck to a stop, then ran back to the spot where the bus had vanished into the canal. He saw a few people come to the surface right away, screaming for him to help. He hesitated; he couldn't swim. In moments, however, other passing motorists started to pull over, and someone went to the nearest phone and called the police.

More heads popped above the surface. Adults on the bus beat at the windows and doors with their bare hands and managed to break four windows, giving them a way out of the sinking bus. They pulled themselves through jagged openings that tore at their flesh, arriving at the surface with bloody cuts and scrambling for a handhold on top of the bus. Some swam for shore, about fifteen feet away.

"When the bus hit the water, it floated what seemed like a few seconds or so. Everyone was screaming and shouting," said Ernest D, "but I got my own self out. I don't swim so good, but I got out that window. When I got on the roof, the bus just sank underneath me."

He was the only member of his family who survived. His mother, brother Harvey, and two sisters, Velma and Corea, all drowned, trapped inside the bus. "I was waitin' for my family to come up from the water," he said. "I didn't see 'em and I kept waitin' and waitin'. Then the policemen come."

In minutes, friends and relatives began to gather on the bank, reaching out hands to help people to the shore and safety. Fifteen people made their way up from the bus, across the canal, and to the waiting arms of their neighbors and family members. It soon became clear, though, that more would not follow them. The majority of the people on the bus had not escaped.

By dusk, divers with helmets had arrived, and a wrecker truck with a crane began the process of bringing the bus out of the canal. When the bus emerged, draining water out of its few open windows, would-be rescuers could see many unconscious bodies inside. Divers went down again and again to find anyone who had begun an escape from the bus but run out of strength. The effort continued through the night until people who could list their family members, friends, and neighbors who had been on the bus confirmed that every passenger had been accounted for.

Ambulances lined up to bring the bodies to a temporary morgue set up in the National Guard Armory in Belle Glade. Families gathered outside to wait their turn to look for their loved ones, filing past the bodies lined up on tarps on the floor as morticians raised the shroud over each, allowing each family to identify their own.

Young Ernest D took on this miserable task alone, as everyone in his family except his stepfather had been on the bus, and his stepfather did not make an appearance at the makeshift morgue. The boy quietly identified his sisters and brother, and then, his work finally finished, he collapsed on the armory floor. Later the Red Cross worked to locate an aunt in Sanford, who arrived in Belle Glade to pick up Ernest D and give him a new home.

The final tally broke the hearts of Belle Glade's residents: Nine men, five women, and thirteen children drowned inside Poor Boy Slim's Bus. The numbers staggered the local media and generated a barrage of questions. Why were there so many children on this bus traveling daily out to the fields? Child labor laws had been in effect since the Fair Labor Standards Act of 1938, prohibiting children younger than twelve from working in the fields unless their parent owned the farm. Yet here were children as young as six years old, their hands stained from harvesting crops all day.

A *Tampa Tribune* reporter put the question to one of the adult workers. "We got no place to keep them," the worker said. "They go with us to the fields. Most of them work."

Something very wrong was happening on this farm.

Truck driver James Sconyers was arrested and charged with manslaughter and improper passing and held on $2,500 bond. The Florida Highway Patrol held firm in its position that Sconyers was responsible for the deaths of twenty-seven people. "We've investigated this matter very thoroughly and this is our firm conclusion," Trooper George H. Emerson of the Highway Patrol told the *Fort Lauderdale News* on May 24. "Both vehicles were traveling north when Sconyers passed the bus on the left and cut in sharply in front of it."

A week later, a judge dismissed the manslaughter charge, replacing it with a lesser charge of failure to give aid following an accident. The judge agreed with the Highway Patrol's assertion that Sconyers had cut in front of the bus, but said that he had not done so to deliberately harm anyone.

The Florida Highway Patrol revealed on Monday, May 20, that bus driver Edgar Lee Anderson's driver's license had been suspended some time ago by the Financial Responsibility Division of the State Insurance Commissioner's Office. So on the day of the accident, Anderson was driving without a Florida license. Anderson, who survived the accident, told a court a few days later that he had a valid Pennsylvania license but no Florida permit. Emerson of the Highway Patrol acknowledged Anderson's lack of a proper license, but added that this fact did not affect "the facts on the cause of the accident." He reiterated that Sconyers's act in cutting off the bus had caused the accident and that Anderson had responded by veering right—the only option available to him in his attempt to disengage from Sconyers's bumper.

Sconyers and Anderson, however, were clearly not the only ones who had broken the law.

Florida State Representative Emmett S. Roberts, who represented Belle Glade, called for the passage of "emergency legislation to close loopholes in our present traffic laws." He arranged for an investigation by the Florida Railroad and Public Utilities Commission to see what could be done to prevent such an accident from happening again.

Florida Governor Farris Bryant stepped into the fray as well, demanding a special report from the Florida State Highway Patrol to determine "if there is any way in which it (the accident) could have been avoided through some action by the state," he said in a news conference. But it took the head of the Migrant Labor Committee of the Florida Committee on Rural Health, Dr. George W. Karelas, to question what so many children were doing on the bus. He vowed to investigate "sanitation, child labor and substandard transportation" for migrant workers, though how an investigation might be conducted remained to be defined. He asked specifically "what little children were doing on the bus" and "if six-year-olds [were] actually working in the fields."

Rep. Roberts joined Karelas in his concern for the workers and their children, telling the media in a prepared statement,

There is tremendous interest nationally as well as statewide in the problems of our migrant agricultural laborers, both in housing and transportation areas ... I sincerely feel that our laws should provide adequate insurance protection for our citizens involved in this type of accident and that every effort should be made to prevent overcrowding, which could contribute to additional loss of life in similar situations.

He referred specifically to the fact that the "death bus," as the media began to call it, had a maximum capacity of thirty-two people, but it was carrying forty-two people on the day of the accident. No law at the time limited the number of people who could crowd onto a bus, so Roberts implied that a new law might address this.

The perennial call for guardrails or another protective barrier between the road and the canal—an outcry that came up every time a major road accident took multiple lives in the Everglades—rose once again in this corner of Florida. Metal guardrails remained beyond the state's budget, however, so trees came up as another solution. They certainly would slow and most likely prevent a vehicle's descent into deep water. Tree roots, however, would grow and distort the already uneven road even further, officials said, so representatives next called for earthen embankments high enough to halt a runaway bus or truck. "The one drawback here is that in many cases there is not enough room between [the road and the canal] for the earthwork," the *Palm Beach Post* mused.

The area's activist organizations had heard all of these excuses before, and they had had enough. The Belle Glade Junior Chamber (Jaycees) issued a resolution that they sent to Governor Bryant and to State Road Board Chairman John R. Phillips.

We feel that the tragic bus accident of May 18 could have been avoided had the repeated requests of the citizens and officials of this area been heeded in their many requests for more adequate roads ... [Publicity] has resulted in confusion, misconception of pertinent factual conditions and clouding of the real issues involved.

The resolution went on to call road conditions in the Everglades "critical" and to underscore that they had been in this shape for more than a decade without any response from the state. At the same time, the State Road Department (SRD) completed a survey of this and other Everglades roads and rated most of them "critical" or "poor," warning that the sugar industry, with its five hundred heavy, sugar-hauling trucks passing over the roads daily, would be hampered in its planned exponential growth if the roads were not improved "as soon as practical."

The solution, the SRD said, included four-lane roads with limited access, preventing slow-moving trucks from bringing traffic to a standstill and eliminating the need for risky lane changes to pass slower vehicles.

After the initial outrage and calls for reform, however, voices quieted and officials found a wide range of reasons not to proceed with reforms. The greatest improvement to Brown's Farm Road turned out to be the addition of "too expensive" steel guardrails between the road and the canal, as well as periodic resurfacing of the two-lane blacktop to eliminate the potholes and cracks.

If an investigation of the migrant workers' employer and his use of underage children during harvests ever took place, the media took no notice. The federal government, however, saw the need to keep the youngest children—from birth to age five—out of the fields where they could be exposed to pesticides, heavy equipment, extreme weather, and other hazards that could affect their long-term development. In 1969, Migrant and Seasonal Head Start became available to migrant worker families, placing children in daycare while their parents worked in the fields. This still did not provide alternative care for school-age children on weekends, like the children on the ill-fated bus who were working on a Saturday; in fact, this is a problem that persists to this day. A loophole in migrant worker laws allows children as young as ten years old to work in the fields during the harvest. Twelve-year-olds can perform nonhazardous farm work outside school hours, and at sixteen they can leave school and work in the fields full time.

It would feel like sad but effective symmetry if those twenty-seven deaths had led to real reforms. Unfortunately, even the shock and grief of losing so many children did not increase the value of the most undervalued people in our society.

10

Forever Lost, Occasionally Found

IT'S EASY ENOUGH TO IMAGINE. YOU TAKE A BOAT INTO THE TEN THOU-sand Islands and lose your way among the confusing waterways, a remarkably uniform parade of hammocks and islands and ever-present walls of mangrove and sawgrass. Or you leave your car for what appears to be a trail and it turns out to be a bug-infested lane of muck that sucks at your feet the way you imagine quicksand would. These things happen to people in the Everglades, though they are the exception rather than the rule. Most of them emerge from the fetid wilderness alive. Some come out in body bags. And some—surprisingly few—are never seen again.

There have been a number of large-scale searches for missing peo-ple in the Everglades. Some of these are suicides—people who have no intention of being found when they move off into deep cover with a bot-tle of pills or a loaded pistol. I have made it a policy not to cover suicides in my books, because I do not want to provide you with the instruction manual for committing such an act yourself. I urge readers to think for a moment about the money wasted in a massive search effort, as well as the unfortunate searchers—dedicated rescue personnel hoping to find you alive—who instead come upon your decomposing body in the wild. A national park suicide is not a clean break if it forces hundreds of people to risk their own lives looking for you.

Occasionally someone uses a national park to attempt to fake their own death. I came across such stories while researching this book, and I want to assure you that these efforts were dismal failures. Perhaps no one is clever enough to pull this off in a national park, and the ones who have tried were caught only after causing their loved ones horrendous grief and pain. I won't glorify these attempts by describing them here.

Instead, let's look at cases in which something truly went terribly wrong, leaving someone lost in the wilderness to perish alone.

THE WRONG TURN

Thomas Wentz had a lot of money, but his friends knew that his driving skills lacked a certain respect for safety. The slight, forty-seven-year-old man, five feet nine inches tall and weighing about 150 pounds, had a love of speed behind the wheel—something he had already demonstrated as he and three friends drove from Norristown, Pennsylvania, to Miami on March 1, 1931.

So threatening was his driving style that none of the friends volunteered to ride with Wentz when he took his battered 1929 Cadillac four-passenger coupe to Homestead on March 6 for repairs. Later his friends described his car's many dents and cracks to police: "right fender smashed, right running board smashed, windshield out, rear window out, front bumper missing," and the right side so crumpled that the door would not close and had to be wired in place. The car's battery sat out in the open on the remaining running board as if warning all potential passengers to reconsider their transportation options.

So on the morning of March 6, Wentz set out on his own for Homestead. He carried about $2,000 in cash in his pockets and checkbooks for the Pennsylvania Company for Insurance on Lives and Granting Annuity, and the Norristown Penn Trust Company. He arrived at a mechanic's shop in Homestead and ordered a number of repairs for the beleaguered auto. When the shop completed his list, he paid the proprietor, got back in his car, and drove northeast toward Miami on the Naranja road.

That was the last anyone heard from Thomas Wentz.

When he did not return, Wentz's three friends thought first that the repairs may have taken longer than anticipated, but when several days passed without word, they notified the police. The search began with a check of the repair shop in Homestead, where officers learned that Wentz had departed from there days before. Theories abounded—had he made a wrong turn and become lost on the confusing dirt roads that led into the swampland? Had he made an unscheduled stop at one of the hunting and fishing lodges on the edge of the backcountry? A check of the Cypress Lodge on the Tamiami Trail revealed that Wentz had not been there; other establishments said the same.

The Dade County Police Department notified all of its patrolmen to check the cars in garages on their beats in Miami, just in case Wentz had ditched his friends and rented himself an apartment in the city for the winter. Like other wealthy individuals looking for a getaway, he may have parked his Cadillac in a garage, closed the door, and quietly gone away for an extended time. His fairly distinctive auto did not show up on anyone's route, however, and as they checked each new theory off the list, officers had to grapple with the possibility that Wentz had become lost in the Everglades on his way back from Homestead.

By this time, the three friends had notified Wentz's family in Pennsylvania, and relatives offered a $10,000 reward for information that might lead to the missing man. This amount was swiftly overruled by Wentz's brother Harry, however, who arrived in Miami around March 16 and met with L. O. Scarboro, Miami's chief of detectives. Harry presented Scarboro with a letter authorizing a reward of $5,000 to anyone who could lead them to Thomas "dead or alive." The rest of the family, hearing of the letter and the lesser reward, withdrew their offer of $10,000, losing the interest of some of the volunteer parties who had leapt into the search.

Harry, attorney John Dettra (who represented Thomas and his company), and Miami detective Sgt. Eddie Melchen spent a day in Melchen's car, driving up and down roads in southern Dade County in hopes of spotting some evidence that Thomas had pulled off somewhere. They found nothing, despite questioning Everglades residents they came across on those country roads. Melchen finally voiced his assessment of the case: Thomas, with his penchant for driving recklessly and too fast, must have come to an unmarked fork where a canal crossed a road. Unaware of such twists and turns along the canals and going too fast to stop suddenly, Thomas must have driven off the road and right into a canal, sinking along with his car to the bottom. Numerous such intersections can be found on Everglades roads, so this could have happened at any one of many places.

By March 21, two weeks after Wentz's disappearance, detectives, police, and volunteers believed they had covered all of the accessible areas a Cadillac could reach. They had also received word that police in Mayfield, North Carolina, had found Thomas Wentz, but the man the police had arrested (presumably for driving a blue Cadillac of the same make, model, and damage level as Thomas's car) turned out to be a traveling watch repairman, A. N. Alexander. Even after his identity came to light, the arresting officers saved face by holding Alexander on a weapons charge because he had two concealed pistols in his possession.

The Miami police saw the possibility of solving this case diminishing, so they decided to invest in a more thorough search method. Officers and a pilot took to the air in a small plane to see if they could find the car in an area it should not have ventured into at all. They canvassed an area west of Homestead, where fewer parties had searched because it was in exactly the wrong direction, but Wentz, unlikely to be carrying a compass, could have gotten confused by the twists and turns of the country roads and not known that he was headed west instead of east.

As they circled an area about six miles from Homestead, Miami-Dade police officer James Barker, scanning the area with binoculars, spotted the blue Cadillac. It stood just off an old logging road in the midst of a marsh, its wheels buried deep in the muck, clearly stuck fast.

The airborne searchers took careful note of the car's position and brought the news to the Dade County police, who went to the spot immediately and found the car. Officers C. C. Jackson and E. A. Richardson looked inside the car and found a hat and eyeglasses on the seat, both of which were identified later as belonging to Thomas Wentz.

Now they could piece together a scenario that might lead them to Wentz: When he left Homestead, he got mixed up about directions and which road he had used to get there and turned the wrong way into the Everglades. Taking one dirt road after another and getting farther and farther from his intended route, he eventually drove right off the road and into the murky marsh. Here, they believed, he hit his head on a number of metal "appliances" fastened to the car's ceiling, disorienting himself even more. He staggered out of the car and into the marsh, and soon vanished in the dense vegetation all around him.

Not a single police officer in Dade County felt up to the challenge of following a cold trail through the sawgrass. They had only one solution: call on the Seminole community for assistance.

The Seminole had a comfortable relationship with governments and law enforcement in Dade and Collier counties, so the call to assist in the search for Thomas Wentz startled no one. Their ability to track game and people through the Everglades was no myth—in fact, they had long since established their superiority in this with the region's police and detectives, making them an important resource in tracking escaped convicts, criminals, and the occasional tourist lost in the backcountry.

Willie and Mack Osceola and John Buck rose to the challenge of finding where Wentz may have gone after he abandoned his vehicle in the muck. Chief Cory Osceola headed up the Seminole search party, bringing several other men whom he knew were expert trackers.

"Cautioning officers to keep untrained trackers from leaving false trails in the Everglades, Osceola and his men carried on their own search in their own way," the AP observed.

The group started their search at Wentz's car, examining the area close to the vehicle. In time they noted footprints that indicated a pointed shoe, the kind only very fashionable men wore. The trail did not reveal itself easily, but the men saw recognizable signs of human disturbance in the area: a bent twig here, a trampled tuft of sawgrass there. They picked their way through the muck until they found a bloodstained handkerchief, then a packet of matches. Wentz had passed this way in his increasingly desperate search for a way out of the swamp.

A particularly pressed-down grassy area could only be a spot where he spent the night, no doubt growing more hungry and thirsty and more disoriented. Here they discovered a pair of sunglasses, probably dropped there during his rest. From here, his trail became fainter.

Feeling that Wentz could not have gone much farther, the Seminole party came back for a third day of searching, March 24, eighteen days after Wentz disappeared. They followed more crushed grasses and bent twigs. By this time they had tracked him for ten miles from the car, yet the trail continued—so they knew Wentz had exhausted whatever meager supplies he might have carried with him.

Then one of the men pushed some stalks of sawgrass apart and found what they had been searching for: Thomas Wentz's partly decomposed body. It lay in the grass barely a mile from Silver Palm Drive between present-day Redland and Princeton, where a farmhouse stood. Had he managed to press on, he could have asked for help there and received food, water, and first aid.

Wentz had crisscrossed his own trail in his wanderings in the swamp, so while his feet carried him more than ten miles, he was really just four miles from his car. Remarkably, he still had nearly $1,100 in his pocket, the rest probably spent in Homestead on car repairs. And he still wore the costly Masonic ring he'd had on when he left his friends.

The police brought the body out of the swamp and into Miami, where Harry Wentz completed the positive identification. An autopsy revealed that Thomas had died of starvation and exposure and had been dead for about ten days when he was found. The coroner saw no evidence of foul play; the death was an unfortunate accident, the result of a few wrong turns made by someone completely unprepared to spend several days tramping through the south Florida backcountry.

True to his word, Harry Wentz paid out the reward money, splitting it between Mack Oakford as the pilot of the airplane ($900); J. D. Barker of the Miami Police Department as the scout ($500); C. C. Jackson ($200) and E. A. Richardson ($200) of Homestead, who found the glasses and hat in the car; and $3,200 among the Seminoles who completed the search: Chief Cory Osceola, Mack Osceola, John Buck, Henry Cypress, and William McKinley Osceola. Wentz also provided another $2,000 to pay for the search plane and to make gifts to eight others who had participated in the search.

THE DISAPPEARING JOCKEY

The funny thing about Al Snider is that once the search for him ended, the media seemed to forget his name.

The first mention of him I came across was in a 1972 article in the *Miami Herald* about searches in the Everglades. The article mentioned the mysterious disappearance eighteen years earlier of a nationally famous jockey, "Junior Bellefield."

A quick Wikipedia search did not turn up anyone by that name, nor did the name appear on any of the lists of famous jockeys available online. I went back to the searchable archives of major newspapers and soon found another *Miami Herald* piece, this one from November 1959, identifying the missing jockey as "Gerry Snyder." This article provided a little more information: The jockey's empty boat had turned up "south of Gopher Key," but the man himself was never found.

So I went back to the lists of famous jockeys . . . and still nothing. Not only had this man vanished from his boat in the Ten Thousand Islands, he had also dropped out of history.

My usual course of action in such cases is to try alternative spellings of the last name, as a misspelled or mistranscribed name can hide a fascinating story forever. I searched using "Snieder," "Sneider," and finally "Snider." That's when I hit pay dirt.

Albert (not Gerry) Snider had established himself as a top professional jockey, a Calgary, Alberta, native who made his name riding in races in the southern United States. His biggest achievements came from his years at Calumet Farm, riding U.S. Racing Hall of Fame inductee Citation and winning nine races astride the horse in 1947, including the Belmont. He continued as Citation's rider in 1948, riding him to victory in the Seminole and Everglades Handicaps at Hialeah Park and then winning the Flamingo Stakes in early March. It looked like this would be a Triple Crown year for the magnificent horse and its highly skilled rider.

After the Flamingo, Snider took a few days off beginning on March 3 and headed into the Everglades with two friends, C. H. "Tobe" Trotter, a horse trainer, and Don Frasier, a Canadian businessman and manufacturer. They departed on a yacht called the *Evelyn K* with B. W. Miller, the yacht's owner; Snider's agent, George Woods; and another passenger, Lawrence Boido sailing for the Florida Keys.

Somewhere offshore from the town of Craig on March 4, Snider, Trotter, and Frasier took Snider's own thirteen-foot wooden tender, equipped with oars and a brand-new outboard motor, a three-gallon reserve tank of gas, plenty of drinking water, life preservers, a coffeepot, a pail for bailing water if they should take any on, and seventy-five feet of rope, and set off to do some fishing. They even had a package of extra sparkplugs along in case the motor conked out on them. While the Evelyn K anchored off Sandy Key, the three men motored here and there, fished to their hearts' content, and rejoined the *Evelyn K* at dinnertime. Everyone bedded down by 10:00 p.m. with plans for more fishing the following day.

Snider and George Woods rose early and took the skiff out once again, pulling up about a mile and a half from the yacht and fishing until lunch. They returned to the *Evelyn K* and had a meal, then took a nap. At 5:00 p.m., Snider, Trotter, and Frazier boarded the skiff once again and motored about a mile and a quarter from the yacht. Boido, Woods, and Miller stayed on the larger boat.

Then, the story goes, the weather changed. The wind picked up and soon blew hard with gusts up to 48 mph. A pelting Florida storm drenched everything in its path as waves rose higher than a small boat could handle. The men still on the yacht scanned the horizon for Snider's skiff, but the rain obscured the view through their binoculars. They had no choice but to wait and hope that the fishing party in its sturdy craft would make its way back through the weather.

When the clouds finally parted, however, the little skiff carrying Snider, Trotter, and Frazier was nowhere to be found.

It didn't take long before a full-scale search got underway for the three men. Lt. Cdr. Richard Baxter of the Coast Guard headed up the rescue operation. Yachts arrived to help and were assigned search areas, and planes from the U.S. Navy base on Key West, the Coast Guard, and a blimp joined the effort, as well as civilian pilots with their aircraft— among them Porter Roberts, another jockey and Snider's personal friend. Roberts went so far as to cancel his races at Tropical Park on the Tuesday after Snider's disappearance so he could continue to fly his private plane over the Ten Thousand Islands to look for his colleague.

The National Park Service launched its own search around Cape Sable and the Shark River area, directed by park superintendent Daniel Beard and his assistant, Marcus Parker. They also joined with Baxter's forces to send trucks to spots they could reach along the southernmost mainland of the park.

For four days, boats, planes, the blimp, and land parties canvassed the islands and the open water, looking for the least indication that Snider and his friends might have beached somewhere and were waiting for rescue. When nothing at all came to light, Baxter and the park service agreed that there was no more to be done.

"Extensive search has disclosed nothing on land or water identified as belonging to these men or their boat," they said in a joint announcement to the media.

The many searchers closed their operations and went back to their bases and their lives, but Dorothy Snider, Albert's wife, did not accept their conclusion that he had drowned in the storm. Struggling through the torment of waiting for word of her husband's fate, she lingered at her mother's home in Miami Springs with her five-year-old daughter, Nancy, and accepted the support of a physician to help her endure the anxiety and fear.

"I know he is alive," she told staff writer Lawrence Thompson of the *Herald*. "He can swim like a fish. He is strong. Dieting to keep his weight down would permit him to live a long time without food. He was in an unsinkable plywood boat equipped with five life saver pillows. I can't believe anything except that he is alive."

Her hopes rose when she received a telephone call from Havana, Cuba, that was disconnected before she could hear the voice at the other end. She clung to the belief that the call had come from Snider and that a fisherman had picked him up from an unspecified key and taken him to Cuba. Police followed up on this lead, but they did not find Snider.

Trotter's family—a wife and four children—suffered through the ups and downs of the search from their Miami home. At one point a report came in from Turkey Key that a pilot had spotted the three men there, but the men turned out to be inhabitants of the island. Pilots and observers reported many stranded skiffs and wrecked boats over the course of the four-day search, but "nothing that in any way, shape or form could have come from the vessel," Baxter told the media. Many reports came in of flares fired from boats, but the skiff Snider and his friends were last seen in had no flares aboard.

On Saturday, March 13, the eighth day since the fishing party's disappearance, fishermen Gus and Rayford Rewis came across an abandoned plywood skiff on a small island near Rabbit Key, ten miles south of Everglades City. The boat had been beached under a clump of mangrove trees—and while the boat was in good condition, its oars and motor were missing.

This discovery set off "one of the greatest air-sea-land searches in South Florida history," as Earl Barber wrote in the *Miami Herald* the following Monday. "Scores of planes, boats and ground parties" headed for the Ten Thousand Islands, braving choppy waters and high winds and scouring dozens of small islands in hopes of finding more clues, and perhaps the missing men themselves.

The Fifth Emergency Rescue Squadron from MacDill Field joined the Coast Guard and Navy planes, as did the Florida Air Pilots Association. Private pilots also arrived with their planes to join the search. "High winds prevented blimps from participating in the hunt, but they were expected to be out today if the weather permits," the *Herald* noted.

A break in the weather on Sunday intensified the search "to a degree so far unparalleled," the paper continued. "Hundreds of calls asking for the latest information on Snider swamped the *Herald*'s switchboard and city desk." The AP reported that "jungle combat teams in amphibious craft" aided in the search on the water and on various islands close to where the plywood boat had been found.

Seaplanes extended the search southward some twenty miles from Everglades City. When one of the seaplanes landed on a tiny island at the mouth of Lostmans River, the pilot discovered another clue: three sets of footprints on the beach, with one set smaller than the others, just as the jockey's foot would be.

The news triggered the order to contact Miami detective Thomas Lipe, who brought two bloodhounds to track where Snider, Trotter and Frazier might have gone from there.

"If Snider and his two companions . . . had landed there they could not have gone far," Sheriff L. J. Thorp told the media. The island had not been searched before this, so search parties had new hope that additional clues would be found here.

The search narrowed even more when a team found "an oar identical with one aboard the 16-foot tender" in the Cape Sable area. By this time as many as five hundred people were in the field looking for the three men, making this the single largest search effort in Everglades history at the time.

But that was the last clue anyone ever found. A day or so later, the search effort came to an end with no further sign of Snider, Trotter, or Frazier.

With hope exhausted and the trio's final moments a complete mystery, there was nothing left to do but try to honor Snider's memory. Eddie Arcaro took Snider's place astride Citation at the Kentucky Derby, the Preakness, and the Belmont, winning the Triple Crown just as Snider had expected to do. Arcaro gave his share of the Kentucky Derby winner's purse—$2,085—to Dorothy Snider and her daughter, and Calumet Farm owner Warren Wright matched the winnings with his own funds, for a total of $4,170 (roughly $41,000 today). Mrs. Snider told the media that she would place the money in her daughter's college fund.

To this day, no one knows what happened to Snider and his friends. Writer Dan Parker with the *Miami Herald*, however, could not let the question go. In scratching his journalistic itch, he pieced together an alternate story, one with sinister overtones that seems every bit as plausible as the simpler explanation that Snider had died in a sudden storm.

It seems that when Snider, Trotter, and Frazier took the skiff out at 5:00 p.m. on March 5, they anchored in less than four feet of water about one-half mile from shore. All three men could swim, so even if the boat capsized in a storm, they should have been able to make it to land. "Trotter knew these waters as well as he knew the Hialeah race track," Parker wrote. "From the yacht, the three who remained aboard could watch Snider casting continuously through their binoculars."

And that's when the story told to the media in March 1948 begins to change.

First, there was no storm. The sun set and dusk came at about 6:30 p.m., making it impossible for the men aboard the yacht to see the little skiff in the dark. Snider, Trotter, and Frazier had planned to return to the *Evelyn K* by 7:00 p.m., but they did not, so Miller switched on every light on the boat to make it easier for the fishing party to see it. This included a revolving searchlight on top of the deck house—a light so bright that the men on the skiff could have seen it from several miles away. In addition to this beacon, three red lights spaced for twelve miles along the shoreline served as navigation aids, flashing to let sailors know exactly where they were in relation to the shore.

At about 8:00 p.m. the breeze picked up, as it often does after becalming boats at sunset. Some of the gusts reached 30 mph, but these were hardly enough to capsize a small boat. After another hour passed without any sign of the skiff, Miller radioed the Coast Guard to begin a search.

Three people who were not on the yacht told investigators that they had seen the skiff before dark that evening. One of them, Capt. Jack Martin, passed the little boat in his own craft a little before 7:00 p.m. and observed the men fishing and the boat under anchor. A mullet fisherman on Sandy Key said he saw the men aboard pull up their anchor as the sun went down and begin to motor toward the yacht. Another motorboat, the *Junalaska*, passed close to the skiff as dusk settled in and its captain told the Coast Guard during the investigation that the skiff was not in distress.

So if there was no storm and all was well at dusk, what happened after the men pulled anchor and started their motor?

It was no secret that all manner of organized crime collected around Miami during racing season every winter, and as Parker noted, "jockeys are constantly being approached by gangland betting syndicates and offered big money to ride to their orders." The horse racing industry knew that Snider "was a straight shooter," but that certainly would not have kept mob henchmen from pressuring him to throw a race. The question weighed even heavier when, two months after his death, the Sniders' maid discovered $4,000 in cash and a check for $295 in an envelope in one of Snider's shirts. "Where this came from has never been explained," Parker noted. Mrs. Snider banked this with the Kentucky Derby money and gave $200 to her maid to reward her for her honesty in turning the cash over to her.

Where did this money come from? Had a mob operative given Snider the money in exchange for a specific outcome in a race? If so, had

Snider taken the money, but later refused to throw a race as he had been paid to do?

Parker posed the climactic question: "Did his honesty cost him his life in that baffling triple tragedy?"

The answer, it seems, will never be known.

LOST IN THE WILD

At six feet six inches tall, twenty-one-year-old Patrick Asa King looked like a difficult man to lose track of, even in the Everglades backcountry. When he loaded his 1953 blue Pontiac sedan at his home in Fort Lauderdale on the morning of January 4, 1966, for a hunting trip in the swampland, driving off at about 8:00 a.m., he went prepared: He carried a shotgun, a rifle, and a revolver along with a tent, a sleeping bag, and other gear.

Patrick worked for his cousin Howard, who owned Beacon Ambulance Service—very much a family business, as Patrick's father, Clarence King, managed the service. The young man drove an ambulance and worked as an attendant as well, earning money for his tuition at Broward Junior College.

For recreation, he particularly enjoyed the J. W. Corbett Game Reserve, so his parents believed that when he drove away that Tuesday morning, he planned to go there. They expected him back that night to be in class at Broward Junior College the following morning, as he had enrolled using his own money and seemed very enthusiastic about beginning the semester there, continuing his degree work in psychology.

But when Patrick didn't show up for class Wednesday morning, the Kings contacted his friends to see if anyone knew of his whereabouts. To their dismay, no one had heard from him since before he went off into the Everglades. Patrick's parents continued for several days to try to find him on their own. "I didn't report him missing for four days because I didn't think he could stand being alone any longer than that and would come back home," Clarence King told the *Fort Lauderdale News* the following week.

By Saturday morning, with no further word from or about Patrick, his parents filed a missing person report with the police.

The police contacted Everglades National Park, and conservation, fresh water, and fish and game commission authorities began a search. Nothing turned up on the ground, however, so searchers took to the air to try to locate the blue Pontiac, the best clue they could hope for in determining where the young man might be. More than twenty-five planes turned out for the effort, working under the direction of mission commander Maj. Edwin Johnson out of Opa-Locka Airport, but they were forced to wait out a period of heavy cloud cover and fog until they could see the ground clearly from the air. Corbett Game Preserve was a primary target, but the searchers did not know for certain where Patrick intended to hunt, so the entirety of South Florida became the search territory—an unwieldy but necessary range.

In the beginning, it appeared that the search had borne fruit. Deputies located an abandoned blue car with a bullet hole through its back window on January 12, twelve miles west of U.S. Route 27, and believed it was Patrick's missing vehicle. A check of the license tags, though, made it clear that the car belonged to someone else: Martin Cassidy, an employee on the Everglades Parkway construction project, who had abandoned the car in the wilderness months before. Police decided that the bullet hole "may have been made by hunters after the auto was abandoned," the *Fort Lauderdale News* reported later that day.

With no new leads, twelve Civil Air Patrol (CAP) planes joined the search under the command of Capt. Earl Haddaway, while planes from North Perry, Fort Lauderdale-Hollywood, and West Palm Beach airports multiplied the number of searchers in the air. "CAP flyers and observers from Broward, Dade, Palm Beach and Hendry counties [flew] low altitude, crisscross patterns for four days . . . over desolate hunting areas of the Everglades from Tamiami Trail north to the upper tip of Lake Okeechobee in a futile search," the *Fort Lauderdale News* reported. In total, the report continued, CAP flew 44 sorties covering more than 800 square miles, spending 81 man-hours in the air. "Senior members . . . and cadets had 127 personnel take part in the search with 29 aircraft, 11 mobile radios and one ground search rescue team on standby." The Fort Lauderdale police and the Hendry County Sheriff's Office both commended CAP's tactics and extensive search capabilities, but even this level of strategic coverage did not reveal any further clues to Patrick's whereabouts.

By Friday, January 14, ten days had elapsed since Patrick's disappearance, and the CAP called off further sorties. Fort Lauderdale police sergeant Bill Capko told the media that he planned to turn the case over to detectives for a more in-depth investigation—apparently with some sense that there might be foul play involved.

Mr. and Mrs. King, who had adopted Patrick when they lost their own child, went home to grieve for the apparent loss of their only son.

Clarence King told *Fort Lauderdale News* staff writer Patty Mummert that he was "at a complete loss" in trying to imagine what might have happened to Patrick. "We don't even know definitely that he went hunting … It's just the only thing we found missing was his hunting equipment." It was late in the hunting season, King noted, with only duck hunting still permitted. "He liked to hunt alone, so he probably didn't take anyone with him if that's where he went."

Patrick had made impulsive trips on his own before, King said, including one to visit his grandparents in Alabama. "But we've been in constant contact with them and with all my friends out of state. No one has been contacted by him."

Then on Tuesday January 19, the Kings' phone rang. A family friend, Mrs. Jean Stamos, had the best news they had ever heard.

Patrick had called the Stamos residence that evening at about 7:00 p.m., asking for Jean's daughter, Lanie. Mrs. Stamos had the presence of mind to insist that Patrick come over immediately.

The young man obeyed and arrived at her home a few minutes later. He was "unstrung and highly nervous," Mrs. Stamos said. "He had no idea people were looking for him … I showed him some newspaper clippings and he became very upset." Patrick told her that he was afraid to go home to his parents right away—not because they would be angry, but because something was not right with him and "he didn't want to shock them," Mrs. Stamos told the *Fort Lauderdale News*.

Patrick said that he had been hunting with a man from Greenville, and that they had traveled to a game preserve in northern Florida near Tallahassee, so he had missed the news coverage of his disappearance and the massive search effort. He said he had been staying with a game warden for the last two days and remembered hunting with a sore back, but he did not remember leaving Fort Lauderdale or why he ended up on the Florida panhandle.

His parents arrived and took him to Broward General Hospital, where police questioned him further the following day. What might have caused Patrick's amnesia episode was not publicized, but it seems clear he had some kind of injury or illness (such as a diabetic episode, which could cause such a memory lapse) early in his trip. The newspapers did note his engagement and wedding the following year, however, an indication that whatever had happened to him was not permanent.

In the Blink of an Eye

If my husband and I had not been in Everglades National Park in March 2011, we never would have known that Roger Kenneth Sawyer had disappeared there on March 5. We spotted a flyer taped to a post when we were on our way to Eco Pond, past the Flamingo Visitor Center and campgrounds.

The black-and-white flyer featured a photo of an older bald man sitting across from the photographer at an open-air restaurant, a bowl of empty seafood shells in front of him. Below the photo, a detailed description became a plea for help.

MISSING
White Male, Approximately 6'2", 180 lbs.,
Bald with grey on sides
Last known to be wearing a green sleeveless tee shirt with
"Got Milt?" printed on it,
Khaki shorts,
A black Hard Rock Cafe baseball hat,
And Crocs with socks.
IF YOU SEE THIS PERSON, PLEASE CALL
EVERGLADES NATIONAL PARK DISPATCH
AT 305-242-7740

More than ten years later, our photo of the flyer popped to the surface as we reviewed our photo inventory to find potential cover shots for this book. I remembered perusing Miami and Homestead media back in 2011, looking for coverage of the search for this man in the park and finding none. Perhaps the case has been solved, I thought at the time. Maybe they'd found him days ago and just haven't taken down the flyers.

That's not what happened.

Roger Kenneth Sawyer, sixty-seven and a retired butcher, traveled to Florida from Oregon on an extended road trip across the country in a motor home with his family. He disappeared from a campground in the Flamingo area on March 5, 2011.

On that afternoon, he and his wife, Paula, had stayed behind in the campground while the rest of the family went to the Flamingo Visitor Center. His family remembered seeing him on the beach at Florida Bay at about 6:00 p.m. When everyone returned to the motor home later in the evening, Roger did not. "He has never been heard from again," says the Charley Project, a missing persons website.

When Roger had not appeared by 8:30 p.m., the family notified authorities at the park. Roger was no stranger to the outdoors, his family said, so it seemed unlikely that he would just wander off and get lost. He was in good health and his mind was sharp. The family had explored the Keys in their motor home before arriving at Everglades National Park, and he had made sure to tell them every day that he was having the time of his life.

"He would often say, 'I know yesterday I said was the best day of my life, but today is the best day of my life,'" his daughter-in-law, Janice Williams, told a reporter at CBS Miami on April 5, a month after Roger had vanished.

The national park's incident team mounted an extensive search with all of the resources it had at its disposal, including Miami-Dade Fire Rescue. "The park service did a stellar job and we were so grateful for all the agencies, and they covered every square inch of the park," Williams said in the CBS Miami report. But they did not find a single sign of Roger's whereabouts or any clue to the reason for or method of his disappearance.

Could someone have taken him out of the park? The only way to get clues to such a thing would be to ask for leads through the media, but the park's incident team made a decision the family did not understand: They kept the media in the dark, with an unnamed spokesperson for the search teams telling the newspaper and television reporters that the family did not want to speak to them. The spokesperson even said that they did not want to provide a photo for publication.

This simply wasn't true, said Williams. "We would have been all too willing to speak with them," she wrote on a comment board on the CBS Miami website. "We feel it would have helped in finding Roger, and we are so grateful to everyone who has been concerned; we wanted them to be able to know what was going on."

The incident team made a decision early on to keep the media out of the search, confirmed Linda Friar, park spokesperson at the time. She also noted that the incident team, not the family, did not want to provide a photo to the media, even though the media had been told that this was the family's decision.

"They wanted to concentrate man hours on the search," Williams said. Indeed, decades of past experience may have left the search team leaders wary of using this avenue to generate leads. A public eager to help can provide hundreds of false leads, monopolizing police and detective time in following up on them all.

This did not stop the media from making inquiries of the park's media relations office, but not a single story about Roger's disappearance appeared in the local newspapers. "They spoke with the rangers' offices, but we don't know what happened there," said Williams. "They may have had their own reasons for keeping the media away."

Ten days of thorough searching turned up nothing, and the family eventually had to return home without any idea of what may have happened to him. Friar told CBS Miami that the park service "is taking a second look at the way the dissemination of information was handled during the search." To this day, no sign of Roger Sawyer has surfaced anywhere.

11

Into the Canal

MANMADE CANALS FORM A GEOMETRIC NETWORK ACROSS THE EVERglades, a part of efforts that began in the 1940s to control the flow of water and prevent flooding. They vary in depth from about fifteen feet to as much as thirty, their water dyed a murky brown by the muck that blankets the entire region—a mix of leaves and roots of the omnipresent sawgrass constantly decomposing in the saturated soil.

Impermeable to sunlight and often deep enough to cover a two-story house, the canals have become the ultimate hiding places for evidence of crimes both petty and capital: automobile theft, insurance fraud, murder. They can hide a car while its owner claims it was stolen and collects the insurance money. They can provide a convenient place for a thief to literally "ditch" a stolen vehicle. And they have become one of the most popular places in the United States to dump a dead body.

Not everyone who dies in an Everglades canal has been murdered, of course. Some choose this watery grave to end their own lives, while others take a wrong turn on a dark road and find themselves immersed in silty, muddy water. Once the water closes in above their head, they can be hidden for days, months, years, or even decades—and judging by the lists of unsolved missing person cases in South Florida, some may never be found at all.

Robert Steward Hall was nearly one of the unfound. On the afternoon of October 6, 1979, after work at the Dade County Water and Sewer Department, he stopped to have a couple of drinks with friends—and a couple of drinks became an all-night binge. He called his wife of twenty-eight years, Beatrice Hall, at about 8:00 p.m. and again at 12:45 a.m., telling her that he was working overtime and would be home shortly after the second call. "He asked me what I wanted for my birthday," she told the AP. "I used to hate for him to come home late because of the canals. I'd tell him, 'One false move on those roads and that's it.' And he would tell me, 'Don't worry about it. My car knows how to get me home.'"

The two calls did not come from the office, of course—Robert made them from two different bars of the five he and his friends patronized that night. His coworker and pal David Buzzard said he last saw Robert at 5:15 a.m. when Robert dropped him off in the parking lot of the Western Sunset Bowling Alley.

"He said, 'I'll see you tomorrow,'" Buzzard told the *Herald*. "As far as I knew, he was going home."

His spirits had been low for some time, Beatrice said, and with good reason: In the previous three years, his mother and twin brother had died, his son Dean had married and moved away, and Robert himself had turned fifty years old. It was a lot to absorb.

Meanwhile, Robert had told his wife and several coworkers that he had been diagnosed with cancer that might be terminal. Robert's doctors, however, said they had never told him that. It simply wasn't true.

"He made up a big old long story," Beatrice said to the *Herald* a year after Robert's disappearance. "I think it was because he thought if I thought he had cancer I would accept his drinking."

He'd taken up drinking late in life after his doctors discovered that he did not have an ulcer as he had believed for decades, but actually had a gall bladder issue. Surgery fixed that problem, freeing him to enjoy alcohol if he chose to do so. After that, he drank often—and he lied about it, his wife told the *Herald*.

When he wasn't home by 6:00 a.m., Beatrice called Buzzard to ask where her husband might be. Buzzard "suggested she wait a while," as he had just left him not an hour before. She waited until 6:00 that evening, and then called the police.

Sometime after 5:15 a.m., Robert and his company car—a white and yellow 1972 Chevrolet Nova—had disappeared. His most recent paycheck for $840 languished uncashed.

"It doesn't make sense," Beatrice told the AP. "We had a happy marriage. No problems." Later she dispelled any thoughts of foul play to Edna Buchanan of the *Herald*: "He didn't have an enemy in this world that I know of. He wasn't into anything that he shouldn't have been into."

In her struggle to come up with a reason why Robert might leave her, Beatrice and her children concocted all kinds of scenarios. Perhaps he had decided to get help for his drinking and had gone off to some kind of rehabilitation center or a veterans' hospital (he had fought in the Korean War and came home with a Purple Heart). Maybe he had been attacked and kidnapped. They consulted psychics, who said Robert was still alive but "confused." None of these explanations seemed like the right one.

Twenty-one years, four months, and two weeks later, the Hall family got some answers—not all of them, but enough to give their story an ending.

Dade and Broward County police periodically perform a task unique to law enforcement in South Florida. They clean out the many canals within their jurisdiction, hauling up the husks of waterlogged cars that have been submerged there for months or even years. Using divers and massive cranes—and, more recently, sonar systems—the police not only clear the waterways for proper drainage, but they also solve a number of crimes by finding cars reported stolen, used in criminal activities, or with their vehicle identification numbers (VINs) filed off.

Fraudsters perpetrate a complex ruse that nets them a tidy profit. They create a fake identity and insure a car under that name, then dump the car in a canal and report the sunken car as stolen. After a police report and an interval of waiting for the car to turn up, the insurance company pays the fake "owner" for the total loss of the vehicle. Even if the car is found later, sitting at the bottom of a canal completely destroys a vehicle, so the loss is total, car or no car.

Finding these cars and connecting them with scams is the job of the Dade County and Collier County Sheriff's Offices, so salvage operations are frequent in Everglades canals. Most of the cars found underwater are fairly recent models, but on February 22, 2001, crews working in the Tamiami Canal along U.S. Route 41 pulled up an early 1970s Chevrolet and took immediate note that it still bore on its doors the logo of the water and sewer department. This made it very unlikely to be part of an insurance scam—this was something else.

The rest of the car had long since lost its paint to algae and rust, but the age and model were easily determined. More important, workers spotted a bulge sticking out of the layers of muck inside the car: dark cloth over something angular that could only be a human knee.

Detectives went to work that night to find a missing person's report that matched the description of this vehicle. They had a number of clues to go on: a wallet with some laminated items that were still readable when the muck had been removed, and a tiny pocketknife that Beatrice Hall had described in the missing person report two decades earlier.

Meanwhile, Robert's son Dean happened to be watching the news that evening when coverage of the surprising find appeared on the screen. A shot of the car being loaded onto a truck startled him into picking up the phone and calling the detectives.

"I knew that car," he later told the *Miami Herald*. "I was in that car lots of times. My dad used to drive me to the bus stop in high school."

The detectives asked for the missing persons case number. Dean knew his mother would have it, so he called her in her new home in Ocala, where she lived near her daughter. Sure enough, she told the detectives, "I've kept it by the phone all these years, waiting for you to call."

Lead detective Angel Valhuerdi and his team started the dirty job of retrieving all of the bones that they could from the wreck, "wearing knee-high rubber boots and latex gloves in the medical examiner's garage," the *Herald* reported. They cut the car into pieces to remove all the mud that remained in it, then took the mud to a box fitted with a screen in the bottom, sifting it much as if they were prospecting for gold. They used a gentle hose spray to wash the dirt away and pick out whatever was not dirt—small things Robert may have carried with him or had in the car, as well as bone fragments. The bones were as black as the muck now, stained so by decades in the canal.

"The skeleton is essentially fully recovered," associate medical examiner Dr. Daniel Spitz told the media. While the lack of soft tissue made it impossible to say what the cause of death might have been and whether Hall was conscious when he went into the canal, Spitz could tell that there had been "no obvious trauma" such as a gunshot, which would have broken bones, or a blow to the head. All of the personal effects the family described were found: glasses, ring, watch, clothing, and boots.

They didn't get answers to all of their questions, Dean Hall acknowledged to the media, but now, at least, they had "something to bury." Sometimes families learn to accept the level of closure they can get, even when it falls far short of telling them all they want to know.

WHERE THE BODIES HIDE

When Apple first introduced Siri, its personal digital assistant, it had at least one morbid Easter egg hidden in the voice recognition programming. Users could ask, "Hey Siri, where can I hide a body?" and Siri would respond with four possibilities: swamps, reservoirs, metal foundries, and dumps. If you chose one of these from the list, "swamps," say, Siri would display a selection of swamps that were "fairly close."

This little game ended in 2014, when iPhone data accessed by police showed that Pedro Bravo, a Florida man, may have asked the Apple assistant to find a place to hide his roommate's body after he strangled him to death. Bravo chose a forest rather than a swamp, but the fact that Siri may have helped him find a choice location to stash the deceased Christian Aguilar sparked Apple to remove this gem from its programming. Now if you ask (and I did), Siri will respond with, "An interesting question," followed by, "I used to know the answer to that."

In South Florida, murderers have never needed an app to tell them where to conceal the evidence of their crimes. For a chilling number of killers, the Everglades ranks high among places to dump remains—in fact, Listverse placed it fourth in the nation in body-dumping popularity among serial killers and less prolific criminals. So the use of the region's backcountry as a center of corpse disposal began long before Siri suggested such a thing, and it is still a popular solution for hiding the evidence.

Take, for example, the dry spring of 1973 when low water in the canal behind the Golden Gates Estates in Naples revealed a white 1964 Ford sticking out of the murk. Passing by at about 7:00 p.m., Allen Johns's sharp eyes caught a glimpse of the watery grave of Alan Stuart

Marsh, forty-one, a resident of Seminole Trailer Park, who had been missing since the previous June. Marsh's skeleton sat in the front seat of the submerged vehicle, wearing the clothes in which he had last been seen. Medical Examiner Courtland Berry's examination of the remains turned up multiple gunshot wounds that had broken through bones.

Who was Marsh, and why would someone want him dead? Working with information gathered from multiple clandestine sources, the police soon found links between the dead man and a number of harassment activities they were tracking in Collier County. The tactics all added up to one thing: emergence of the Ku Klux Klan in this corner of southwest Florida.

"The motive for the killing may have been leadership of the Klan in this area," Cecil Farrell of the *Naples Daily News* reported. Police had become aware of Klan activity in 1973 when a local youth shelter that harbored children of color became the target of numerous attacks, from rocks thrown through windows to phone calls suggesting to the supervisors that they "get out of town." In the most serious attack, someone cut a hole in a window screen and poured in a "volatile liquid," presumably gasoline, and ignited it. This forced the supervisors to evacuate all twenty-three children in the building, ranging in age from four months to thirteen years.

Police were deep into their investigation of this possible Klan activity, using a number of potential members as informers, when Marsh's body turned up. "The Marsh murder sort of slowed things down," an officer told Farrell. "A lot of potential members got scared after that and backed out." The organization's active recruitment efforts stopped as well. Clearly word had got around that working with the cops could be fatal.

The careful investigation continued, however, and in June 1974, police arrested Kenneth Ray Jenkins, twenty-four, of Knoxville, Tennessee, and local resident George Lewis Thornton, forty-one, and charged them with first-degree murder. Both men made a deal that they would plead guilty to second-degree murder in court in exchange for sentences of not more than twenty-five years.

Judge William Lamar Rose made it clear that he knew what had brought the two men to this day. "You were trying to organize the

Klansmen and wanted to straighten that old fellow out. There's no question that you did straighten him out—straightened him right out of this world."

Marsh's killers did their best to hide their crime, but they were outsmarted by drought, something simple and out of their control. Many bodies in the canals never surface, however, and others—dozens, perhaps hundreds, of cases like this one—never get solved. A December 5, 1977, article by Lee Melsek in the *Pensacola Journal* lists case after case in which the discovered body was unidentified and the cause of death "undetermined." My own research turned up a long list of unsolved killings as well, far too many to pursue in this book and most with no clue to their identity or the last moments of their lives.

Why do so many bodies end up here? Authorities list a wide range of reasons, beginning with a high incidence of drug traffic in the region. Many of the bodies that can be identified turn out to be somehow related to the drug trade, perhaps the result of a deal going wrong. This became especially prevalent in the 1980s and 1990s as Miami rose to prominence as a drug smuggling capital.

Others have nothing to do with drugs—as far as police can tell. The killers do their deed elsewhere and transport the bodies to the swamps to conceal them forever, knowing that the harsh conditions will help a body decompose quickly, rendering it virtually impossible to identify. Even if a skeleton or a pile of bones comes to light later, it may never be linked to the killer who took its life.

And then, of course, there are alligators here. The enormous reptiles will eat decomposing bodies if they happen across them, digesting the remains of murder victims or leaving them completely unrecognizable. "Alligators are opportunistic feeders and will eat animals that are readily available to them," says Tammy Sapp of the Florida Fish and Wildlife Conservation Commission (FWC). "They prefer to go after prey they can overpower easily. Opportunity is the primary factor that causes an alligator to pursue prey."

So if a human body part happens to float by, an alligator will indeed eat it. In June 2016, fishermen spotted two alligators eating what was obviously part of a human body in the Southwest Ranches district near

U.S. Route 27. The remains "appeared to have been in the canal for some time," Davie Police captain Dale Engle told the *South Florida Sun-Sentinel*. The conclusion: This was a found meal for the reptiles, not one they had hunted themselves. Alligators may indeed participate in the dispatch of bodies, but most bodies that are found have not been ravaged by alligator teeth.

Whether or not these crimes can be solved has a great deal to do with the skill and thoroughness of the killer. Such was the case of seventeen-year-old Marissa Karp, a Broward County resident whose killers shot her, wrapped her body in a sheet, crammed it into a plastic garbage bag, and threw the garbage bag into the L-28 canal near mile marker 52 as they drove west on Alligator Alley. A fisherman on an airboat found the bag on August 10, 2002, but it took more than a month for medical examiners to identify her body because of rapid decomposition. Once they did, a torrent of family and agency finger-pointing in the media overshadowed the early stages of the search for her killer.

Marissa had spent much of her teen years in the foster care system, after her mother died of asthma when Marissa was thirteen. Her father remarried shortly thereafter, and Marissa became "too violent and disruptive to handle," he told the *Fort Lauderdale Sun-Sentinel* on the day of her funeral. In 1998, Gary Karp committed his daughter to University Pavilion Hospital in Tamarac, a short-term facility for crisis management, when she had suicidal thoughts and "out of control behaviors," the *Sun-Sentinel* reported.

After Pavilion, she was removed from her "typical Jewish family" and sent to live with one relative after another, as well as friends of the family including Linda Spedalere, who took in Marissa for several months in 2000.

"I used to sit on the phone when she'd beg him to come home," Spedalere told the *South Florida Sun-Sentinel* when Marissa's body was identified. "He did not want Marissa. She was a lost little girl."

Marissa went to shelters and facilities as far off as Vermont, and eventually came under the care of the Florida Department of Children and Families. Her evaluations at the various shelters noted that she suffered from a psychiatric disorder for which she was prescribed medication that she often refused to take, as well as depression and other issues. She spent a good deal of her time running away from the shelters in which she had been placed—even though records suggest that she had been fairly happy in one of them, the Brown's Harbor shelter in Pembroke Pines. This was the last supervised place she lived before she ran at the end of January 2002. It's not illegal to be a teen runaway in Florida, so she was free to do as she wished, judging for herself whether she was safe in her circumstances.

"The law needs to allow an agency to pick up a child and when they do, to keep the child in their custody," Gary Karp said to *Sun-Sentinel* reporters.

Friends who saw her shortly before she died said that she was waiting for the day she turned eighteen, when she would "come into some money" and have the opportunity to set herself up in an apartment and work toward her graduate equivalency diploma. By then she had begun frequenting neighborhoods even her street friends advised her to avoid. The last time anyone saw her, she was getting into a car with a man in his forties. Her body turned up in the canal a few weeks later.

To this day, no one has been prosecuted for Marissa's murder. A Bahamian man with whom she had lived, Randolph Almanto Coakley, became a "person of interest" in the case (and in another murder) before he left Florida for his native island, but even as authorities in Florida worked toward his extradition, he was murdered in the Bahamas. The case remains unsolved.

The police had better luck with another incident, even though they began the investigation with a lot less to go on.

Imagine that you're out on a peaceful fishing trip with a buddy in the Francis S. Taylor Wildlife Management Area and you cast your line across a tranquil canal. When you reel in your line, you can tell you've hooked something with some weight, though it doesn't seem to be struggling. When it comes out of the water, you see it's something in a grocery bag . . . and when you look inside, the object looks back at you.

It's a decomposing human head.

Two anglers came across this horrific find near mile marker 35.7 on Alligator Alley as they fished there on April 28, 2007. They managed to compose themselves enough to call the Broward Sheriff's Office and met homicide investigators on the bank of the canal to turn over the evidence. No doubt they were glad to wash their hands of this affair as police began a search for the identity of the unfortunate victim.

The killer had left a glaringly obvious clue: The head was contained in a Waldbaum's shopping bag, a supermarket chain located only in New York City's five boroughs, Long Island, and downstate New York—a solid clue that the killing may have some connection with that area. The Broward Sheriff's Office contacted police in New York City and Long Island, alerting them to the find.

Just a week later, a detective in Port Orange, Florida, called police in Suffolk County on Long Island to inquire about a blue 1988 Dodge Dakota pickup truck that sheriffs had pulled over for a traffic stop on May 1, with a license plate that matched a missing person report. Sure enough, the truck was registered to a Lorraine Hatzakorzian of Mastic, New York, whose mother had reported her missing on April 21. Two men who worked as tree trimmers, Paul Bryan Trucchio, 33, and Robert Mackey, 39, who lived in Port Orange, were driving the truck. The detective had an interest in Trucchio and Mackey because Douglas Stine, a man who had shared a hotel room at the Fairview Inn with them in May, had walked into the Port Orange Police Department of his own accord and reported that these roommates bragged to him about murdering a woman they called a "crack head."

Not only had they killed her, they boasted, but they cut her body apart with "pole saws and other tree trimming equipment" and dumped her body in the Everglades. He'd also seen them clean a blue 1988 Dodge truck inside and out with bleach.

Another man in the room at the time, Lewis Caroleo Jr., corroborated Stine's story, making Trucchio and Mackey prime suspects for the woman's murder.

Trucchio, it turned out, was Hatzakorzian's ex-boyfriend, and she had driven down to Florida from New York with the two men. No one knew what went wrong, but when Hatzakorzian tried to escape the two men, Mackey "jumped into the bed of the truck and beat [her]," the *Miami Herald* reported. Caroleo added that the two killers tried to burn her body after dismembering her, but found this much more difficult than they expected. They resorted to depositing her in pieces in the canal. Later, they took the extra step of destroying the truck, crushing the plates, and throwing them into Rose Bay. Divers later recovered the plates, a critical clue in linking the men with the crime.

With these solid leads to the head's identity, it took nothing more than a DNA test to confirm that this was indeed what remained of Lorraine Hatzakorzian. Both suspects denied any knowledge of the crime, but their boasts to the other men, the discovery of pole saws in their hotel room, and the physical evidence of Hatzakorzian's head all gave the lie to their claim.

"Lorraine could have remained another missing person," said Veda Coleman-Wright, spokesperson for the Broward Sheriff's Office, to the *Herald* on August 21, 2007. "Without the discovery of the head, all the people they bragged to would have thought they just made it all up." The two killers were each sentenced to thirty years in prison and are serving their time in Florida—though they have attempted to have their sentences commuted because they claim they actually killed Hatzakorzian in South Carolina, leaving Florida with no jurisdiction in the case. So far, this tactic has not resulted in their release.

Would that more murderers slipped up the way these two did. Florida's law enforcement files remain cluttered with cases that cannot be solved, triggered by human remains that refused to remain hidden despite the best efforts of their concealers, the appetites of alligators, and the peculiarities of the Everglades.

12

When Alligators Attack
(Which Isn't Often)

IF YOU HAVE READ THIS FAR, IT WILL HAVE BECOME ABUNDANTLY CLEAR that there are far more threatening forces in the Everglades than alligators. When people tell me that they have never visited South Florida, however, they invariably say that they are afraid they will be attacked by "an alligator or a crocodile or whatever they have down there."

So let's set the record straight before we learn the stories of a few people who have had a violent encounter with an alligator.

First, both American alligators and American crocodiles live in the Everglades—in fact, it's the only place in the world where both species reside. The state of Florida hosts about 1.3 million alligators, none of which are looking at you and thinking, "Mmm, lunch." These large reptiles are opportunistic feeders, eating animals that are easy prey and within their immediate vicinity—exclusively animals that are smaller than they are, such as "fish, snakes, turtles, birds and small mammals" so they can overpower them without much of a fight, according to Tammy Sapp at the FWC.

When they hunt, they usually do so in water. This being so, your best defense against them is simple: Stay out of bodies of water that may contain alligators.

By contrast, only about one thousand American crocodiles live in Florida. Crocodiles can't live where it gets cold, so crocodile colonies are much larger farther south and outside the United States—in fact, the northernmost place they have been found is Tampa Bay. (Alligators, on the other hand, are in every county in Florida.) You can tell the difference between alligators and crocodiles in several ways, but the most obvious at a glance is that alligators have a squared-off, *U*-shaped snout, while crocodiles have a pointier, *V*-shaped snout. Some other tips: Alligators are grayer while crocodiles are green, brown, or black; also, a crocodile's jaw exposes its top and bottom teeth, while the alligator's jaw exposes only its top teeth. Once you have seen both species, you will find it fairly easy to tell them apart. Chances are, however, that you will encounter a crocodile only while on a boat tour of the Everglades backcountry.

Crocodiles see humans as creatures to fear, so they will not approach you. Again, stay out of the water where crocs are known to live, and you will have no reason to dread them.

The FWC keeps records of every known human encounter with these animals. From 2009 to 2019, the state of Florida averaged seven unprovoked alligator bites per year that were "serious enough to require professional medical treatment," according to the FWC's April 2019 fact sheet, the most recent one available. Even with the significant human population growth in Florida in recent years, there has been no upward trend in alligator attacks. "The likelihood of a Florida resident being seriously injured during an unprovoked alligator incident in Florida is roughly one in 3.1 million," the FWC assures us.

In fact, since 1948, just twenty-five alligator-bite incidents in the entire state have ended in death for the human victims—that's one every three years or so. For the most part, these have occurred in residential areas with ponds or canals, or in parks where people swim or snorkel. Eight of these deaths took place within the region dominated by the Everglades.

Experts note that as more residential development takes place in previously undeveloped areas close to the Everglades, more alligators and humans will come into conflict. New housing and commercial developments create basins and trenches from which construction soil comes. Turning these areas into stormwater retention ponds or canals is a legal requirement for building new housing tracts, and these bodies of water then become prime habitat for alligators. And if the ponds and canals connect with existing creeks, lakes, and other waterways, the alligators then have an easy transportation network to explore, and they move into areas that are not already dominated by large alligators, establishing their own territory.

This means the animals are everywhere: in and along canals, around lakes and ponds, and more numerous the farther south you go. They lounge as ominous curiosities in the most visited areas of Everglades National Park: Anhinga Trail, Eco Pond, Royal Palm, Paurotis Pond, and Shark Valley, although in the park they take little notice of humans for the most part, going about their business as tourists snap photos of them. Attacks in the park are very rare and do not end in death—in fact, none of the deadly incidents to date took place inside the park, so you can rest easy in the knowledge that the odds are in your favor if you choose to visit this spectacular place.

In many cases, the unfortunate victims were swimming or snorkeling in inland waters, unwittingly presenting themselves as easy targets for these opportunistic feeders.

Take, for example, the case of Kevin Albert Murray, a forty-one-year-old resident of North Port, near Fort Myers. On July 15, 2005, at about 7:00 p.m., he had just finished mowing a lawn in Port Charlotte when he decided to take a quick swim to cool off.

Hardly had he jumped into the nearby canal when a twelve-foot alligator came right for him, biting his right arm and thumb and pulling him underwater. Someone must have heard him cry out or even seen him go under, because they called the Charlotte County Sheriff's Office at 7:17 p.m., and by 7:40, state trappers Tracy Hansen and Bo Davis reached the spot where Murray had gone into the water. While they searched for Murray and the alligator, the animal came to the surface on the opposite side of the canal, its jaws clamped around Murray's right arm as it dragged the man's lifeless body into some bushes.

Hansen, Davis, and two additional officers moved quickly, getting into a boat and crossing the canal to edge close to the alligator. Seeing them coming, the alligator released Murray's arm. They retrieved the dead man's body and brought it to shore, then attempted to bait the alligator using two cow lungs on ropes held just over the water. The alligator showed no interest and vanished under the surface.

The trappers got out flashlights and turned them on, shining them into the water—and in a few seconds they saw the alligator's eyes glittering back at them. Now they knew they were close enough to try a more effective tactic: Hansen took aim with a crossbow and shot the alligator with a dart attached to a rope, effectively harpooning the reptile. The dart hit its target and held. They pulled the alligator to within four feet of the boat, put a gun to its head, and pulled the trigger.

But "the bullet only stunned him," Hansen later told Sarah Lundy of the *Fort Myers News-Press*. Nonetheless, it gave them the opportunity they needed to tie a noose around the stunned alligator's head and start pulling it toward the shore. By the time they reached the bank, the alligator had come to its senses and was struggling against the noose, but they then shot the alligator again, killing it this time. They loaded the beast into a truck and took it to Lakeland for a necropsy and to examine its stomach contents to determine if it had actually consumed any part of Murray.

Murray's death had come a year after an alligator attack that took the life of landscaper Janie Melsek, fifty-four, an incident that led to an overhaul of alligator policy on Sanibel Island.

As Melsek quietly trimmed vegetation around a backyard pond on Sanibel, an 11-foot 9-inch alligator rose up out of the pond, grabbed her right arm, and dragged her into the water. She fought the 457-pound animal and would have been killed on the spot had it not been for the quick action of a neighbor, Jim Anholt, who heard her screams and ran over to help. He called police and held her head out of the water, doing his best to resist the alligator until they arrived.

"It was kind of a tug of war," Anholt told the *Fort Myers News-Press* later. Three police officers joined him and struggled with the alligator for five minutes, finally winning the battle and pulling Melsek out of its jaws.

By this time emergency medical technicians were on the scene as well. They began controlling her bleeding and treating her wounds, well aware of the risk of infection from alligator bites.

Police, meanwhile, took the opportunity to shoot the alligator in the head. Even in death, the alligator put up a struggle, its sheer size making it tough to remove from the pond. Six men worked to pull the dead animal to shore and put it in a truck, sending it to the FWC for a necropsy.

Melsek's injuries were so severe that doctors amputated her right arm below the elbow. She also suffered bites on her buttocks, back, and inner thighs, making it unlikely that she would escape the body's inevitable response to severe alligator bites—an infection known as systemic inflammatory response syndrome. She died two days after the attack as trauma surgeons worked to combat the spreading inflammation.

This could have been the end of the story, but Melsek's death touched off a tinder pile of anger and fear among Sanibel residents. The island had its own set of rules for dealing with alligators, an animal that had been on the national endangered species list as recently as 1987. Sanibel rules protected alligators over four feet long unless they became aggressive—usually because tourists fed them, causing them to lose their wariness of humans and to associate people with food. After that large alligator killed Melsek, however, the city council agreed their policy had to be broadened to protect human residents. Two weeks after the landscaper's death, the council voted unanimously to allow the city to hire trappers to kill an alligator more than four feet long "if it makes people feel unsafe." This brought the island in line with rules established by the FWC, which the rest of the state already followed.

In the next two months, residents reported forty-four alligators that needed to be removed from their neighborhood, and trappers and police made quick work of them. Even with this aggressive level of scrutiny and capture, however, only two months later another death on the island underscored the need to be vigilant around these enormous reptiles.

Friends called twenty-year-old Michelle Reeves a free spirit, "the kind of person who would go swimming at two in the morning," said Paul Voss, one of her professors at Georgia State University. "She was intelligent and thoughtful. She had a very probing mind and a very sharp though subtle sense of humor."

Reeves had a talent for writing poetry, an ability with wordplay that brought her to the attention of the Atlanta Poets Group, an exclusive set of writers who encouraged one another's work. It was unusual for someone so young—a junior at Georgia State—to have the kind of command of language and originality of thought that she did, said Mark Prejsnar, a founding member of the group, to Kevin Lollar of the *Fort Myers News-Press*. "We are not an open group at all," he said. "We're very much a closed group . . . She started out very shy, but once she got to know us, we found out she was a lot of fun. She was a very spontaneous person."

Which may be how Reeves ended up in a small lake on Sanibel Island on Sunday, September 26, 2004, in the middle of the night and became the island's next victim of a deadly alligator attack.

Michelle had told her grandfather, James Reeves, how happy she was to be back "with the water again" and how she wanted to swim in the lake near her grandparents' home. Jim Reeves had cautioned her repeatedly about alligators and how dangerous they were, especially in neighborhoods like this one where some people fed them. "I don't know how we could have cautioned her more strongly," he said to the *News-Press*. "I'm sure on that night there was a bright moon and it was very inviting, and she probably was seduced by the scene. She probably thought, 'Nothing is going to harm me tonight.'"

The last time anyone saw her was 2:30 a.m. When she had not appeared for breakfast by 10:00 a.m., her grandfather called the police. They discovered her body floating face down in the lake, her right arm missing below the elbow, and punctures from alligator teeth in her body. An autopsy revealed that she had drowned as a result of the attack.

Trappers captured a 7-foot 11-inch alligator in the lake later that morning and removed it from the island. A necropsy performed by John French, a top nuisance alligator trapper in the area, found Reeves's hand and lower arm in the animal's stomach.

Barely a week after Reeves's death, as the *Fort Myers News-Press* took on the topic of the rising number of alligator attacks in its readership area, French mused at the different reactions of people who understood the danger that alligators could pose in a neighborhood, and those who felt that wild animals should be protected at any cost. "You've got some people who are tickled to death to see you when you come to get the gator," he said to Byron Stout, writer for the *News-Press*. "Then there are those others . . ." He referred specifically to newcomers to the area who have "seen Steve Irwin on television and know all about alligators. If you're not careful you can get perturbed."

The Florida west coast has no monopoly on alligator attacks, as residents of Sunrise discovered on Tuesday, May 9, 2006. At about 7:00 p.m., Yovy Suarez Jimenez, a twenty-eight-year-old resident of Paradise Village Mobile Home Park in Davie, west of Fort Lauderdale, put on jogging shorts, a running top, and Nike jogging shoes and went for a run. Jimenez was studying biological science at Florida Atlantic University and often jogged after class, sometimes walking her dogs along the path beside her.

She ran along an eight-foot-wide gravel path by the North New River Canal in West Broward and stopped under a bridge to talk to her mother on the phone. Yovy mentioned that she was feeling down, her mother told WFOR-CBS4 Miami later in the week, and she said she offered to come and pick Yovy up, but her daughter turned her down. Then the line went dead, probably just a cellular glitch in the midst of the call.

Someone walking by later told police that he had seen someone who looked like Yovy "sitting with her feet near the canal." This became the only clue to what may have happened next.

No one heard from Yovy that night, but by the next afternoon, when she still had not checked in with her family and she did not answer her phone, they began to worry—and when television news that evening reported that a body had been found in the canal, they raced to the scene. The family found they now had the grim task of identifying the mangled body of Yovy Suarez Jimenez from police photos.

Yovy died of "traumatic injuries sustained by an alligator attack," said Dr. Joshua Perper, Broward County medical examiner. After a thorough examination of the body, he put together this scenario: The alligator, perhaps seeing Yovy's feet swinging over the water, came up on land and attacked her, "severing her arms, and biting her legs and her back." The beast then dragged her into the canal. "In my opinion, she died very fast," he said, noting that blood loss and shock would have hastened the process.

The young woman may not have realized that alligators tend to hunt in the evening, or that her feet dangling over the water could have looked like small enough prey to catch with a snap of the jaw.

Broward County had made a planned effort not to develop the area along this canal, to protect the water supply by maintaining its natural state. Water in the Everglades decreases at this time of year, so alligators head east in a search of more habitat, making this particular spot a favorite among Florida's alligator hunters. As many as ten times more alligators can come to this canal in spring than are usually there, University of Florida ecologist Frank Mazzotti told the *Miami Herald* in their coverage of Jimenez's death.

None of this activity would be considered unusual for this time of year, but everyone from the medical examiner to professional conservationists reacted with shock at the sheer viciousness of the attack.

"I do not recall an alligator attack of this kind ever taking place in Broward or Miami-Dade," Perper said.

This made the capture of this particular alligator an urgent problem. Trappers set to work using a pig lung dangled over the water to lure the animal out. When the alligator swallows this bait, they explained to the press, the trapper pulls up next to the alligator in a boat and snares it with a noose around its neck. He can then use the handle of the snare to pull the alligator into the boat, tape its mouth with duct tape, and tie its legs. The only way to be sure the right alligator has been caught is to kill it and examine the contents of its stomach for evidence, so any alligator of the right size—eight to ten feet long, based on the bite marks on Jimenez's body—would be destroyed before its guilt could be determined. In this case, trappers caught a 9-foot 6-inch alligator, and a necropsy revealed that it had swallowed Jimenez's arms. Perper concluded that the alligator attacked her on land and dragged her into the water.

More than a year passed before another alligator targeted a human being in the Everglades. Justo Padron did not go out of his way to antagonize an alligator, but he managed to do so just by swimming in its waters.

Described by the police as a career criminal with a long rap sheet including arrests for burglary, robbery, drug possession, and more, Padron had served a six-year sentence in prison for burglary, and had been arrested as recently as April 2007 for selling cocaine to an undercover police officer. He managed to get off with eighteen months' probation, but in September he moved without notifying his probation officer, triggering a bench warrant for his arrest on September 24. He then evaded law enforcement for six weeks, but could not help but get into trouble again.

On November 8, 2007, Padron and a partner, Heriberto Rubio, drew the attention of a local tribal police officer as they attempted to steal a car from the parking lot at the Miccosukee Resort and Convention Center. The police gave chase and captured Rubio quickly, but Padron took a calculated risk: He jumped into a nearby lake to swim for it.

What happened next was not disclosed to the media, but we can assume that Padron's sudden splash aroused the interest of an alligator, which may have mistaken him for much smaller prey in the dark. The alligator grabbed him in its jaws and held on, and Padron could not escape.

When police divers found his body in the lake the following afternoon, there was little question what had happened. The medical examiner classified the death as an accident and left it at that, and Miccosukee police said no more about it. They did bring in a professional trapper to find the offending alligator, though, and he returned with two, one of them 9-foot 3-inches long and the other just over 7 feet long. Both were removed from the lake permanently.

A more recent death from an alligator attack happened in Davie, and while no one saw what happened, a necropsy filled in the blanks in the story.

Shizuka Matsuki, a forty-seven-year-old Plantation resident, took her dogs for a walk on a path around a pond at Silver Lakes Rotary Nature Park on Friday morning, June 8, 2018. When she did not come home, a search began—and it led first to the trapping and killing of an alligator in the pond. FWC personnel found Matsuki's arm in the alligator's stomach, and they found her body in the park at 9:49 p.m. that night.

Whether her dogs drew the alligator's attention—one of them had had a bloody encounter with the alligator, but escaped—or she herself had somehow attracted its interest, it led to the worst possible outcome.

This focused litany of deaths may make the risk seem much greater than it actually is. "Most alligators are naturally afraid of humans and serious injuries caused by alligators are rare in Florida," says Sapp of the FWC. Alligators lose their fear of humans only when people feed them, but feeding them is illegal. So the more people understand the need to keep their distance from these animals, the fewer violent incidents we'll have to examine in such detail in the future.

Gliding on Air: Airboat Deaths

FEW MODES OF TRANSPORTATION ARE SO FIRMLY LINKED WITH A national park as airboats are with the Everglades. Airboats' ability to glide along the surface of fairly shallow water makes these sturdy—albeit noisy—contraptions the go-to method of reaching the region's extensive backcountry, from the mangrove swamps in the Ten Thousand Islands to areas deep within the towering sawgrass. No trip to South Florida can be complete without an airboat tour, especially if children are involved, and the chance to see large wading birds, turtles, and alligators up close from the safety of a watercraft can be positively irresistible. For many visitors, airboats may be the only way they will experience the Everglades in all its splendor.

When the first airboats appeared in the Everglades in the 1940s, they were the sole property of frog hunters who sought the amphibians' tasty hind legs, providing these "giggers" with unencumbered passage through the peculiar conditions of South Florida's waterways. An airboat's ability to glide over shallow water provided a more effective means of transport than a labor-intensive rowboat, or a motorboat with an outboard motor that extended down into the water. The airboat's above-the-surface propulsion device—an airplane propeller—does not become entangled in vines below the water's surface the way an outboard motor's propeller can, and a flat-bottomed craft doesn't have a centerboard, keel, or other structure that could catch in underwater vegetation.

Soon tourists took an interest in these curious crafts, and the airboat tour industry took off. Until very recently, airboat tour operators were not required to be licensed, and there were no special regulations or rules for setting up an airboat tour business. Visitors had no way to know which were the safest and most experienced, though Everglades National Park authorizes just three airboat tour companies to take passengers into the backcountry: Coopertown Airboats, operating since the 1940s; Everglades Safari Park, in business since the 1980s; and Gator Park Airboat Tours—all of which dock their boats at facilities along the Tamiami Trail. Private airboats are not permitted in the park, in part to steer tourists toward skilled, experienced guides who know how to pilot their boats.

Airboat tour proprietors are quick to quip "Haven't lost anyone yet" if asked questions about safety—and for the most part, they speak the truth. My research turned up only five fatal accidents involving airboats in the Everglades from 1955 to 2021, making them much safer than driving the Tamiami Trail or Alligator Alley, where dozens of accidents take place every year. (Other parts of the state have seen additional airboat accidents and deaths.) Some nonfatal accidents have left passengers with serious injuries, including the loss of a limb in collisions with propellers.

Until very recently, just about anyone could buy an airboat, take a few hours of training, and set themselves up in business giving tours. Taking an airboat ride was very much a caveat emptor situation, in which tourists who did not ask many questions of a tour operator occasionally found themselves in an unexpectedly dangerous situation.

On March 6, 1955, two fourteen-foot airboats took a total of sixteen passengers into the wilderness from Coopertown, a former Seminole village converted to a roadside rest stop on the Tamiami Trail. (This rest stop is now the current site of Coopertown Airboats.) Back in the early days of Everglades tours, the trips had less to do with observing wildlife and much more to do with the thrill of gliding over the shallow water in a speeding craft. Airboats revved up their 75 hp engines to reach speeds above 40 mph and create a sense of flying through the wild, much to the delight of passengers looking for a true Everglades adventure.

On this particular day, John Cooper piloted one of the boats, while Harry Riggs drove the other. They both left from the same spot but at different times, zipping over the water and through vegetation so dense that they could not see what approached from the next lane over.

Hardly had Cooper gone a few hundred feet when both boats emerged from sawgrass at a curve in the narrow waterway, on a collision course at over 40 mph. The pilots swerved, but had no time to slow down. In a roar of snapping wood and rending metal, the boats collided, throwing pieces and passengers into the air to land hard in the knee-deep water.

Somehow the boats remained upright, trapping some of the passengers underneath them while the boats' propellers continued to spin.

"It happened in a split second," Riggs told the *Miami Herald* from the emergency room in Doctors' Hospital. "We couldn't do a thing. God! It was awful." Cooper's boat, he said, was "coming like a bullet," though he didn't go so far as to guess its speed.

Owen Boyle, 58, visiting from Rapid City, South Dakota, became the unluckiest of the passengers. The force of the collision hurled him from his seat and directly into a spinning propeller. He landed "trapped beneath the hull of a boat, with his legs grotesquely snagged inside the craft," the *Herald* said the following day. The propeller wound killed him instantly.

Nearby, the propeller slashed Mrs. Neal Cramer, a winter visitor from Topsfield, Massachusetts, and cut a large gash in her side. She was rushed to the hospital in a private car and immediately went into surgery as doctors attempted to close the gash, but she died from her wound before the day was out. Her husband had cuts and bruises and was admitted to the hospital.

In all, fifteen of the passengers suffered injuries—everyone but twelve-year-old Wayne McDaniel, who had come with his parents for the sightseeing ride. Mr. and Mrs. J. J. McDaniel sustained minor injuries, but Wayne managed to escape "without even a scratch," the *Herald* said.

Remarkably after such a spectacular accident, no one called for new rules governing airboats. The sightseeing public accepted this as a one-time occurrence and went on taking airboat rides across the river of grass.

The next time someone died on an airboat ride, the circumstances were strikingly similar to the 1955 crash, but they did not involve a tour company. Instead, six men in their thirties on a fishing expedition would have benefitted from a better way to communicate, should such a thing have been available at the time.

The men camped for the weekend on November 8, 1958, at an established site in the backcountry with two airboats at their disposal. On Saturday, they split into groups of three and took the two airboats out onto the water. As one of the boats glided along a waterway, the boat hit a clump of swamp grass and jolted, throwing Max L. Goode forward. He hit his head on the bow of the boat and cut his face severely enough that the two men with him, Charles Roberts and Joseph M. Malzohn, brought him to Jackson Memorial Hospital in Miami for treatment.

This meant that the three men did not get back to camp that night, so in the morning the other three men decided to go out looking for them. On Sunday at about 9:00 a.m., Thomas S. Nunn, George McFarland, and Richard Thaysen got into their airboat and set out at a speed of about 35 mph to find their friends.

As they came around the curve at 40 Mile Bend, the boat carrying the first three men appeared in the marsh channel as if out of nowhere. The two boats crashed head-on, one of them running right over the bow of the other and sending all six men flying through the air and into various jagged parts of the wrecked boats. One of the propellers sliced through Thaysen's hand and left him with severe damage. Goode suffered internal injuries, while Roberts, Nunn, and McFarland were treated at hospitals and released the same day. Roberts remembered sailing through the air and over the propeller. "I could see those twisting blades as I was falling downward," he told a reporter from the *Orlando Sentinel*. "The Lord was with me." He landed in water and muck and did not sustain a serious injury.

But those spinning propellers caught Malzohn in midair and sliced through his body. He died instantly.

The following year, another private airboat user lost his life in seconds as he and three other men worked to push a boat over a dike about fifteen miles west of Terry Town. Thirty-one-year-old Fred Mohrhardt and his friends were each piloting their own airboat for a deer hunting outing on Saturday, December 12, 1959, but when they reached a dike between ponds, they hopped off their boats and inched the boats over one at a time by pushing them from behind. Three of the boats slid over the dike without incident, so they all got behind Fred's boat to heft it over as well, its motor still running and the propeller whirring at high speed in front of them to add its propulsion to their effort.

This had not been a problem with the first three boats, but on this fourth one, Fred slipped on a clump of wet grass and lost his footing. He then careened into a bush as the airboat slid backward. Startled by his fall and trapped by the branches, he could not escape the whirling propeller.

"His body was badly mangled by the propeller, and he was almost decapitated," Deputy Sheriff Theo York told the *Palm Beach Post*. The blades severed his right hand from his body as well. Mohrhardt died at the scene.

After this accident, many airboats were fitted with a protective housing for their propeller to prevent such a grisly death from occurring. No law requires this housing, however, so some airboats still operate without this added safety measure.

Many airboat accidents have resulted from inexperience in piloting the vessels. People renting an airboat for the first or second time may not be aware that the flat aluminum hull can rise out of the water vertically if it crosses its own wake, or if it crosses waves created by other motorboats. The elevated bow can then flip the boat over, plunging its passengers and pilot into the water—and if the boat continues to circle upside-down with its propeller running, the blades can maim or kill anyone caught under or near the boat.

This kind of inexperience led to an accident in a canal near Andytown on Father's Day in 1962, when John L. Sullivan, 37, and his sons—Charlie, 5, and Larry, 7—went out on an airboat to do "something special" for the holiday. Sullivan had borrowed the twelve-foot airboat from a brother-in-law, Charles Arnold, as a treat for his boys, piloting it himself for the second time ever. "He was a good woodsman and fisherman," Arnold told the *Fort Lauderdale News*. "He knew what to do in the water."

Sullivan wanted the outing to include his three daughters and his wife Betty Jean as well, but Betty turned down the invitation, telling him "it was better for just the father and sons to go," the *News* reported.

Sullivan and the boys rode up and down the canal and then came back in to the landing—but Sullivan took the turn too fast. The little boat tipped, teetered for a moment, and then capsized.

Father and two sons jumped off the boat as it turned over in the water, and a witness, Earl Chambers, saw their heads come up to the surface in seconds. Then Sullivan and his younger son vanished into the muddy canal and did not bob up again. Larry swam for shore and made it, pulling himself out of the water as more help arrived. Two highway patrolmen, Sgt. O. D. Arnett and Trooper L. F. Thomas, dropped their gun belts on the shore and dove into the canal to attempt to rescue Sullivan and Charles. In the opaque water with no diving gear, however, they could not find them.

What happened? When divers found the bodies later that afternoon, both were entangled in the vegetation that grew underwater along the canal's bottom and sides. Sullivan was a "powerful swimmer," Arnold said, but he could not overcome this kind of impediment. The divers found his body about eight feet from the canal bank.

Accidents like these continue to be an issue for airboats, though fatalities in recent years have been higher in Central Florida than in the Everglades. One thing is very clear: Most accidents involve private airboats, not those operated by reputable tour companies. So it makes sense to inquire about any tour company's safety record before boarding an airboat, especially if you're more attracted to brightly lit signs and flashing lights than to the longevity of the business or its pilots' level of experience.

Not every fatality is the result of spinning propellers or head-on collisions, however. In one case, an unexpected breakdown reminds us of how important it is to make proper preparations before venturing into the wilderness, especially if there's a chance you might be out for longer than a half-hour airboat ride.

Cristina Menendez, a twenty-four-year-old graduate student in biology at Florida International University (FIU), went out monthly into the Everglades to collect water samples for her research. On Thursday, July 23, 1998, she departed from the lab at FIU's Southeast Environmental Research Project at about 8:00 a.m. to test the water that flows into the Everglades from nearby farms—part of a project for the Miccosukee Tribe Water Resources Division.

She met her airboat pilot near the Tamiami Trail. Eric James Cypress was himself a hydrologic technician with Miccosukee's Water Resources Department, so he knew what Menendez needed to do that day and where the best places would be to test the water. They set out on the boat in a bright, sunny area with no sources of shade, working their way northward toward Alligator Alley.

They had nearly reached the northern road when their boat became stuck in the vegetation and muck, and no amount of pulling or pushing could free it.

"That happens to us a lot," said Ron Jones, director of the project at FIU. "It's the Everglades. Generally, you talk about how many times you get stuck a day. If the researchers aren't able to dislodge the boat themselves, they call for help."

Menendez and Cypress made the call at about 4:00 p.m., using their radio to ask for someone to come and get them. Then they waited in the late afternoon heat and humidity with not a millimeter of shade in sight. Both of them became dehydrated, then severely so, and likely developed symptoms of heat-related illness: a fast pulse, nausea, vomiting, muscle cramps, weakness, headache, dizziness, and confusion. This may be why they both left the boat, going off in different directions.

When helicopters found the boat at 7:30 p.m., they also discovered Menendez's lifeless body nearby, face down in the water. Some five hundred yards away, they came upon Cypress bushwhacking through the grasses and brush, hot, dehydrated, and disoriented.

"Not staying with the vessel was a mistake," said John F. Long, owner of Old-Fashion Airboat Rides farther north, in an interview with the *Miami Herald*. "If I was out there, I would call someone and have them come get me." This is precisely what Menendez and Cypress tried to do at first, though their later decision to leave the vessel, made when both were likely confused by dehydration and exposure, may have lengthened the time it took to locate them.

This tragedy triggered a long-overdue outcry over the lack of regulations for airboat pilots. While pilots of other kinds of watercraft had to be licensed and were required to adhere to strict safety standards, airboat pilots had no such requirements.

In 1998 when the Menendez incident occurred, the U.S. Coast Guard already required airboat drivers to adhere to the same licensure requirements as any Florida watercraft operator. Pilots of airboats that carried six paying passengers or fewer had to obtain an Operator of Uninspected Passenger Vehicle License, and to do so they had to take a course on navigation and emergency procedure, among other topics. These licenses, however, were required of vessel pilots only on "navigable" waters, or streams, creeks, rivers, and so on that connect to major water bodies like oceans and lakes. Most of the Everglades is not considered navigable, so airboat operators in this area did not have to have licenses.

Neither the state, local law enforcement, nor the Coast Guard regulates speed on Everglades waters, a lack of institutional control linked to one of the most publicized deaths on an airboat there. Jason Goode, a thirty-year-old local firefighter who loved the South Florida wilderness, took a friend's racing airboat out for a test drive on December 5, 2004. Goode intended to open his own airboat tour business, and he had spent countless hours on airboats over the years while saving up the startup money. He had experience with these boats, and he knew what their limits were. Perhaps this is why he opened up the throttle on this one and tried to make it fly.

Witnesses said Goode must have been speeding along at 70 or 80 mph; some said he may have been going even faster. Even so, the boat should have been able to handle it, they would say later, as it was built specifically to travel at high speeds.

No matter what special engineering the boat had, it could not handle that kind of velocity. At about 4:00 p.m., as Goode flashed down a canal near 40 Mile Bend about twenty-one miles west of Krome Avenue and about ten miles north of the Tamiami Trail, he caught air under the hull, bouncing the bow up and over his head. The boat flipped 360 degrees and landed upright—but in the course of the somersault, it threw Goode into the water.

Miami-Dade Fire Rescue arrived quickly and loaded Goode into a helicopter, but he had sustained serious head injuries that soon ended his life. He died at Miami Memorial Hospital later that day.

A similar incident two years later may have involved high speed as well. Details never became clear in the case of Ryan Anthony Carraway, a twenty-six-year-old airboat driver piloting a one-passenger craft on April 1, 2006. Much as Jason Goode did, Carraway caught some air under the bow of his boat, making it somersault into the air. He was severely injured and died shortly thereafter, but whatever may have caused the boat to flip in the Francis S. Taylor Wildlife Management Area was not revealed to the media.

One more accident, however, led to the first real, systemic change in the airboat tourism industry.

Elizabeth "Ellie" Goldenberg had just graduated from the University of Miami when she, her parents, and her sister decided to take an airboat tour on May 13, 2017. They chose River of Grass Adventures, leaving from a Shell gas station at Dade Corners in Miami. They were riding with pilot Steve George Gagne, who guided the boat over the established trail used by this tour company through the Francis S. Taylor Wildlife Management Area.

The ride began with a ten-minute glide through the area before Gagne came to a stop to provide information about the Everglades, the wildlife, and what they might see on the tour. Soon Gagne started forward again, but within five minutes, in a marshy area north of U.S. Route 41, while attempting to pass an airboat that had broken down and blocked the trail ahead of them, Gagne lost control of the boat. The boat rolled onto its left side, throwing everyone aboard into the water.

Ellie Goldenberg was caught face down under the engine cage. The marsh was shallow, but she could not raise her face out of the water to breathe. For ten minutes she remained stuck fast while her sister and mother tried to free her, but it took assistance from passengers on several other boats to raise the craft just enough to pull her out from under it.

Her mother, Renee Flax-Goldenberg, was a physician, and she began CPR on her daughter immediately, even as the young woman was lifted into another airboat. She kept this up while the second boat transported Ellie thirty miles to a boat ramp, where she could be transferred to a hospital. Despite her efforts, Ellie died a short time later at Kendell Regional Medical Center. The report lists drowning as her cause of death.

Renee and David Goldenberg, Ellie's father, escaped with non–life threatening injuries, though Ellie's sister Dana sustained second-degree burns on her left shoulder and received treatment at the hospital. Gagne was not injured.

The FWC opened an investigation of the incident, and it took barely a week before airboat tour operators, the South Florida Wildlands Association (SFWA), and the media began calling for stiffer regulations for airboat owners, pilots, and tour companies. When this accident happened, airboats were not required to have seat belts, airbags, or even windshields, making ejection because of a sudden maneuver a virtual certainty, said Matthew Schwartz, SFWA director, to the *South Florida Sun-Sentinel.*

While the accident that killed Ellie Goldenberg may have been a "freak," Schwartz said, there was no way to stop the airboat she was riding in when the broken-down airboat suddenly appeared in the trail ahead of them. "Airboats don't stop abruptly. There's no brake on an airboat to stop abruptly. He had to hit something to make it stop—and the passengers would continue to move at the speed [they were] traveling at the time."

The incident report issued by the FWC revealed that Gagne had used marijuana within twenty-four hours of operating the boat and had high levels of THC in his system. This led to a criminal investigation, but Gagne was not charged in Ellie Goldenberg's death because authorities "could not testify that his normal faculties were impaired," according to a statement from court prosecutor Laura Cespedes. Gagne retired from the airboat industry after the incident and refused to talk to the media about what happened.

David Goldenberg decided to turn the tragedy of his daughter's death into an opportunity to make meaningful change. As he told the *Miami Herald* on February 2, 2018, once he learned that "anyone can do whatever the hell they want" in the airboat tourism industry, he began working with representatives in the Florida State Legislature. His calls and emails to Florida legislators led to a movement to pass Ellie's Law,

HR 1211, and a companion law in the Florida Senate, SB 1612. The law requires standards for airboat operator courses, certification for pilots in CPR and first aid, and fines if tour operators do not comply. The Goldenbergs live in Pennsylvania, but David continued to work with legislators in Florida on the twin bills until they passed.

"When someone you love dies, you try and make sense of it, though there is no sense," he said to the *Herald*. Ellie's Law will "prevent some other parent from having to endure what we did, some other child from having to go through what she did."

Ellie's Law passed in 2018. Today airboat operators must complete a course with twenty-four hours of instruction—eight of those in class, and the rest on the water. The courses cover state and federal boating requirements, navigation rules, environmental and ecosystem awareness, and causes and prevention of airboat accidents. Passing a fifty-question final exam is required as well. Course instructors must have at least 120 hours of experience actually operating an airboat over the previous three years, as well as no felony convictions for the last five years. The new rules went into effect on July 1, 2019.

While David Goldenberg told the *Miami Herald* that he would like to see stiffer penalties for violating the new rules, he called the law "a step in the right direction." A stronger marijuana law would be more satisfying as well, he said. "Just because there's no marijuana law in Florida yet is not a good enough reason" for Gagne to have escaped prosecution, he noted.

Today's airboat passengers still need to be smart consumers of this service, selecting the most reputable airboat tour companies with the safest track record. The three named above as authorized tour operators within park boundaries are an excellent place to start in choosing a vendor for your own adventure.

Epilogue

HOW TO STAY ALIVE IN THE EVERGLADES

Are you ready to make the commitment to seeing all that the Everglades has to offer—its river of grass, mangrove swamps, dense forests, secluded waterways, fascinating wildlife, and open vistas—and living to tell the tale?

It's easier than you may think after reading this book. By taking some entirely reasonable precautions and following a few simple rules, your visit to the Everglades can be as peaceful and filled with wondrous sights as you wish.

Here are basic guidelines to help you, gathered from the advice of law enforcement, national park rangers, and all manner of experts on the special features of South Florida's wilderness.

On Land

- Stay on designated trails. There are not many places where you can wander off and get lost in the Everglades, as much of the land is impenetrable except on roads and well-marked trails. You can see plenty of marvelous sights from these established routes, so there is no need to try to bushwhack your way through dense growth. Watch for signs and markers to be sure you're heading in your intended direction—and always carry a map.

- Take fences and barriers seriously. There are no high ledges or precipices in the Everglades, but there are places where the dry land ends and water and muck begin, much of which provides a home for snakes, alligators, and other wildlife. Fences, guardrails, and barriers are there for your protection, *not* to keep you from enjoying your surroundings. The moment you step beyond a boundary, you risk injury.

- Know your limits. We come to the wilderness on vacations to take on greater challenges than we have ever tried before, often venturing into completely unfamiliar territory. Be sure that you understand the kinds of skills required to complete your adventure successfully. Hiking a three-mile trail in 90 degree heat and 90 percent humidity is a very different experience from walking around a Midwestern neighborhood in August, for example. Paddling a canoe or kayak all day through a maze of waterways can become dizzying and confusing—and exhausting for your arms and back. Go with someone who has the requisite experience to be sure you get home safely, and take all the necessary precautions, from carrying the right gear to recognizing that the challenge may be too great.

- Know facts from fiction. Everything from old movies to reality TV have led us to view the Everglades as a terrifying place filled with dangers, but most of these are just stories. There is no quicksand here, alligators do not actively hunt human beings, and "deadly sawgrass" may leave you with a few paper cut–like scratches, but it certainly can't kill you.

On the Road

- Watch out for traffic. When you stop at a pull-off along the side of a road, keep an eye out for oncoming traffic and fast-moving vehicles, just as you would on any busy street. Drivers gazing out over a spectacular view may not see you on the road, so watch out for people who are not watching out for you.

- If you're driving, watch the road. Cars slow down and stop unexpectedly on scenic roads. In the Everglades, any vista may be a place for birders or wildlife watchers to stop suddenly, pull over, and get out of their cars. Keep an eye out for unexpected pedestrians.

- Pass with utmost care. Every bend in the road can be a spot where a car may be coming toward you at top speed. Head-on collisions are common here on roads with one lane moving in each direction. Don't pass unless you have a clear view of what's ahead.

- Obey speed limits. The long, straight roads across the Everglades have speed limits, though some drivers see them as polite suggestions. High speeds are one of the main causes of accidents on these roads. Resist the temptation to put pedal to the metal, no matter how sunny and pleasant the ride may be.

Snakes

- Remember there are venomous snakes here—in particular, Florida cottonmouths, eastern coral snakes, dusky pigmy rattlesnakes, and eastern diamondback rattlesnakes—though you are unlikely to encounter them unless you venture out into the wilderness.

- Let them know you're coming. On a trail, make noise to alert snakes that you are in the vicinity, as they have little interest in people and will steer clear of you if given the chance.

- Watch where you step. If you come across a snake on a trail, do not attempt to pick it up or handle it in any way, and don't try to step over it. Wait for it to move off the trail. If it doesn't look like it's going to move, turn back. If you must step off the trail, look first to be sure there are no snakes where you put your feet.

- Do not wait to get treatment for a bite. Deaths from snakebite are exceedingly rare here, but a bite from a venomous snake in the Everglades has the potential to kill you within hours. In the very unlikely event that a snake bites you, call 911 immediately and tell them you've been bitten by a snake. The Miami-Dade Fire Rescue Venom Response Program maintains the largest antivenom bank in the country, so hospitals here will have access to exactly what you'll need to survive the bite.

Alligators

- Leave alligators alone. Generally, an alligator will not approach you. No matter what you may have seen in TikTok videos or selfies, these shy creatures see no benefit in a relationship with human beings.

- If the alligator's hissing, you're too close. Maintain a safe distance of at least fifteen feet from the animal. If you are at least fifteen feet away and it's still hissing, move farther away.

- Do not harass alligators. It seems ridiculous that this needs to be said, but do not attempt to tease an alligator, kick it, touch it, throw things at it, or poke it with a stick. Harassing an alligator is illegal in Florida, so you can be arrested for behaving foolishly with one. While they may look slow and lazy, alligators can move very fast when provoked.

- Pay attention to your surroundings. Keep an eye out near freshwater features like canals, ponds, streams, and lakes. Avoid areas of dense vegetation around water. If you see an alligator, put distance between the alligator and you as quickly as possible.

- Do not feed alligators. It is illegal to feed an alligator in Florida. Alligators that take food from humans come to associate humans with food and become more aggressive around people. Do not contribute to this.

- Skip the selfie. Turning your back on an alligator and inching in closer for a selfie is a bad idea. While there are no actual cases (that I know of) of a person being attacked from behind by an alligator while taking a selfie, there is no way for the animal to know what your intentions are when you make this potentially threatening move. Other national parks have plenty of stories of people being gored by buffalo, elk, or moose when a tourist tries to get in close for a photo, and Everglades National Park could be next. Don't take the chance on becoming a viral video.

- If you fish, throw your scraps in a trash can. When you leave fish scraps around, you attract alligators, which may then become accustomed to hanging around where fish scraps are plentiful. This amounts to feeding an alligator, which can have dire consequences.

- Swim only where it's safe. If an area has signs posted that warn of possible alligators, it means that one or more alligators have been sighted there. Do not swim or enter the water where you see these signs. An alligator can mistake your hand or foot for a fish and try to catch it, resulting in a severe bite.

- Swim in daylight. Alligators are more active at night, so stay out of the water after dark.

- Never leave children unattended. Do not let your children run around near water or play on the edge of a pond or stream without supervision. A tiny hand or foot in the water can be seen as prey by an alligator.

- Keep your pets away from alligators. Alligators may attack small dogs and cats that they know they can overpower quickly. Walk your pet some distance away from a pond or stream, even if there is a paved path along the water.

- If an alligator charges you, run away in a straight line. Do not run in a zigzag pattern, as this makes it easier for the alligator to catch you. Run directly away from the animal.

Airboats

- Choose a well-established and licensed tour company. Most airboat accidents happen on privately owned boats or on boats with inexperienced operators. Tour companies with a long history of operation will have pilots who are well trained and who have passed the tests required by the Florida Fish and Wildlife Conservation Commission. Check with the Everglades National Park website at www.nps.gov/ever/planyourvisit/guidedtours.htm to see which airboat businesses are authorized to tour inside the park, as these companies have been carefully vetted by park administration.

- Ask questions. It is absolutely reasonable to ask your tour operator about your pilot's experience level and the tour company's safety record. If your pilot appears to be under the influence of alcohol, marijuana, or drugs, do not get on the boat.

- Avoid the propeller. Keep your hands and feet away from the propeller, as that whirling propeller blade can maim or kill. Keep long hair away from the propeller as well.

- Wear sunscreen. It can seem cool and windy while you're cruising on an airboat at 30 mph, but you're still exposed to the sun's rays. A sunscreen above SPF 30 is a good idea.

- Consider noise protection. Airboats are loud and you'll be sitting right in front of the motor and propeller. Ear plugs will protect your hearing.

- Bring water and snacks. It's rare that an airboat breaks down in the wilderness, but if it does, you may have to wait a while for rescue. Water and salty snacks can help keep your electrolytes balanced under the hot sun.

Backcountry

- Don't boat or hike alone. If you're heading into the Everglades backcountry, bring a friend. The lure of solitude in the wild may be very attractive, but lone hikers and boaters can go missing for weeks, months, or even indefinitely. Hiking, camping, and boating with at least one other person can make the difference between a great day in the wilderness and a misadventure that ends in tragedy.

- Let someone know where you're going. If you're not hiking or boating in one of the national parks in South Florida, you may not have a ranger with whom to file your plans. Make sure someone knows where you intend to go and print them a Google map with your intended route. Tell them when to expect you back as well, so they know when to start searching for you if you don't return on time. This information can mean the difference between a safe arrival at home and vanishing into the wilderness forever.

- If you have any questions, ask a ranger. If you are going to explore Everglades National Park or Big Cypress National Preserve, talk to rangers at the visitor center about where you plan to go and what they know about your intended route. Rangers know which trails may be compromised by weather events, where flooding or impassable mud may be a problem, what areas might be on fire, and what other hazards may be in store. If they warn you not to take a certain route, think very seriously about changing your plans. Likewise, if people coming back from a particular route tell you that they encountered dangerous conditions, don't go that way.

- Pack for every possibility. Every time you step out on a trail or climb into a canoe, there's a chance you'll encounter situations that require an abrupt change of plans. Maybe you miss a turn and find yourself lost in the wilderness. Perhaps a storm front moves in without warning or someone in your party sustains an injury. Any of these circumstances can extend your time outdoors, turning a day hike or paddle into an overnight stay or forcing you to seek cover off trail.

Remember: You won't be the first person to feel compromised in the backcountry—in fact, it happens often enough that there's a checklist of things you should have with you every time you go out. The list is known as the "Ten Essentials"—that is, ten items that can help you take control of your situation and make it back home in one piece. The Ten Essentials were first developed by the Mountaineers, a club for hikers and climbers founded in the 1930s, and they've since updated the list in their book,

Mountaineering: The Freedom of the Hills, in which they group individual items to provide a more thorough list. If you carry all of these things with you on every hike or paddle, you'll be ready for most of the things nature throws at you.

- navigation tools: a good map and compass (for backcountry hiking, consider adding a GPS beacon that you can use to alert rescuers to your location if you become injured)
- sun protection: sunscreen and sunglasses
- insulation: extra clothing and a poncho
- illumination: a flashlight or headlamp
- first-aid kit
- fire starter: a lighter or waterproof matches
- repair kit and tools (I add a roll of duct tape to this one)
- nutrition: more food than you think you'll need
- hydration: more water than you think you'll need
- emergency shelter: a space blanket or ultralight tarp

In addition, parks recommend that you carry an emergency whistle, so you have a way to alert others in the area if you or your hiking partner is injured and needs assistance.

Finally, insect repellent is an absolute must in the Everglades. Mosquitos are not active year-round, but you can encounter them in any season around sunrise and sunset and in areas of shade or high grass. There are forty-three species of mosquitos in the Everglades, but take heart—only thirteen species bite. Bug sprays with a high percentage of DEET are the most effective here. Wearing long sleeves and long pants during the buggiest season (summer) can help you avoid a lot of bites.

Keep in mind that while your smartphone may provide maps, a bright light, and life-saving contact with the rest of the world, it will run out of power in the great outdoors and you'll have nowhere to charge it, so bring extra batteries or a solar charging device.

What About Crime?

There is a lot of murder in this book, but you may have noticed one thing that links almost all of these crimes: In just about every case, the victim knew his or her assailant. These were not random crimes against visitors who happened to be in the right place at the wrong time.

As a tourist in the Everglades, you have little to fear from criminals. Even so, you can avoid potentially dangerous situations the same way you do at home: by paying attention.

- Don't create temptations. Don't leave your valuables in your car, wear expensive jewelry, or leave your purse or wallet unattended. At night, stay in places that are well lit, and go out in pairs or groups. Don't wander off into dark paths or alleys.

- Pay attention to the people you see. If someone makes you uncomfortable, put some distance between you and them as quickly as you can.

- Don't look like a target. Criminals looking for a random victim generally do not choose confident, alert people who appear able to defend themselves. Stay focused, aware, and assertive. Try not to look distracted, meek, and unsure of yourself. Instead of using a purse that dangles from your arm or shoulder, carry your wallet and identification in a pocket, a waist pack worn in front, or a concealed pouch.

- Be careful with controlled substances. You may be on vacation, but staggering around drunk or high makes you an easy target for someone looking to hold you up. Bars, pubs, parties, and the like are lots of fun, but make sure you are sober enough to take care of yourself when you are ready to leave.

- Trust your instincts. If you feel like something isn't right but you can't put your finger on what's wrong, steer clear of it. Have your phone in your hand so you can press the emergency call button if you need to.

I urge you to explore this South Florida paradise just as Nic and I have on countless occasions, to experience the expanses of water and grass, the abundant wildlife, the stunning foliage and flowering plants, the night sounds and skies, and the one-of-a-kind ecosystem that make this such a fascinating and compelling part of Florida. Leave the congested beaches and flashy cities behind and find your way to a Florida that shows us how a vast wilderness can take care of itself for eons, if left to its own devices. Just follow a few simple precautions, and you will make certain that your visit here is memorable for all the right reasons. The Everglades awaits you. Find your way here.

References

INTRODUCTION: IT'S NOT WHAT YOU THINK

Associated Press, "Babbitt Seals Swampland Buy," *Florida Today*, February 12, 1998, B-1, www.newspapers.com/image/174948663/?terms=death%20%22Everglades%20National%20Park%22&match=1.

Daytona Gazette-News, "The End of the Everglades," June 29, 1901, 4, www.newspapers.com/image/76294221/?terms=death%20Everglades&match=1.

Detroit Free Press, "Florida's State Land Opening," January 9, 1910, 15, www.newspapers.com/image/118653393/?terms=death%20everglades&match=1.

Miami News, "Exhibition Farm and Two Dredges Will Help," August 13, 1909, 1, www.newspapers.com/image/297523048/?terms=death%20everglades&match=1.

Tampa Bay Times, "Bush Signs Law to Help Restore Everglades," May 17, 2000, 44, www.newspapers.com/image/327301570/?terms=Everglades%20death&match=1.

CHAPTER 1: THE DESPERADO OF CHATHAM BEND

Arkansas Gazette, "Belle Starr's Husband," February 21, 1889, 4, www.newspapers.com/image/138023343/?terms=%22E.A.%20Watson%22&match=1.

Arkansas Gazette, "Captured and Jailed," September 19, 1889, 5, www.newspapers.com/image/134042449/?terms=%22E.A.%20Watson%22&match=1.

Arkansas Gazette, "Charged With the Murder," February 9, 1889, 1, www.newspapers.com/image/138022970/?terms=%22E.A.%20Watson%22&match=1.

Charles W. Tebeau, *The Story of Chokoloskee Bay Country* (Coral Gables, FL: University of Miami Press, 1955), 77–81.

Coastal Breeze News, "The Story of Edgar J. Watson: The Infamous Businessman & Serial Killer," December 17, 2020, www.coastalbreezenews.com/opinion/columnists/the-story-of-edgar-j-watson-the-infamous-businessman-serial-killer/article_e53a5f09-ff02-5b4f-9273-a0753cfbf46e.html#tncms-source=login.

Daily Arkansas Gazette, "Insufficient Evidence," February 24, 1889, 1, www.newspapers.com/image/138023424/?terms=%22E.A.%20Watson%22&match=1.

Fort Pierce News, "Some State Happenings," March 25, 1910, 8, www.newspapers.com/image/61701213/?terms=%22Leslie%20Cox%22escape&match=1.

Fort Smith Elevator, "Trial of E. A. Watson," March 2, 1889, 4, www.newspapers.com/image/30430780/?terms=Belle%20Starr&match=1.

Gainesville Daily Sun, "Mike Tolen, a Prominent Farmer Residing," March 26, 1908, 5, www.newspapers.com/image/98488370/?terms=%22Mike%20Tolen%22&match=1.

Indian Citizen, "A. E. Watson, Accused of Murdering Belle Star," Atoka, OK, March 16, 1889, 2, www.newspapers.com/image/611444084/?terms=Belle%20Starr&match=1.

John O'Connor, "The Legend of Chokoloskee," *Oxford American*, November 9, 2015, https://main.oxfordamerican.org/magazine/item/695-the-legend-of-chokoloskee.

Kansas City Gazette, "Belle Starr," Mo., March 7, 1889, 4, www.newspapers.com/image/367228395/?terms=Belle%20Starr&match=1.

Nixon Smiley, "Witness Was Lynched—Murders Unsolved," *Miami Herald*, October 27, 1968, 4D, www.newspapers.com/image/621683576/?terms=death%20%22Ten%20Thousand%20Islands%22&match=1.

Ocala Banner, "Mike Tolen, a Prominent Columbia County Farmer," April 3, 1908, 9, www.newspapers.com/image/194784512/?terms=%22Mike%20Tolan%22&match=1.

Peter Matthiessen, *Shadow Country Trilogy: Lost Man's River* (New York: Modern Library, 2008).

Richard D. Arnott, "Belle Starr," historynet.com, www.historynet.com/belle-starr.htm.

Tahlequah Arrow, "Belle Starr," Okla., February 21, 1889, 4, www.newspapers.com/image/657441346/?terms=Belle%20Starr&match=1.

Tampa Tribune, "Big Murder Trial in Madison Today," December 14, 1908, 5, www.newspapers.com/image/326021365/?terms=%22E.J.%20Watson%22&match=1.

Tampa Tribune, "Death in Cane-Mill," January 14, 1904, 1, www.newspapers.com/clip/70613641/bob-daniels-dies-working-for-e-j/.

Tampa Tribune, "Farmer Murdered as His Brother Was Last Summer," March 25, 1908, 1, www.newspapers.com/image/325748178/?terms=%22Mike%20Tolen%22&match=1.

Tampa Tribune, "Two Men and Woman Are Murdered in Lee," October 25, 1910, 1, www.newspapers.com/image/326590932/?terms=%22Ellen%20Smith%22&match=1.

Weekly Tribune, "Murderers of Three Killed by Posse Resisting Arrest," Tampa, FL, October 27, 1910, 1, www.newspapers.com/image/327943598/?terms=E.%20J.%20Watson&match=1.

CHAPTER 2: PLUMAGE TO DIE FOR

Audubon Florida, "History of Audubon in Florida," https://fl.audubon.org/about-us/history.

Daily Miami Metropolis, "Guy Bradley Was Instantly Killed," July 15, 1905, 1, www.newspapers.com/image/297518434/?terms=Guy%20Bradley&match=1.

Daily Miami Metropolis, "Guy Bradley Was Wounded," July 14, 1905, 8, www.news papers.com/image/297518408/.

Frank M. Chapman, *Bird-Lore*, vol. 11 (New York: MacMillan Company, 1909), https://play.google.com/books/reader?id=1Am-kDi2WIkC&pg=GBS.PR1& hl=en.

Lindsey Williams and U. S. Cleveland, *Our Fascinating Past: Charlotte Harbor, The Early Years* (Punta Gorda, FL: Charlotte Harbor Area Historical Society, 1993).

Miami Daily Metropolis, "Smith Ordered His House Burned," July 21, 1905, 8, www .newspapers.com/image/297520323/?terms=Guy%20Bradley&match=1.

Miami Evening Record, "Plumer's Revenge," August 9, 1905, 1, www.newspapers.com/ image/615651846/?terms=Guy%20Bradley&match=1.

Miami Evening Record, "The Bradley Murder," July 17, 1905, 1, www.newspapers.com/ image/615651124/?terms=Guy%20Bradley&match=1.

Miami Metropolis, "The Slayer of Guy Bradley Was Acquitted," December 6, 1905, 1, www.newspapers.com/image/299794122/?terms=Guy%20Bradley&match=1.

Morning Post, "Tragedy of the White Heron, Victim of Women's Vanity," August 21, 1905, 8, www.newspapers.com/image/446291227/?terms=Guy%20Bradley& match=1.

Muncie Morning Star, "Dies to Save the Birds," August 12, 1905, 5, www.newspapers .com/image/249672279/?terms=Guy%20Bradley&match=1.

New York Herald, "Victim of a Plot," August 9, 1905, 5, www.newspapers.com/image/ 279120745/?terms=Guy%20Bradley&match=1.

Stuart B. McIver, *Death in the Everglades: The Murder of Guy Bradley, America's First Martyr to Environmentalism* (Gainesville: University Press of Florida, 2003).

Times-Tribune, "First American Martyr to Bird Protection," September 22, 1905, 9, www.newspapers.com/image/533544266/?terms=Guy%20Bradley&match=1.

U.S. Fish and Wildlife Service, "Lacey Act," www.fws.gov/international/laws-treaties-agreements/us-conservation-laws/lacey-act.html.

William Sounder, "How Two Women Ended the Deadly Feather Trade," *Smithsonian Magazine*, March 2013, www.smithsonianmag.com/science-nature/ how-two-women-ended-the-deadly-feather-trade-23187277/.

CHAPTER 3: THE MURDEROUS KING OF THE EVERGLADES

Daytona Daily News, "John Ashley, Desperate Chief of So. Florida Outlaw Gang Run Down By Posse," February 26, 1915, 1, www.newspapers.com/image/ 612575124/?terms=%22John%20Ashley%22&match=1.

Fort Myers News-Press, "Ashley Is Lodged in Jail," February 26, 1915, 1, www.news papers.com/image/216538257/?terms=%22John%20Ashley%22&match=1.

Fort Myers News-Press, "Asks Government Aid," January 18, 1912, 3, www.newspapers .com/image/211101851/?terms=%22Desoto%20Tiger%22&match=1.

Fort Myers News-Press, "Murder Trial Next Week," November 13, 1914, 1, www.news papers.com/image/216534047/?terms=%22Desoto%20Tiger%22&match=1.

Miami Herald, "Abandoned Search for John Ashley," November 18, 1914, 1, www.news papers.com/image/616151480/?terms=%22Desoto%20Tiger%22&match=1.

Miami Herald, "Bob Ashley, Notorious Bandit, Shot and Killed Deputy Sheriff Hendrickson In Cold Blood," June 3, 1915, 1, 5, 7, www.newspapers.com/image/616182216/.

Miami Herald, "F.E.C. RY. Offers Reward of $500," February 11, 1915, 8, www.newspapers.com/image/616041981/?terms=%22Train%2033%22&match=1.

Miami Herald, "John Ashley, Alleged Slayer of Desoto Tiger, Gets Away," November 15, 1914, 8, www.newspapers.com/image/616150314/?terms=%22Desoto%20Tiger%22&match=1.

Miami Herald, "John Ashley on the Stand, Testified in Own Defense," April 4, 1915, 2, 5, www.newspapers.com/image/616155589/.

Miami Herald, "Red Lantern Death Signal to 4 Bandits," November 3, 1924, 1, 2, www.newspapers.com/image/616375035/?terms=%22John%20Ashley%22&match=1.

Miami Herald, "Reward of $500 Has Been Offered for John Ashley," November 16, 1914, 2, www.newspapers.com/image/616150819/?terms=%22Desoto%20Tiger%22&match=1.

Miami Herald, "Ten Jurymen Were Tentatively Accepted," March 30, 1915, 3, www.newspapers.com/image/616152184/?terms=%22John%20Ashley%22&match=1.

Miami News, "Ashley is Sentenced to Die on the Gallows for Murder of Desoto Tiger," April 9, 1915, 1, www.newspapers.com/image/298514422/?terms=%22John%20Ashley%22&match=1.

Miami News, "Ashleys Indicted for Stuart Bank Robbery," March 12, 1915, 2, www.newspapers.com/image/298513795/?terms=%22John%20Ashley%22&match=1.

Miami News, "Ashley's Fate in Hands of Jury by Tonight, Closing Arguments Made," April 5, 1915, 1, 2, www.newspapers.com/image/298514337.

Miami News, "Jury Trying Ashley for Murder Unable to Arrive at Verdict," July 1, 1914, 2, www.newspapers.com/image/298218154/?terms=%22Desoto%20Tiger%22&match=1.

Miami News, "Offers Reward for Capture of John Ashley," January 11, 1912, 1, 4, www.newspapers.com/image/297346503/.

New Smyrna Daily News, "John Ashley Still Eludes Pursuers," November 20, 1914, 3B, www.newspapers.com/image/15310604/?terms=%22Desoto%20Tiger%22&match=1.

Orlando Evening Star, "Ashley Gang Has Become Terror to People of Lower East Coast," February 25, 1915, 2, www.newspapers.com/image/340859755/?terms=Boynton%20shot&match=1.

Orlando Evening Star, "Jailor and Policeman Killed by Bob Ashley Trying to Free Brother," June 10, 1915, 6, www.newspapers.com/image/340801394/?terms=%22Desoto%20Tiger%22&match=1.

Orlando Evening Star, "John Ashley Tries to Break Out of Jail," November 18, 1915, 6, www.newspapers.com/image/340820633/?terms=%22John%20Ashley%22&match=1.

Orlando Evening Star, "The Escape of an Indian Slayer," November 19, 1914, 4, www.newspapers.com/image/340843831/?terms=%22John%20Ashley%22&match=1.

Orlando Sentinel, "Government Took Hand in the Capture of Indian Slayer," May 2, 1914, 3, www.newspapers.com/image/313659838/?terms=%22Desoto%20Tiger% 22&match=1.

Tampa Times, "Ashley Gave Himself Up," May 1, 1914, 13, www.newspapers.com/ image/325815607/?terms=%22Desoto%20Tiger%22&match=1.

Tampa Times, "Ashley Gave Himself Up," May 1, 1914, 1B, www.newspapers.com/ image/325815607/?terms=%22Desoto%20Tiger%22&match=1.

Tampa Times, "Indians Ask Reward Be Offered for Murderer," January 16, 1912, 3, www.newspapers.com/image/325520928/?terms=%22Desoto%20Tiger%22& match=1.

Tampa Tribune, "John Ashley Guilty," April 6, 1915, 11, www.newspapers.com/image/ 326024369/?terms=%22John%20Ashley%22&match=1.

Tampa Tribune, "Murder of Indian, Desoto Tiger, Caught," April 29, 1914, 9, www.news papers.com/image/326525962/?terms=%22Desoto%20Tiger%22&match=1.

Tampa Tribune, "Slayer of Desoto Tiger Is Hounded," January 11, 1912, 11, www.news papers.com/image/326559530/?terms=%22Desoto%20Tiger%22&match=1.

CHAPTER 4: HURRICANES WITH NO NAMES: 1926 AND 1928

Associated Press, "325 Known Dead, 4,000 Injured on East Coast," *Orlando Sentinel*, September 21, 1926, 1, www.newspapers.com/image/223058995/?terms=hurricane %20Moorehaven&match=1.

Associated Press, "500 Killed in Florida; Damage in Millions," *Miami Herald*, September 20, 1926, 2, www.newspapers.com/image/616541140/?terms=hurricane% 20Moorehaven&match=1.

Carter W. Hodding, *Stolen Water: Saving the Everglades from its Friends, Foes, and Florida* (New York: Atria Books, 2004), 8.

E. Blake, C. Landsea, and E. Gibney, "The Deadliest, Costliest, and Most Intense United States Tropical Cyclones from 1851 to 2010 (and Other Frequently Requested Hurricane Facts)," National Weather Service, National Hurricane Center, Miami, FL, August 2011, www.nhc.noaa.gov/pdf/nws-nhc-6.pdf.

Eliot Kleinberg, *Black Cloud: The Great Florida Hurricane of 1928* (New York: Carroll & Graf, 2003).

Fort Lauderdale News, "Influenza Breaks Out at Clewiston with Forty Cases," September 22, 1928, 1, www.newspapers.com/image/229875987/?terms=hurricane% 20Everglades&match=1.

Helen Hill, "Miami Beach Cityscape: The Collins Avenue Story," http://funandsun .com/1tocf/allgosf/mbf/collinsave.html.

Henry Reno. "Workers Say Few Died in Pelican Bay." *Miami Herald*, September 27, 1928, 1, 11, https://www.newspapers.com/image/616548599/

Jack Falconnier, "Moore Haven Now Sepulcher; Storm Ruined Lake Town," *Tampa Bay Times*, September 23, 1926, 1–2, www.newspapers.com/image/314689807.

Miami Herald, "Beginning to Realize," August 6, 1928, 4, www.newspapers.com/image/ 616551460/?terms=hurricane%20Everglades&match=1.

Miami Herald, "Moore Haven Situation is Declared Critical," October 3, 1926, 6, www .newspapers.com/image/616544721/?terms=%22Governor%20Martin%22%20% 22Moore%20Haven%22&match=1.

Miami Herald, "Relief Trains Rushed to Hurricane Area," September 20, 1926, 1, 2, www.newspapers.com/image/616541140/?terms=hurricane%20Moorehaven& match=1.

Miami Herald, "Restoration Ordered," October 3, 1926, 6, www.newspapers.com/image/ 616544721/?terms=%22Governor%20Martin%22%20%22Moore%20Haven% 22&match=1.

Miami News, "Pelican Bay's Toll May Rise Over 400 Dead," September 23, 1928, 1, www.newspapers.com/image/301933431/?terms=death%20everglades&match=1.

Palm Beach Post, "Tropical Storms Moving Up Coast May Strike City," September 17, 1926, 1, www.newspapers.com/image/133337185/.

Pensacola News Journal, "Continued vigilance of Red Cross groups helps stricken area," September 28, 1926, 1, www.newspapers.com/image/352745920/?terms=hurri- cane%20Moorehaven&match=1.

Pensacola News Journal, "Faith Retained in Florida by Men of Vision," November 8, 1926, 8, www.newspapers.com/image/352899007/?terms=hurricane%20Moore- haven&match=1.

Pensacola News Journal, "People Ask Assurance of Protection from Future Flood Waters," September 30, 1926, 1, www.newspapers.com/image/352745936/?terms =hurricane%20Moorehaven&match=1.

Pensacola News Journal, "Swam 3 Miles with Baby on Back; 2 Were Drowned," Sep- tember 24, 1926, 1, www.newspapers.com/image/352745880/?terms=hurricane% 20Moorehaven&match=1.

Ralph Wallace, "Death in the Everglades," *St. Louis Post-Dispatch*, September 27, 1945, 3D, www.newspapers.com/image/138427727/?terms=death%20Everglades& match=1.

Richard Blaisdell, "Moore Haven Toll of Death Is Set at 125," *Tampa Times*, Septem- ber 20, 1926, 1–2, www.newspapers.com/image/332748008.

Tallahassee Democrat, "Threat of Epidemic Stalks Everglades as Greatest Menace," September 21, 1928, 1, www.newspapers.com/image/244384028/?terms=death% 20everglades&match=1.

Tampa Bay Times, "Rehabilitation of Moore Haven Will Start This Week," November 4, 1926, 3, www.newspapers.com/image/315026322/?terms=hurricane%20Moore- haven&match=1.%20%20https.

Tampa Tribune, "Fisherman Saves 19 from Lake at Height of Hurricane's Fury," Sep- tember 21, 1926, 2, www.newspapers.com/image/332392702/?terms=hurricane& match=1.

Tampa Tribune, "Sufferers in Flood Demand Lower Level for Lake Okeechobee," Sep- tember 23, 1926, 1, www.newspapers.com/image/332393421/.

Tampa Tribune, "Survivors Facing Forcible Removal to Avoid Disease," September 23, 1926, 1, www.newspapers.com/image/332393421/.

Tampa Tribune, "Typhoid Epidemic Imminent Over Lower East Coast," September 23, 1926, 1, www.newspapers.com/image/332393421/.

Travers Green, "Seven Victims in Sebring Morgues Awaiting Burial" and "First Moore Haven Dead Brought from Flooded Territory," *Tampa Tribune*, September 21, 1926, 1 and 3, www.newspapers.com/image/332392684.

Truman Felt, "Burial Parties Declare 1,800 Bodies Found," *Miami News*, September 21, 1928, 1, www.newspapers.com/image/301932653/?terms=hurricane%20Everglades&match=1.

CHAPTER 5: RUNNING RUM: DEATH OF A POLICE CHIEF

Associated Press, "Alleged Buying of Testimony to Be Investigated," *Bradenton Herald*, November 22, 1932, 1, 5, www.newspapers.com/image/682754797/?terms=%22W.E.%20Hutto%22&match=1.

Associated Press, "Collier Sheriff and Others Named in Liquor Charges," *Tampa Tribune*, October 14, 1932, 1, www.newspapers.com/image/332603096/?terms=%22W.E.%20Hutto%22&match=1.

Bradenton Herald, "Negro Sought in Death of Officer," December 29, 1931, 8, www.newspapers.com/image/682763418/?terms=death%20everglades&match=1.

Fort Myers News-Press, "Collier County Jury Begins Its Murder Inquiry," January 26, 1932, 1–2, www.newspapers.com/image/219684823.

Fort Myers News-Press, "Davis' Testimony Injects 'Blonde Man' Into Murder," May 3, 1932, 1, 5, www.newspapers.com/image/219532721/.

Fort Myers News-Press, "Hutto Murder Trial Starts Again Today in Collier County," May 2, 1932, 1, www.newspapers.com/image/219532696/?terms=%22Robert%20Brown%22&match=1.

Fort Myers News-Press, "Negro, Acquitted in Hutto Murder Trial, Goes Free," May 7, 1932, 1, 5, www.newspapers.com/image/219532823/.

Fort Myers News-Press, "Negro, Acquitted in Hutto Trial, Goes Free," May 7, 1932, 1, 5, www.newspapers.com/image/219532837/.

Fort Myers News-Press, "Negro Gives New Story of Hutto Murder in Trial," May 5, 1932, 1, 4, www.newspapers.com/image/219532781/.

Fort Myers News-Press, "Negro Is Arrested in Hutto Slaying," December 30, 1931, 1–2, www.newspapers.com/image/220506321.

Fort Myers News-Press, "Negro Still Insists He Was Kidnapped by Slayers of Officer," January 10, 1932, 1, www.newspapers.com/image/219683444/?terms=%22W.E.%20Hutto%22&match=1.

Fort Myers News-Press, "Seminole Tells Jury Negro was Killer of Hutto," May 4, 1932, 1–2, www.newspapers.com/image/219532744/.

Fort Myers News-Press, "Special Grand Jury to be Called to Investigate Slaying of Police Chief W. E. Hutto at Everglades," January 17, 1932, 1, www.newspapers.com/image/219684110/?terms=%22W.E.%20Hutto%22&match=1.

Fort Myers News-Press, "Strayhorn Says Freeing of Davis Was a Surprise," January 25, 1932, 1, 6, www.newspapers.com/image/219684746/.

Fort Myers News-Press, "Warrant Issued for Negro Held in Hutto Death," January 2, 1932, 1, www.newspapers.com/image/219682817/?terms=%22W.E.%20Hutto%22&match=1.

Miami Herald, "Everglades Officer Victim of Unidentified Motorist," December 25, 1931, 1, www.newspapers.com/image/617427311/?terms=death%20everglades&match=1.

Miami Herald, "Seven Are on Trial as Five Are Freed," May 10, 1933, 2, www.newspapers.com/image/617423429/?terms=%22W.E.%20Hutto%22&match=1.

Miami News, "Negro Re-arrested after His Release," January 7, 1932, 3, www.newspapers.com/image/298367549/?terms=%22W.E.%20Hutto%22&match=1.

Mrs. Foster K. Floy, "Everglades," *Fort Myers News-Press*, June 31, 1930, 5, www.newspapers.com/image/221086554/?terms=%22W.E.%20Hutto%22&match=1.

Mrs. Foster K. Floy, "Everglades," *Fort Myers News-Press*, June 4, 1930, 2, www.newspapers.com/image/221066225/?terms=%22W.E.%20Hutto%22&match=1.

Mrs. Foster K. Floy, "Everglades," *Fort Myers News-Press*, May 1, 1930, 2, www.newspapers.com/image/216977132/?terms=%22W.E.%20Hutto%22&match=1.

Orlando Evening Star, "Five Are Held in Slaying of Chief," October 23, 1932, 1, www.newspapers.com/image/289922501/?terms=%22W.E.%20Hutto%22&match=1.

Orlando Evening Star, "Five Are Held in Slaying of Chief," October 23, 1932, 1, www.newspapers.com/image/289922501/?terms=%22W.E.%20Hutto%22&match=1.

Chapter 6: Unintended Consequences: Deaths on the Tamiami Trail

Associated Press, "20 Trapped in Bus Drown," *Tampa Times*, January 25, 1937, 1, 3, www.newspapers.com/image/332782175/.

Associated Press, "Safer Tamiami Highway Urged after Accident," *Tampa Bay Times*, January 27, 1937, 9, www.newspapers.com/image/315330591/.

Associated Press, "Survivors Tell of Terror in Everglades Bus Tragedy," *Tampa Times*, January 25, 1937, 1, 4, www.newspapers.com/image/332782175/.

Fort Myers News-Press, "17 Die as Bus Runs in Canal Out of Miami," January 26, 1937, 1–2, www.newspapers.com/image/219843170.

Fort Myers News-Press, "Eye Witnesses Here Tell of Bus Disaster on Trail," January 26, 1937, 1–2, www.newspapers.com/image/219843170.

Fort Myers News-Press, "Mounted Officer Killed on Trail," January 19, 1929, 1, www.newspapers.com/image/216561220/?terms=Tamiami%20death&match=1.

Fort Myers News-Press, "War Roads in Florida," August 2, 1940, 6, www.newspapers.com/image/220416389/?terms=%22Tamiami%20Trail%22%20guard%20rails&match=1.

Fort Myers News-Press, "Woman Killed in Accident on Tamiami Trail," March 25, 1929, 1, www.newspapers.com/image/216566952/?terms=body%20Everglades&match=1.

Henry O. Reno, "17 Drown in Bus, 3 Are Unidentified," *Miami Herald*, January 26, 1937, 1, 9, 10, www.newspapers.com/image/617128856/.

Miami Herald, "Jury Blames Bus Company for Tragedy," January 30, 1937, 1, www
.newspapers.com/image/617130143/?terms=bus%20disaster%20%22Tamiami%
20Trail%22&match=1.

Miami Herald, "Miamian Dies in Everglades Motor Crash," June 8, 1929, 1, www.news
papers.com/image/616572204/?terms=death%20everglades&match=1.

Miami Herald, "Mounted Patrolman Killed in Collision," January 20, 1929, 1, www
.newspapers.com/image/616575222/?terms=Patrol%20Officer%20Irwin&
match=1.

Miami Herald, "Too Much Speed?" January 30, 1937, 6, www.newspapers.com/image/
617130178/.

Miami News, "Third Person Dies in Trail Accident," April 4, 1938, 20, www.newspapers
.com/image/298465294/?terms=%22Tamiami%20Trail%22%20guard%20rails&
match=1.

National Park Service, "Tamiami Trail: Next Steps," www.nps.gov/articles/tamiami-
trail-next-steps.htm.

Tampa Bay Times, "2 Bus Victims Are Identified," January 27, 1937, 1, 6, www.news
papers.com/image/315330289/.

Tampa Times, "First Pictures of Bus Wreck on Tamiami Trail in which 17 Lost Lives,"
January 26, 1937, 1, www.newspapers.com/image/332782419/?terms=bus%
20disaster%20%22Tamiami%20Trail%22&match=1.

Tampa Tribune, "Bus Accident Starts Move to Guard Highway," January 27, 1937, 4,
www.newspapers.com/image/327195506/?terms=bus%20disaster%20%22Tami-
ami%20Trail%22&match=1.

Tampa Tribune, "Fatal Accident Held Unavoidable by Coroner," June 9, 1929, 3, www
.newspapers.com/image/332488563/?terms=%22Waddie%20A.%20McCreary%
22&match=1.

William Stuart Hill, "Dream Is Realized by Tamiami Trail," *Miami Herald*, April 26,
1928, 14, www.newspapers.com/image/616658665/.

CHAPTER 7: MURDER OF A MOONSHINER

Bradenton Herald, "WPB Man Is Sought in Moonshiner's Death," December 12, 1958,
2, www.newspapers.com/image/717116862/?terms=Moonshiner%20body&
match=1.

Brian Osbourne, "Warrant to Be Issued Today Charging Holzapfel with Killing of
Harvey," *Palm Beach Post*, October 7, 1960, 1, www.newspapers.com/image/
133675450/?terms=Floyd%20Holzapfel&match=1.

Ed Pfister, "A Blunder Made on Suspect?" *Miami Herald*, December 14, 1958, 47, www
.newspapers.com/image/618388445/?terms=%22Lew%20Gene%20Harvey%22&
match=1.

Ed Pfister, "Law Joins Forces on Canal Murder," *Miami Herald*, November 22, 1958, 21,
www.newspapers.com/image/619077841/?terms=%22Lew%20Gene%20Harvey%
22&match=1.

Ernie Hutter, "Chillingworth Bid Fortune to Live—Died Calmly with His Wife in Ocean," *Palm Beach Post*, October 6, 1960, 1, 2, www.newspapers.com/image/ 133675295.

Fort Lauderdale News, "Holzapfel Has Admitted Killing Chillingworths," October 6, 1960, 1, 10, www.newspapers.com/image/230446834/?terms=Floyd%20Holzap-fel&match=1.

Ian Trontz, "Racketeering, Revenge and Little Remorse," *Palm Beach Post*, May 3, 1996, 1, 12, www.newspapers.com/image/134637341/.

Jack Ledden, "Peel Denies Plot Charge," *Palm Beach Post*, March 25, 1961, 1, 5, 6, 7, www.newspapers.com/image/133664654/.

Jim Bishop, Admitted-Slayer Holzapfel May Be Miscalculating in Testifying Against Joe Peel," *Tampa Tribune*, March 9, 1961, 2B, www.newspapers.com/image/ 331476954/.

Jim Bishop, "Joe Peel Sits Fascinated As Ex-Pals Indict, Re-Indict Him in Chilling-worth Case," *Tampa Tribune*, March 21, 1961, 9, www.newspapers.com/image/ 329652835/.

Miami Herald, "Accused Moonshiner Gang-Murder Victim," November 15, 1958, 2, www.newspapers.com/image/619068904/?terms=%22Lew%20Gene%20Harvey% 22&match=1.

Miami Herald, "Holzapfel Surrenders, Makes Bond," January 6, 1959, 3, www.news papers.com/image/618553666/?terms=Floyd%20Holzapfel&match=1.

Miami Herald, "Miles Admits Death Plot," December 20, 1960, 1, www.newspapers .com/image/619385970/?terms=Floyd%20Holzapfel&match=1.

Miami Herald, "Nation Asked to Seek Canal Killer Suspect," December 12, 1958, 3, www.newspapers.com/image/618388103/?terms=%22Lew%20Gene%20Harvey% 22&match=1.

Miami Herald, "Two Palm Beach Killings Linked?" November 16, 1958, 43, www.news papers.com/image/619069106/?terms=%22Lew%20Gene%20Harvey%22& match=1.

Miami News, "Holzapfel Named As Slayer," October 6, 1960, 1, 8, www.newspapers .com/image/301000158/.

Miami News, "Man Surrenders in Forgery Case," January 6, 1959, 5B, www.newspapers .com/image/298675063/?terms=Floyd%20Holzapfel&match=1.

Orlando Evening Star, "Holzapfel Arraignment Due Monday," October 8, 1960, 1, www .newspapers.com/image/290452167/?terms=Floyd%20Holzapfel&match=1.

Palm Beach Post, "Chillingworth Death Laid to Pair," November 4, 1960, 1, 6, www .newspapers.com/image/132382328/.

Palm Beach Post, "Lew Harvey Out on Bond When Killed," November 5, 1958, 1, www .newspapers.com/image/133608055/?terms=%22Lew%20Gene%20Harvey%22& match=1.

Paul Wilder, "Jury Convicts Joe Peel in Chillingworth Murder, But Spares His Life," *Tampa Tribune*, March 31, 1961, 1, www.newspapers.com/image/329710944/.

Paul Wilder, "They Cracked the Chillingworth Case," *Tampa Tribune*, April 9, 1961, 3E, www.newspapers.com/image/329736024/?terms=Floyd%20Holzapfel& match=1.

Paul Wilder, "Undercover Agent Says Peel Plotted To Kill Holzapfel," *Tampa Tribune*, March 21, 1961, 1, www.newspapers.com/image/329652153/.

Ray Linders, "Chillingworth Mystery Ranks by Itself," *Miami Herald*, October 5, 1960, 1A, 18A, www.newspapers.com/image/619089458.

Sam Tranum, "Last of Judge's 1955 Killers Dies in Obscurity," *South Florida Sun-Sentinel*, May 30, 2004, www.sun-sentinel.com/news/fl-xpm-2004-05-30-0405300171-story.html.

Tampa Tribune, "Confessed Killer Says Peel Plotted Murder of Judge," March 9, 1961, 1A, 2B, www.newspapers.com/image/331476954/.

Time, "Crime: The Scoutmaster and the Judge," November 16, 1960, http://content.time .com/time/subscriber/article/0,33009,711938,00.html.

Tom Smith, "Luck Runs Out on 'Lucky'—He Got the Chair," *Miami Herald*, May 4, 1961, 1, 2, www.newspapers.com/image/619530545/.

"Murder Suspect to Give Self Up?" Miami Herald, December 28, 1958, 31, www.news papers.com/image/618480864/?terms=%22Lew%20Gene%20Harvey%22& match=1.

CHAPTER 8: COMMERCIAL AIRLINE DISASTERS

Ardy Friedberg, "We'll Continue the Search Until They Call It Off," *South Florida Sun-Sentinel*, May 15, 1996, 4, www.newspapers.com/image/238772434/?terms=Ever glades%20body&match=1.

Arnold Markowitz, "81 Survive Plane Crash; Death Toll Jumps to 96," *Miami Herald*, December 31, 1972, 1, 14, www.newspapers.com/image/625496433/.

Associated Press "Lost Jet Had Troubled Past," *Fort Myers News-Press*, May 13, 1996, 7, www.newspapers.com/image/217590934/?terms=Everglades%20body&match=1.

Associated Press, "Airliner Wreckage Site Put Under Heavy Guard," *Tampa Times*, February 13, 1963, 1, 4, www.newspapers.com/image/328968964/.

Associated Press, "Investigators Probe Cause of Air Crash," *Longview Daily News*, Washington, February 13, 1963, 1, www.newspapers.com/image/575559047/?terms=death%20Everglades&match=1.

Aviation Safety Network, Flight Safety Foundation, "Friday, December 29, 1972, 23:42, Lockheed L-1011-385-1 TriStar 1," https://aviation-safety.net/database/record .php?id=19721229-0.

Aviation Safety Network, Flight Safety Foundation, "Tuesday, 12 February 1963, 13:50, Boeing 720-051B, Northwest Orient Airlines," https://aviation-safety.net/data base/record.php?id=19630212-0.

Aviation Safety Network, Flight Safety Foundation, "Tuesday, March 25, 1958, 00:06, Douglas DC-7C, Braniff International Airways," https://aviation-safety.net/ database/record.php?id=19580325-1.

Bert Collier, "26 Experts Studying Clues in Crash of Braniff Plane," *Miami Herald*, April 12, 1958, 1C, www.newspapers.com/image/619686376/?terms=%22plane%20crash%22%20Everglades&match-1.

Bill Bondurant, "Sudden Deaths Cut Happy Holidays," *Fort Lauderdale News*, February 13, 1963, 14A, www.newspapers.com/image/271939265/?terms=death%20Everglades&match=1.

Bob Swift, "Engineer Tells Story of Braniff Crash," *Miami Herald*, March 31, 1958, 1, www.newspapers.com/image/619063377/?terms=death%20everglades&match=1.

Boston Globe, "Recorder: Electronic Clue in Flight Death," January 14, 1973, 1A, www.newspapers.com/image/435555119/?terms=death%20everglades&match=1.

Bureau of Aircraft Accidents Archive, "Crash of a Lockheed L-1011-385 TriStar 1 in the Everglades National Park: 99 killed," www.baaa-acro.com/city/everglades-national-park.

Bureau of Aircraft Accidents Archives, "Everglades National Park: Crash of a Boeing 720-051B in the Everglades National Park: 43 killed," www.baaa-acro.com/city/everglades-national-park.

Christopher Cubbison, "Probe Considers Pilot's Activities Before Crash," *St. Petersburg Times*, January 3, 1973, 1, 5, www.newspapers.com/image/317663152/.

David Cázares, "SabreTech Fined $11 million," *South Florida Sun-Sentinel*, August 15, 2000, 1D, www.newspapers.com/image/239220389.

Don Bedwell, "Glades Jet Probe Focuses on Crew," *Miami Herald*, March 6, 1973, 2A, www.newspapers.com/image/622781806/.

Don Bedwell, "TriStar Logged 11,116 Mishap-Free Hours," *Miami Herald*, December 31, 1972, 15A, www.newspapers.com/image/625496681/?terms=death%20Everglades&match=1.

Fort Myers News-Press, "Swamp Swallows Jet," May 12, 1996, 1, www.newspapers.com/image/217585561/.

Gene Miller, "Did Doomed Plane Stall in Severe Turbulence?" *Miami Herald*, June 20, 1963, 2B, www.newspapers.com/image/619594828/?terms=%22Northwest%20Orient%22%20705&match=1.

Gene Miller, "Witness: A Glow, then Screaming in the Dark," *Miami Herald*, December 31, 1972, 15A, www.newspapers.com/image/625496681/?terms=death%20Everglades&match=1.

George Bennett, "A Dive, a Splash . . . Then Nothing," *Palm Beach Post*, May 12, 1996, 1, 20, www.newspapers.com/image/134602140/?terms=Everglades%20body&match=1.

Haines Colbert and Milt Sosin, "9-Death Air Crash Probed," *Miami News*, March 25, 1958, 1, 2, www.newspapers.com/image/298292967.

Ina Paiva Cordle, "Sentencing for SabreTech in ValuJet Trial Delayed," *Miami Herald*, June 6, 2000, 1C, www.newspapers.com/image/643788274/.

James Buchanan and Gene Miller, "9 in Braniff Liner Killed, 15 Survive," *Miami Herald*, March 26, 1958, 1, 2, www.newspapers.com/image/619061984.

James Buchanan, "Death Toll Mounts to 103 in Glades Crash," *Miami Herald*, January 2, 1973, 26, www.newspapers.com/image/625305562/.

Jay Maeder, "Spunky Stewardess Led Carols to Boost Morale," *Miami Herald*, January 1, 1973, 26, www.newspapers.com/image/625305132/.

Jim Greenhill, "Searchers Face Horrific Challenge," *Fort Myers News-Press*, May 12, 1996, 1, 7, www.newspapers.com/image/217585561/.

Joanne Cavanaugh, "To Indians of Glades, Death Isn't a Curiosity," *Miami Herald*, May 25, 1996, 1, 15, www.newspapers.com/image/643677136/.

Julie Vorman, "Grim Search for Plane Is Slow," *Pittsburgh Post-Gazette*, May 25, 1996, 5, www.newspapers.com/image/89635968/?terms=Everglades%20quicksand&match=1.

Ken Kaye, "ValuJet Revisited," *South Florida Sun-Sentinel*, August 24, 1997, 2G, www.newspapers.com/image/238720352/?terms=%22valujet%20592%22&match=1.

Knight-Ridder News Service, "It Was Like a Fireball of Dirt and Debris," *Fort Myers News-Press*, May 12, 1996, 7, www.newspapers.com/image/217585843/.

Miami Herald, "Jet Probe Still Asks 'Why?'" May 5, 1963, 1B, www.newspapers.com/image/619601431/?terms=%22Northwest%20Orient%22%20705&match=1.

Miami Herald, "Toll Was Second Worst in U.S.," January 5, 1973, 18, www.newspapers.com/image/625193244/.

Miami Herald, "Young Plane Looters Escape Jail Terms," May 1, 1958, 1D, www.newspapers.com/image/619100416/?terms=Braniff%20plane%20crash%20Everglades&match=1.

Miami News, "3 Small Fires Guide Path to Wreckage of Jetliner," February 13, 1963, 1, 13A, www.newspapers.com/image/299299578/.

Miami News, "Why 66 Minutes Ticked Off before Searchers Moved," February 13, 1963, 1, www.newspapers.com/image/299302615/.

Mike Baxter, "Rescue Armada Mobilized within Half Hour," *Miami Herald*, December 31, 1972, 15A, www.newspapers.com/image/625496681/?terms=death%20Everglades&match=1.

Miller Davis, "Pray God It Was Fast," *Pensacola News*, February 13, 1963, 1, 2, www.newspapers.com/image/263445912.

Milt Sosin, "Bad Engine Hinted in Braniff Crash," *Miami News*, May 7, 1958, 1D, www.newspapers.com/image/298086946/?terms=Braniff%20plane%20crash%20Everglades&match=1.

Milt Sosin, "Tower Queried TriStar Crew, Got OK Minute before Crash," *Miami News*, January 18, 1973, 1, www.newspapers.com/image/302120902/.

National Transportation Safety Board "Aircraft Accident Report: In-flight Fire and Impact with Terrain, ValuJet Airlines Flight 592, DC-9-32, N904VJ, Everglades, Near Miami, Florida, May 11, 1996," Washington, DC, August 19, 1997, www.ntsb.gov/investigations/AccidentReports/Reports/AAR9706.pdf.

Pensacola News, "Rescuers Sift Ruins," February 13, 1963, 1, 2, www.newspapers.com/image/263445912.

Sallie James, "Tiny Clues Needed to Help ID Victims," *South Florida Sun-Sentinel*, May 14, 1996, 5, www.newspapers.com/image/238772238.

Sandy Murdock, "FBI for 21 Years Have Vigorously Pursued Mechanic Suspected in the ValuJet Crash (110 dead) But . . ." *JDA Journal*, April 12, 2018, http://jda

solutions.aero/blog/fbi-21-years-vigorously-pursued-mechanic-suspected-valujet
-crash-110-dead/.

Sanford Schnier and Dale Pullen, "Witnesses Describe Plane's Flaming End," *Miami News*, March 25, 1958, 4A, www.newspapers.com/image/298292971.

Siobhan Morrissey, "Crash Scene Shows Little Evidence of Large Tragedy," *Palm Beach Post*, May 12, 1996, 1, 21, www.newspapers.com/image/134602140/?terms=Ever glades%20body&match=1.

Stephen Nohlgren, "Plane Crash Takes Seconds; Memory Lingers Longer," *St. Petersburg Times*, June 9, 1996, A17, www.newspapers.com/image/ 403184164/?terms=Everglades%20quicksand&match=1.

Tampa Times, "Plane Victim's Daughter Died in Gulf Crash," February 13, 1963, 1, 4, www.newspapers.com/image/328968964/.

Tampa Tribune, "FAA to Take Harder Look at ValuJet," May 13, 1996, 1, www.news papers.com/image/340379258/?terms=Everglades%20body&match=1.

United Press International, "Air Crash Hearings Finished," *Fort Lauderdale News*, May 9, 1958, 12A, www.newspapers.com/image/229884415/?terms=Braniff% 20plane%20crash%20Everglades&match=1.

United Press International, "Ill-Fated Jetliner Said to Have Broken Up in Air," *Bristol Herald Courier*, Tennessee, February 15, 1963, www.newspapers.com/image/ 584837218/?terms=death%20Everglades&match=1.

United Press International, "Vigil Was Tearful, Anxious at Chicago," *Tampa Times*, February 13, 1963, 4, www.newspapers.com/image/328969002.

William R. Amlong, "No Hint of an Emergency Found on Plane's Tapes," *Miami Herald*, January 1, 1973, 1, 26, www.newspapers.com/image/625305043/.

Chapter 9: The Worst Highway Tragedy and What It Revealed

APMReports, "The Children in the Fields," August 14, 2019, www.apmreports.org/ episode/2019/08/14/the-children-in-the-fields.

EveryCRSReport.com "Child Labor in America: History, Policy, and Legislative Issues," www.everycrsreport.com/reports/RL31501.html#_Toc372703200.

Joe Sullivan, "Bus Tragedy Blame Eyed," *Fort Lauderdale News*, May 24, 1963, 2C, www .newspapers.com/image/271677884/?terms=bus%20accident%20Everglades& match=1.

Joe Sullivan, "Manslaughter Dropped in Bus Tragedy," *Fort Lauderdale News*, May 31, 1963, 12A, www.newspapers.com/image/271712115/?terms=bus%20accident% 20Everglades&match=1.

Palm Beach Post, "Bus Tragedy Sparks Call for Investigation," May 21, 1963, 1, 2, www .newspapers.com/image/134173804.

Tampa Bay Times, "Roads Called 'Shameful,'" June 11, 1963, 8, www.newspapers.com/ image/316804386/?terms=bus%20accident&match=1.

Tampa Tribune, "Canal Death Toll Hits 27," May 20, 1963, 3, www.newspapers.com/ image/330450919/?terms=bus%20accident%20Everglades&match=1.

Tom Smith, "Glades Roads Blamed for Tragedy," *Miami Herald*, June 30, 1963, 1B, www.newspapers.com/image/619612204/?terms=bus%20accident&match=1.

Tom Smith, "Multi-Million-Dollar Plan Urged for Glades Roads," *Miami Herald*, July 6, 1963, 1B, www.newspapers.com/image/619610663/?terms=%22Tom%20Smith%22&match=1.

United Press International, "27 Florida Workers Drown in Bus Crash," *Tampa Bay Times*, May 19, 1963, 1, www.newspapers.com/image/330450919/?terms=bus%20accident%20Everglades&match=1.

CHAPTER 10: FOREVER LOST, OCCASIONALLY FOUND

Associated Press, "Hope Dims for Jockey, Others," *Tacoma News Tribune*, Washington, March 19, 1948, 32, www.newspapers.com/image/733777014/?terms=%22Albert%20Snider%22%20Everglades&match=1.

Associated Press, "Indians Find Body of Miami Man in Glades," *Tampa Bay Times*, March 25, 1931, 3, www.newspapers.com/image/315027178/?terms=%22Thomas%20Wentz%22&match=1.

Associated Press, "Indians Get $3,200 Reward in Body Hunt," *Tampa Times*, April 7, 1931, 9, www.newspapers.com/image/333497161/?terms=%22Thomas%20Wentz%22&match=1.

Associated Press, "Man Wrongly Identified as Missing from Miami," *Tampa Tribune*, March 21, 1931, 1, www.newspapers.com/image/332404097/?terms=%22Thomas%20Wentz%22&match=1.

Associated Press, "Missing Man Is Found Dead in Everglades," *Tampa Times*, March 24, 1931, 1, www.newspapers.com/image/333489766/?terms=Everglades%20missing&match=1.

Associated Press, "Reward Money Distributed in Miami District," *Fort Lauderdale News*, April 7, 1931, 2, www.newspapers.com/image/229803603/?terms=%22Thomas%20Wentz%22&match=1.

Associated Press, "Seek 5 in Missing Boat," *Wilmington Morning News*, Delaware, March 8, 1948, 4, www.newspapers.com/image/160827842/?terms=%22Albert%20Snider%22%20Everglades&match=1.

Associated Press "Search Ends: Indians Find Body of Man," *Fort Myers News-Press*, March 24, 1931, 1, www.newspapers.com/image/221068103/?terms=death%20everglades&match=1.

CBS4 News, "No Trace of Man Missing 30 Days in the Everglades," April 5, 2011, https://miami.cbslocal.com/2011/04/05/no-trace-of-man-missing-30-days-in-everglades-park/.

Charley Project, "Roger Kenneth Sawyer," https://charleyproject.org/case/roger-kenneth-sawyer.

Earl Barber, "Bloodhounds Join Snider Hunt—3 Footprints on Tiny Island Spur Search," *Miami Herald*, March 15, 1948, 1, www.newspapers.com/image/617901120/?terms=Snyder%20missing%20Everglades&match=1.

Fort Lauderdale News, "Air Search Launched for Youth," January 11, 1966, 7, www .newspapers.com/image/272440840/?terms=%22Patrick%20Asa%20King%22& match=1.

Fort Lauderdale News, "CAP Cancels Hunter Search," January 15, 1966, 10, www .newspapers.com/image/272456709/?terms=%22Patrick%20Asa%20King%22& match=1.

Fort Lauderdale News, "Lost Hunter Back Home," January 20, 1966, 1B, www.news papers.com/image/272658759/?terms=Patrick%20King&match=1.

Fort Lauderdale News, "Lost Youth Lead False," January 12, 1966, 21, www.newspapers .com/image/272442182/?terms=%22Patrick%20Asa%20King%22&match=1.

Kansas City Star, "Missing at Sea [photo caption]," March 9, 1948, 12, www.newspapers .com/image/655784245/?terms=%22Albert%20Snider%22%20Everglades& match=1.

Lawrence Thompson, "Search Is Abandoned for Snider and Friends," *Miami Herald*, March 10, 1948, 1, www.newspapers.com/image/617895340/.

Mark Boardman, "Another Trail of Tears," *True West*, October 4, 2017, https://truewest-magazine.com/another-trail-tears/.

Miami Herald, "Roberts Hunts Pal," March 10, 1948, 1, www.newspapers.com/image/ 617895340/?terms=%22Albert%20Snider%22%20Everglades&match=1.

Miami News, "Added Reward Adds to Posse Hunting Wentz," March 16, 1931, 1, www.newspapers.com/image/297480796/?terms=%22Thomas%20Wentz%22& match=1.

Miami News, "Al Snider Memorial Fund to Build Springs Church," December 11, 1948, 4, www.newspapers.com/image/297701290/?terms=%22Albert%20Snider% 22%20Everglades&match=1.

Miami News, "Indian Couple to Go 'Hiepies,'" March 27, 1931, 1, 2, www.newspapers .com/image/298960786.

Miami News, "Search Given Up for 'Glades Hunter'," January 14, 1966, 1, www.news papers.com/image/302064434/?terms=%22Patrick%20Asa%20King%22& match=1.

Miami News, "Wentz Search Is Continued in This Area," March 20, 1931, 1, www.news papers.com/image/297481153/?terms=%22Thomas%20Wentz%22&match=1.

Palm Beach Post, "Foul Weather Hampers Search," January 12, 1966, 8, www.newspapers .com/image/135219397/?terms=%22Patrick%20Asa%20King%22&match=1.

Patty Mummert, "He Doesn't Like to Stay Alone," *Fort Lauderdale News*, January 14, 1966, 1B, www.newspapers.com/image/272450070.

Tom Morgan, "Gopher Key Find Stirs Rumors of Cannibals, Giants," *Miami Herald*, November 22, 1959, 2B, www.newspapers.com/image/619256946/?terms= jockey%20missing%20Everglades&match=1.

Tom Morgan, "Man, Two Sons Missing in Glades; Boat Found Adrift," *Miami Herald*, May 31, 1972, 1C, www.newspapers.com/image/625354120/?terms=Richard% 20Wagner%20Everglades&match=1.

United Press International, "Fate, Which Brought Tragedy, Smiles on Al Snider's Widow," *Anniston Star*, May 18, 1948, 9, www.newspapers.com/image/115186090/?terms=Albert%20Snider&match=1.

United Press International, "Widow of Jockey to Get Earnings If Horse Wins," McCook Daily Gazette, April 10, 1948, 5, www.newspapers.com/image/726002553/?terms=%22Albert%20Snider%22%20Everglades&match=1.

CHAPTER 11: INTO THE CANAL

Ani Martinez, "Head Found in Canal Is from Slain Woman," *Miami Herald*, August 21, 2007, 3B, www.newspapers.com/image/656252802/?terms=Paul%20Bryan%20Trucchio&match=1.

Arnold Markowitz and Tere Figueras, "Bones Found in Sunken Car Are Those of Dade Foreman," *Miami Herald*, February 23, 2001, B8, www.newspapers.com/image/666185555/?terms=%22Robert%20Hall%22&match=1.ll%22&match=1.

Associated Press, "Robert Hall Just Dropped From Sight One Day," *Florida Today*, Cocoa, FL, October 25, 1979,p. 6B, www.newspapers.com/image/125382266/?terms=%22Robert%20Hall%22&match=1.

Caroline Moss, "Murder Suspect Allegedly Asked Siri Where He Could Hide a Dead Body," Business Insider, August 13, 2014, www.businessinsider.com/murder-suspect-asks-siri-where-to-hide-dead-body-2014-8.

Cecil Farrell, "Two Plead Guilty in Marsh Killing," *Naples Daily News*, June 4, 1974, 3, www.newspapers.com/image/19054688/?terms=%22George%20Lewis%20Thornton%22&match=1.

Edna Buchanan, "October 'Night Out' Was His Last Round," *Miami Herald*, March 23, 1980, 1B, 6B, www.newspapers.com/image/628683360/.

Elizabeth Yetter, "10 Popular Places Murderers Dump Bodies in the US," Listverse, https://listverse.com/2015/10/28/10-popular-places-murderers-dump-dead-bodies-in-the-us/.

Farrell, Cecil. "Ku Klux Klan: Does It Exist Here?" *Naples Daily News*, April 12, 1974, 1, www.newspapers.com/image/18986355/?terms=%22Alan%20Stuart%20Marsh%22&match=1.

Fort Myers News-Press, "Body in Canal," May 31, 1973, 2B, www.newspapers.com/image/212828279/?terms=%22Alan%20Stuart%20Marsh%22&match=1.

Fort Myers News-Press, "Guilty Pleas Entered," June 4, 1974, 8, www.newspapers.com/image/221590906/?terms=%22George%20Lewis%20Thornton%22&match=1.

Ihosvani Rodriguez, "Quest to Find Teen's Killer Strikes a Chord," *South Florida Sun-Sentinel*, May 7, 2013, 1A, 9A, www.newspapers.com/image/265703719/.

John Holland, "Family, Friends Recall Runaway Found Slain," *South Florida Sun-Sentinel*, October 4, 2002, 5B, www.newspapers.com/image/284593052/?terms=Marissa%20Karp&match=1.

Juan Ortega and Sallie James, "Two Tree Trimmers Charged with Killing," *South Florida Sun-Sentinel*, August 21, 2007, 7B, www.newspapers.com/image/285677008/?terms=%22Lorraine%20Hatzakorzian%22&match=1.

Lee Melsek, "Gruesome Secrets of Murder Lie Concealed in Everglades," *Pensacola Journal*, December 5, 1977, 10, www.newspapers.com/image/265317538/?terms=death%20Everglades%20alligator&match=1.

Megan O'Matz, John Holland, and Shannon O'Boye, "Slain Girl's Grieving Father Plans to Push for Reforms," *South Florida Sun-Sentinel*, September 28, 2002, 18B, www.newspapers.com/image/284583185/?terms=Marissa%20Karp&match=1.

Miami Herald, "Body Is Found in Drain Canal," May 28, 1973, 1B, www.newspapers.com/image/622768982/?terms=%22Alan%20Stuart%20Marsh%22&match=1.

Miami Herald, "Bullet Recovered in Marsh's Body," May 31, 1973, 1B, www.newspapers.com/image/622772608/?terms=%22Alan%20Stuart%20Marsh%22&match=1.

Miami Herald, "Remains in Canal Are a Human Head," April 30, 2007, 3B, www.newspapers.com/image/655585281/?terms=head%20found%20in%20canal&match=1.

Mike Clary, "Gator Horror Not the First for Everglades," *South Florida Sun-Sentinel*, June 1, 2016, A1, www.newspapers.com/image/265544479/?terms=alligator%20eating%20human%20remains&match=1.

Naples Daily News, "Canal Yields Body," May 29, 1973, 2A, www.newspapers.com/image/31380962/?terms=%22Alan%20Stuart%20Marsh%22&match=1.

Naples Daily News, "Recovered Body Shows Bullet Holes," May 30, 1973, 1, www.newspapers.com/image/19209192/?terms=%22Alan%20Stuart%20Marsh%22&match=1.

Wanda DeMarzo, David Green, and Carol Marbin Miller, "Girl Died of a Single Gunshot; No Evidence of Sexual Assault," *Miami Herald*, September 27, 2002, 1B, 2B, www.newspapers.com/image/646849994.

Chapter 12: When Alligators Attack (Which Isn't Often)

Byron Stout, "Living with Alligators: Problems Grow with Population," *Fort Myers News-Press*, October 11, 2004, 1, 3, www.newspapers.com/image/220718060.

Florida Fish and Wildlife Conservation Commission, "Human-Alligator Incidents Fact Sheet," https://myfwc.com/media/1776/human-alligatorincidentfactsheet.pdf.

Florida Fish and Wildlife Conservation Commission, "Human-Alligator Incidents Fact Sheet," myfwc.com/media/1776/human-alligatorincidentfactsheet.pdf.

Fort Myers News-Press, "Public Service Set for Gator Victim," July 29, 2004, 3B, www.newspapers.com/image/220623740/?terms=%22Janie%20Melsek%22&match=1.

Howard Cohen and Martin Vassolo, "Body of Woman Attacked by Alligator Has Been Found," *Miami Herald*, June 10, 2018, 3, www.newspapers.com/image/654446712/?terms=%22Shizuka%20Matsuki%22&match=1.

Kevin Lollar, "Friends Remember Gator Victim as Talented Poet, Free Spirit," *Fort Myers News-Press*, September 28, 2004, 15, www.newspapers.com/image/219618888/?terms=%22Michelle%20Reeves%22%20alligator&match=1.

Miami Herald, "Alligator Mauls Landscaper," July 23, 2004, 3B, www.newspapers.com/image/651256735/?terms=%22Janie%20Melsek%22&match=1.

Orlando Sentinel, "Death Spurs New Gator Policy," August 5, 2004, www.orlandosentinel.com/news/os-xpm-2004-08-05-0408050149-story.html.

Roberto Santiago, Diana Moskovitz, and Darran Simon, "Trappers Stalk a Killer Gator," *Miami Herald*, May 12, 2006, 1, 2, www.newspapers.com/image/654223871.

Sarah Lundy, "12-foot Alligator Kills Man in Canal," *Fort Myers News-Press*, July 16, 2005, 1, 3, www.newspapers.com/image/221580518.

Scott Hiaasen and Adam H. Beasley, "Suspect Killed by Alligator a Wanted Career Criminal," *Miami Herald*, November 15, 2007, 3B, www.newspapers.com/image/656679310/?terms=Justo%20Padron&match=1.

CHAPTER 13: GLIDING ON AIR: AIRBOAT DEATHS

Bill Bondurant, "Father's Day Event Fatal to Dad, Son," *Fort Lauderdale News*, June 18, 1962, 1, 12, www.newspapers.com/image/271776929/.

Elizabeth Koh, "Man Whose Daughter Died in an Airboat Accident Hopes a New Law Stops More Tragedies," *Miami Herald*, February 2, 2018, A4, www.newspapers.com/image/654584651/?terms=airboat%20death%20Everglades&match=1.

Elizabeth Koh, "New Airboat Regulations after UM Grad's Death," *Miami Herald*, June 23, 2018, A3, www.newspapers.com/image/654448209/?terms=Ellie%27s%20Law&match=1.

Fort Myers News-Press, "Fort Myers Man Dies in Boat Crash," April 3, 2006, 6, www.newspapers.com/image/221162016/?terms=Ryan%20Carraway&match=1.

Henry Pierson Curtis, "Airboat Death Trial Moves Ahead," *Osceola Sentinel*, April 22, 1994, 2, www.newspapers.com/image/233001379/?terms=airboat%20death&match=1.

Lisa Huriash and Mike Clary, "Details Emerge in Fatal Airboat Crash," *South Florida Sun-Sentinel*, May 17, 2017, 1, 9, www.newspapers.com/image/301502856/.

Lisa J. Huriash, "Airboat Driver Won't Be Charged In Fatal Accident," *South Florida Sun Sentinel*, March 22, 2018, A1, A10, www.newspapers.com/image/409202450/.

Miami Herald, "Glades Airboat Crash, One Killed, 16 Injured," March 7, 1955, 1, 2, www.newspapers.com/image/620120529.

Miami News, "Two Air Boats Hit, Man Dies," November 10, 1958, 8, www.newspapers.com/image/298326248/.

Orlando Evening Star, "Swamp Boat Smash Kills 1," November 10, 1958, 7, www.newspapers.com/image/290568495/?terms=Joseph%20Malzohn&match=1.

Orlando Sentinel, "Air-Boats Hit, 1 Killed, 5 Hurt," November 10, 1958, 15, www.newspapers.com/image/223045659/?terms=Joseph%20Malzohn&match=1.

Orlando Sentinel, "Man Dies When Airboat Flips," December 6, 2004, B3, www.newspapers.com/image/268837936/?terms=%22Jason%20Goode%22&match=1.

Palm Beach Post, "Airboat Death Caused by Man Slipping," December 13, 1959, 6, www.newspapers.com/image/129977951/?terms=airboat%20death&match=1.

Rick Jervis, "Airboats' Operation Loosely Regulated," *Miami Herald*, August 1, 1998, 2B, www.newspapers.com/image/642103301/?terms=airboat%20death%20Everglades&match=1.

References

Tampa Bay Times, "Researcher Dies on Everglades Trip," July 25, 1998, 4B, www.news
    papers.com/image/327274933/?terms=%22Cristina%20Menendez%22&match=1.
United Press International, "Glade Wreck Kills 1, Hurts 5," *Palm Beach Post*, Novem-
    ber 10, 1958, 1, www.newspapers.com/image/133606473/?terms=Joseph%
    20Malzohn&match=1.

Index

of illegal, 70; Prohibition and, 69, 70, 80–81. *See also* moonshiner; rum running

Allen, A. F., 65

Alligator Alley, xx, 182–84, 198, 203

alligator attacks, xx, 187, 196; as cause of death, xiii; FWC on, 188; Jimenez, Y., death from, 193–94; Matsuki death from, 195; Melsek death from, 190–91; Murray death from, 189–90; Padron death from, 194–95; Reeves, M., death from, 191–92; Sanibel island alligator rules after, 191

alligators: body dumping feeding by, 181–82; crocodiles compared to, 187–88; Everglades safety on, 212–13; French on danger of, 192–93; media on ValuJet Flight 592 and, 145; as opportunistic feeders, 181, 187

Almquist, Roy W., 124, 130

American Legion, Moore Haven relief from, 56, 57

American Ornithologists' Society, on plumage hunters bird slaughter, 18

American Red Cross: on hurricane of 1928 death toll, 67; hurricane of 1928 relief, 64; on illness from polluted water, 57–58; on Moore

Haven home restoration, 60–61; Moore Haven relief from, 56, 57

Anderson, Edgar Lee, 149, 152

Anderson, Ross, 107–8

Anholt, Jim, 190

Apple Siri, body hiding request, 179

Arcaro, Eddie, 167

Army Corps of Engineers flood control project, xviii

ARTCC. *See* Air Route Traffic Control Center

Ashley, Bob: Ashley, John, hiding with, 33, 35; Hendrickson shooting by, 43; Riblett shooting by, 43–44; robbery indictment, 40; shooting death of, 43–44

Ashley, Ed, 45

Ashley, Frank, 45

Ashley, Joe, 29, 34–35; arrest of, 40; robbery spree of, 38

Ashley, John, 47; Baker, B., escape by, 36–38; Branning as trial judge for, 37, 42; at *Caloosahatchie* dredge, 30; Chaffin encounter with, 34; deputies encounter with, 33–34; disappearance into Everglades by, 32–33; Gramling as prosecuting attorney, 40–42; guilty sentence for, 42; hunting, trapping, and fishing of, 29;

Prohibition, 69, 70, 80–81
propeller of airboats, protective
    housing for, 201
Puerto Rico, hurricane of 1928
    damage to, 63

Raposa, Becky J., 134
Raymond, Will, 7
RCC. *See* Rescue Coordination
    Center
Reed, Jim: Belle Starr marriage
    to, 2; police death of, 2;
    stagecoach robberies of, 2;
    Starr, T., relationship with, 2
Reed, John, 144
Reeves, James "Jim," 192
Reeves, Michelle, 191–92
regulations, for airboats, 203–4,
    206–7
Repo, Donald L., 132, 138
Rescue Coordination Center
    (RCC), of Coast Guard,
    135–36
Rever, Christine, 129
Rewis, Gus, 166
Rewis, Rayford, 166
Reynolds, Dutchy. *See* Melvin,
    Duchy
Riblett, J. R., 43–44
Richardson, E. A., 162
Riddle, Callie, 96
Riggs, Harry, 198–99
Riley, Bart, 81
Ritter, Halsted L., 81

roads: Everglades safety
    on, 210–11; SRD on
    Everglade, 154
Roberts, Charles, 200
Roberts, Emmett S., 152–53
Roberts, Gene, 20, 23
Roberts, Porter, 164
Rogers, Elizabeth, 92
Rogers, Vincent, 86–87, 90, 92
Roosevelt, Theodore, 19
Rose, A. J., 41–42
Rubio, Heriberto, 195
rum running, 71–82; Caribbean
    and, 69; of Davis, J. H., and
    Brown, R., 69; Hutto capture
    and arrests in, 70; police
    officer death, 69. *See also*
    Hutto, W. F.

SabreTech: criminal charges filed
    against three employees
    and, 147; FAA on, 146;
    NTSB on ValuJet Flight
    592 blame, 146–47; oxygen
    generators removal and
    replacement, 140
San Cartier, Thomas M., 122–23
Sanibel island, alligator rules
    of, 191
Santini, Adolphus, 7
Sapp, Tammy, 181, 187, 196
Save Our Everglades Trust Fund,
    Bush and, xix
Sawyer, Paula, 173